THE
EUROPEAN
AUTOMOBILE
INDUSTRY

THE
EUROPEAN
AUTOMOBILE
INDUSTRY

JAMES M. LAUX

TWAYNE PUBLISHERS / NEW YORK

Maxwell Macmillan Canada / Toronto

Maxwell Macmillan International / New York Oxford Singapore Sydney

The European Automobile Industry
James M. Laux

Copyright 1992 by Twayne Publishers

Twayne Publishers
Macmillan Publishing Company
866 Third Avenue
New York, New York 10022

Maxwell Macmillan Canada, Inc.
1200 Eglinton Avenue East
Suite 200
Don Mills, Ontario M3C 3N1

Macmillan Publishing Company is a part of the Maxwell Communication Group of Companies.

Library of Congress Cataloging-in-Publication Data

Laux, James Michael. 1927-
    The European automobile industry / James M. Laux.
        p. cm.
    Includes bibliographical references and index.
    ISBN 0-8057-3800-2. − ISBN 0-8057-3801-0 (pbk.)
    1. Automobile industry and trade – Europe – History. I. Title.
HD9710.E82L38   1992
338.4'76292'094 – dc20   91-43223
                                                                              CIP

The paper used in this publication meets the minimum requirements of American National Standard for Information Sciences – Permanence of Paper for Printed Library Materials, ANSI Z39.48-1984. ∞ ™

10 9 8 7 6 5 4 3 2 1 (alk. paper)

10 9 8 7 6 5 4 3 2 1 (pbk.: alk. paper)

Printed in the United States of America.

CONTENTS

TABLES AND ILLUSTRATIONS

TABLES

FIGURES

MAPS

PREFACE

This book traces the history of the automobile industry in Europe from its origins around 1890 in Germany and France through the following century. Its focus is not, primarily, the technology of the cars and trucks, nor does it deal with racing or styling. It is concerned with motor-vehicle making as a business. Although there are a number of histories of individual firms, a few studies of the industry in specific European countries, and a handful of accounts with a world scope, no recent work is devoted to Europe as a whole. Here most of the attention is devoted to the industry in four countries that have constituted the heartland of European automaking since the 1890s – Germany, France, Britain, and Italy – but as the industry developed elsewhere, such as in the Soviet Union and Sweden, the discussion broadens.

In any book compromises must be made. To keep this one to a reasonable length, much interesting information had to be omitted. Reducing the p. 111 map of the 1939 German autobahn network so that it would fit on a single page has rendered the city names illegible; the road network, however, the important thing, is clear enough.

* * *

I take pleasure in acknowledging the help of many people, most especially my wife, Barbara, and my friend and colleague Frank Kafker. Assistance also came from many others, including Patrick Fridenson, R. J. Overy, Daniel Henri, Yves Cohen, Otto Nübel, Peter Lessmann, Gerald Bloomfield, T. C. Barker, R. A. Whitehead, John Morrow, Jr., Jay Yocis, Sally Moffitt, Bruce Ryan, and Richard Schade. At Twayne, I thank Leslie Hannah, Carol Chin, and Barbara Sutton. Finally, I am much indebted to Dan Gottlieb and Tom White and their genial and expert associates at the Interlibrary Loan office of the University of Cincinnati Library.

1

THE AUTOMOBILE IS BORN

The gasoline automobile was born in the mid-1880s when two lines of technical development converged: lightweight road carriages and the internal combustion engine. Road vehicles go back a long way, of course, and from the 1760s on there were many efforts to apply steam power to move them. The weight and complexity of these steam carriages limited their acceptance, and efforts in the 1880s to power cars by electric batteries met with even less success. A newcomer was the internal combustion engine, feasible for transportation only after the appearance of the petroleum industry in 1859.

Many Europeans experimented with using illuminating gas and petroleum as fuels for mechanical transport through internal combustion in the 1860s and later; notable among these were Etienne Lenoir in Paris, Nicholas Otto in Cologne, Dugald Clerk in Scotland, Enrico Bernardi in Italy, and Edouard Delamare-Deboutteville in Normandy. The first successes of major consequence in applying lightweight gasoline engines to vehicles came in southwestern Germany. In Mannheim in 1886, Carl Benz, a small manufacturer of stationary gas engines, attached a four-stroke gasoline engine of his own design to a large tricycle and drove it successfully. Benz's slow-running (250 rpm) engine produced less than 1 horsepower (hp) and ran the vehicle by means of a belt transmission and two side chains to the rear wheels. Although troubled by his machine's low power and uncertain electric ignition, Benz persevered and finally sold his first car early in 1888 for 2,000 marks ($475). Early one August morning that year Berta Benz, the enterprising wife of the inventor, impatient over her husband's caution, bundled their two sons, ages 15 and 13, into an improved model and, without Carl's permission, set out to drive it some 45 miles to her home in Pforzheim. Although the engine now supplied 1.5 hp, they had to push the 600-pound tricycle up hills and make some minor repairs. Berta and her boys reached their goal as night fell. A few days later

1

they drove back to Mannheim.[1] A woman and two boys had accomplished the first long-distance gasoline automobile trip.

Although Carl Benz often is styled the "father" of the motorcar, his compatriot Gottlieb Daimler made similar progress during this period. An academically trained engineer, Daimler worked for a time with Nicholas Otto at the Deutz company, making gas engines in Cologne. He struck out on his own in 1882, trying to perfect a small gasoline engine for vehicles. Working near Stuttgart, Daimler and his skillful assistant, Wilhelm Maybach, devised a high-speed (700 rpm) engine with ignition by an incandescent tube heated by a small gas burner. In 1886 they tried it out on a rudimentary motorcycle and two years later demonstrated a more powerful engine in a four-wheeled carriage.

Carl Benz and Gottlieb Daimler were slow to market their inventions. First they had to improve their solutions to certain technical problems. A major challenge was transmitting the engine's power to the wheels, an issue that has occupied engineers' attention for a century, with each generation offering new approaches. Other problems were cooling the engine, suspension, brakes, and tires. None of these was a simple matter, but European engineers found satisfactory solutions to them by the early years of the twentieth century.

Gottlieb Daimler wanted to produce gasoline engines; he was not very interested in working on road vehicles that might use them. His firm, Daimler Motor Company, concentrated during the 1890s on supplying engines for boats, for tramways, for stationary purposes, and for road vehicles. In 1890 it manufactured 82 engines; in the year ending March 1896 it sold 201, of which only 33 were for motor vehicles.[2]

In Mannheim, Benz aimed from the first to develop a motorcar and was the only German producer with a significant output until the twentieth century. At first he continued making small numbers of powered tricycles, selling most of them through his agent in Paris, Emile Roger. Benz finally introduced a four-wheeled car in 1892 and sales began to rise. From 1888 through 1893 Benz sold 69, just 15 of these in Germany and most of the rest in France. Sales at Benz rose to 67 in 1894 and 135 in 1895. Automobiles had become a serious business and in 1895 the company set up a department for their manufacture separate from the gas-engine operations. The auto department, housed in two small buildings, employed about 70 workers. By 1898 the Benz company had sold a total of 1,132 cars – 334 in Germany and 509 in France.[3]

These numbers suggest the strong French interest in automobiles. In fact, French engineers and businessmen seized upon devices pioneered by Germans, especially the high-speed gasoline engine, and took them farther and faster, making their country the center of the early automobile industry. The original connection began in 1887, when Daimler's company licensed the highly respected Paris machine-building firm of Panhard & Levassor (P & L) to manufacture its engines. In the following year Daimler and Emile Levassor persuaded Armand Peugeot to use some of the French-made Daimler engines. Members of the Peugeot family operated several metalworking establishments near the town of Montbéliard, close to the Swiss frontier. In the 1880s Armand Peugeot had begun manufacturing bicycles and, like many other bicycle makers over the next few years, soon began to wonder about motorizing these vehicles. He bought a few Daimler engines made by P & L and his engineers fit one to a quadricycle in 1890. Peugeot sold four of these lightweight cars in 1891. Emile Levassor also brought his firm into this new business, using Daimler engines in a heavier vehicle of his own design. The first P & L car sales (six) also came in 1891. These automobiles were the first to have what would become the classic arrangement: engine in front driving the rear wheels. The P & L catalog of 1892 (its first) listed one chassis with four different body styles. Prices ranged from ƒ4,100 ($790) upward, with a ƒ400 ($77) supplement for solid rubber tires rather than steel ones.[4] Through 1895 Peugeot sold a total of 169 cars and P & L 164, compared with Benz's 271 (135 exported to France) over these years.

Closely related to the early growth of the European automobile industry was the bicycle. Developed first in France in the 1860s, British firms soon dominated this trade. The market for the earliest bicycles, with their very high front wheel, remained limited to athletic young men until the introduction of the safety bicycle in the mid-1880s. This type had wheels of equal size and a chain drive, which made it much more user-friendly. Almost anyone could now ride it. After the appearance of a second major innovation, pneumatic tires in the early 1890s, bicycles became the fashion for middle- and upper-class young men and women. As more and more producers entered the business, prices dropped, the market expanded, and a bicycle boom ensued in Europe and North America in 1895-97.

In a variety of ways bicycles led directly to automobiles. Many technical aspects carried over into car design and manufacture: ball bearings, chain drive, pneumatic tires, and the manufacture of standardized parts by single-purpose cutting tools or stamping presses. As will be seen, a large number of early automobile producers came to the industry from bicycle making. Bicycles also accustomed people to individual mechanical transport and encouraged tinkerers to apply some sort of mechanical power source to them. Methods to publicize and market bicycles also were adopted by automakers: annual shows that featured new models, races between cities or on enclosed tracks, specialized weekly and monthly publications financed by manufacturers' advertising, a system of dealers and repair shops, and installment buying.

From the mid-1890s until after the First World War, France led the European automobile industry. France was not the European leader in other industrial sectors, such as steel, electrical equipment, chemicals, or machine tools, during these years. How then can one explain French leadership in the motor business? In part it was the fortuitous event that two substantial metalworking establishments (P & L and Peugeot) jumped into the business very early and used their engineering and production experience, their financial resources, and their marketing skills to win a head start. Also, P & L and most of the other early French firms such as De Dion-Bouton, Clément, Darracq, and Renault were located in Paris. This centralization in the country's largest market for expensive consumer goods and in the center of French journalism made it easy for auto manufacturers to publicize their cars and for buyers to visit factories and showrooms. Paris also was the largest center of French light metalworking and carriage making. This provided an extensive pool of skilled workers, and, of salient importance, many small workshops that could and did begin fabricating large batches of automobile components for the automakers.

In none of the other European countries were all these factors present at the beginning of the industry. In Germany well-established firms other than Benz hesitated to enter the business, and the industry there was very dispersed. In Britain one sees similar dispersal, and established companies, even bicycle producers, entered the business slowly. In Italy no established company plunged into the industry at an early date.

In addition, although all rural roads had gravel or dirt surfaces in this period, the French network was in much better condition than that of Germany or Italy, and even of Britain. The quality of French roads encouraged intercity motor racing as a form of publicity, and the purchase of cars by small-town residents.

Poor roads, the early dispersal of the industry, and false starts with electric and steam cars also held back the American automobile industry, but Americans' high average income and the willingness of American automakers to seek out a market for low-priced cars took them into the lead by 1905.

2

THE FRENCH SET THE PATTERN

The automobile industry developed first in France, and grew quite rapidly from 1898 on.[1] After the turn of the century, motorcar manufacturing in Britain began to expand, followed a few years later in Germany and Italy. In the United States automobile production began climbing after 1899, surpassed France in 1904, and totaled more than all of Europe in 1908 (see Table 2.1).

EARLY MANUFACTURERS AND PUBLICITY

In France the growing success of Panhard & Levassor and Peugeot in the mid-1890s was paralleled by a rash of publicity about the new machines. The first extended trip had taken place in 1891, when two Peugeot engineers drove a car from the company's works to Paris, 260 miles, then followed the season's major bicycle race from Paris to Brest and back, and finally drove the car to a buyer near Mulhouse in German Alsace, a journey totaling 1,200 miles, far eclipsing Berta Benz's trip of 90 miles three years earlier. In 1894 a Paris newspaper sponsored a promenade of the new horseless vehicles from Paris to Rouen, 78 miles. Fourteen of the 21 cars used gasoline engines (13 Daimler and one Benz) and seven employed steam. All of the gasoline cars finished the trip within the time limit, but only one of the steamers. Steam never recovered from this defeat in France.

The next summer the industry's promoters staged a real automobile race, a run nonstop from Versailles (just outside Paris) to Bordeaux and back, about 730 miles. Again the gasoline vehicles proved their superiority. Of the nine cars that finished within 100 hours, six used French-made Daimler engines, two had Benzes, and one machine, built back in 1880, had a steam engine. The single electric car dropped out. After these two defeats only one significant steam-car producer persevered, Léon Serpollet, along with a few constructors of

TABLE 2.1 AUTOMOBILE PRODUCTION, 1898-1914

Year	France	Britain	Germany	Italy	Europe	U.S.
1898	1,500					
1899	2,400					
1900	4,800					4,192
1901	7,600		884	125		7,000
1902	11,000			185		9,000
1903	14,100	2,000	1,450	225	17,775	11,325
1904	16,900	4,000		375		22,830
1905	20,500	7,000		850		25,000
1906	24,400	10,000	5,218	2,000	41,618	34,000
1907	25,200	12,000	5,151	2,500	44,851	44,000
1908	25,000	10,500	5,547	2,300	43,347	65,000
1909	34,000	11,000	9,444	3,500	57,944	130,000
1910	38,000	14,000	13,113	4,000	69,113	187,000
1911	40,000	19,000	16,939	5,280	81,219	210,000
1912	41,000	23,200	22,773	6,670	93,643	378,000
1913	45,000	34,000	20,388	6,760	106,148	485,000
1914				9,210		569,054

Italicized numbers are author's estimates.

Sources:

France: J. Laux, *In First Gear* (Montreal: McGill-Queen's University Press, 1976), 210.

Britain: Society of Motor Manufacturers and Traders, *The Motor Industry of Great Britain, 1932* (London, 1932), 32 for 1907ff.

Germany: H. C. von Seherr-Thoss, *Die deutsche Automobilindustrie* (Stuttgart: Deutsche Verlag, 1974), 557.

Italy: ANFIA, *Automobile in cifre, 1982* (Turin, 1982), 5 for 1911ff.

U.S.: National Automobile Chamber of Commerce, *Facts and Figures of the Automobile Industry* (New York, 1933), 4.

steam trucks. The winner of the Paris-Bordeaux race, Emile Levassor driving one of his P & L cars, negotiated the route in 49 hours for an average speed of 15 mph. This event ratified the French lead in automobiles, for the only other formal contest in 1895 came in Chicago in November and was much less impressive. This race covered just 52 miles and only three of the six starters finished, two of them Benzes.

The Paris-Bordeaux race saw the introduction of a major improvement for automobiles, the pneumatic tire. Like carriages, early cars mounted steel or solid rubber tires. The pneumatic tire, reinvented in Belfast, Ireland, by John Boyd Dunlop in 1888 for use on bicycles, was adopted on these machines as soon as simple methods of attaching it to the wheels were devised. The tire consisted of a rubber tube, which contained the air, inside a canvas and rubber casing. In France the Michelin rubber company of Clermont-Ferrand pioneered in bicycle tires. Edouard and André Michelin soon experimented with pneumatic tires for motorcars as well, and the first major demonstration was their entry in the 1895 Paris-Bordeaux race. The tires showed such obvious advantages that within a few years nearly all French passenger cars drove on pneumatics. In France the average price for a tire and tube from 1900 to 1902 was $49; by 1911-13 the quality had improved and the price had fallen to $33. In the British Isles, Harvey du Cros' Dunlop company of Dublin, Ireland, and then Coventry, England, had exploited Dunlop's invention vigorously for bicycles but fell behind with motorcars and made its first pneumatics for them only in 1902.[2]

Comte Albert de Dion was one of the French entrepreneurs drawn into the automobile industry by the experiments and publicity of the early 1890s. The comte and his talented associate, the mechanic Georges Bouton, entered a small steam-powered tractor pulling a carriage in the 1894 Paris-Rouen demonstration. De Dion helped organize the Paris-Bordeaux race the next year, but his two steamers did not finish. This failed to discourage him, for Georges Bouton now unveiled a new gasoline engine. Air-cooled, with electric ignition, and operating at 1,500 rpm, twice the speed of the Daimler type, it was a great technical achievement. The De Dion-Bouton firm used these very reliable engines to power a tricycle and when the engine's output was raised to 1.25 and then 2.75 hp these machines sold very well. In 1900 the large size sold for about $365, compared with a bicycle at $39, a small Renault car at $675, and a high-quality P & L car at $2,300.

Through 1901 De Dion-Bouton may have sold some 15,000 tricycles and another 10,000 engines separately. These machines certainly accustomed many French people to powered individual transport and prepared the market for full-sized motor cars. And not just French people, for in addition to selling engines to two dozen other French automobile producers, De Dion-Bouton supplied them to British, German, Italian, and American auto firms, licensed widely the manuufacture of its tricycle, and saw still other firms make close copies of it. As Daimler had provided a first-class engine design for the very early

days of the auto industry in France, so De Dion-Bouton a decade later
gave it another boost there and in the rest of Europe.

Comte de Dion promoted the new industry in other ways. He was
the prime mover in organizing the Automobile Club de France in 1895,
an organization primarily devoted to the racing and touring aspects of
motorcars, and in forming the first French automakers' trade association in 1898.

In France automobile journalism also appeared during these years,
first with columns in bicycle periodicals, and then in 1894 *La Locomo-
tion automobile* was the first in a flood of magazines specializing in the
new sport and business. In 1900 a daily, *L'Auto*, launched publication.
Annual shows to publicize and sell cars began in 1894. The Paris Auto
Show in 1898 drew over 300 exhibitors of cars, parts, and accessories
and 140,000 visitors. These numbers are surprisingly high considering
that there were hardly more than 2,200 cars circulating in France at the
end of 1898, but they demonstrate the broad interest in the new trade.
The intercity races had continued: Paris-Marseille-Paris in 1896, Paris-
Bordeaux in 1897, and Paris-Amsterdam-Paris in 1898, along with many
shorter contests.

The earliest buyers of cars in France and the rest of Europe were
wealthy sportsmen, interested in novelty and speed, and engineers, in-
trigued by the new mechanical devices. Soon clients from other social
groups joined them, including businessmen, physicians and other professionals, prosperous rural landowners, and traveling salesmen. These
people hoped that replacing horse-drawn carriages with cars would
help them in their occupations, as well as give them more options for
their leisure time. Then, in the few years before the First World War
when greater numbers of inexpensive cars became available, some independent craftsmen and government employees – especially teach-
ers – began to come into the market.[3]

Cars were sold and repaired at the factories in the very early days,
but soon the manufacturers contracted with agents or dealers to represent them. Sometimes, as in the case of Peugeot, the automaker established its own branches in major cities to ensure reliable treatment of
customers. Manufacturers promised their dealers exclusive selling
rights in their territories and sold cars to them at 10 to 20 percent below the list price. Dealers paid a fraction of the car's cost with their order and the rest on delivery. Frequently they sold cars of several makes.

Automobile dealers often came to the business from the bicycle trade and many of the commercial arrangements were adopted from the practices used there or in the sale of other durable consumer goods such as furniture and pianos, or of farm machinery. The customer usually paid one-third down with the order and the rest upon delivery. Although installment selling of passenger cars over one or two years did appear in Europe early in the new century (it was well known in the furniture trade), it was not common until after the war.

Drivers bought gasoline in tin cans that held 10 liters on the Continent, two imperial gallons in Britain. They found them in bicycle shops and grocery stores. The gasoline pump, developed in the United States by Sylvanus Bowser, began to appear in Europe just before the war. The French price for gasoline generally was equivalent to 42¢ per American gallon.

TAXES AND SAFETY

Following the well-worn principle of taxing anything that moves, the French government in May 1898 began to tax automobiles. The annual rate was the same as for horse-drawn carriages. It ranged from $4.83 for a two-seater registered in a small town to $21.24 for a car with three or more seats registered in Paris and was halved for vehicles used in agriculture or in certain professions. In 1900 the tax was revised to reduce the base rate level but add $1 for each rated horsepower. (In France horsepower is *cheval vapeur*, abbreviated CV.) This began the policy eventually adopted all over Europe of taxing cars according to their power as calculated by the size of their engines' cylinders. This arbitrarily determined fiscal or taxable horsepower always fell below the experimentally derived brake horsepower. Early in the twentieth century the annual tax in Paris for a mid-priced car was about $29 (150*f*) or 1.6 percent of the cost of the car. In 1910 the tax on cars with 13 fiscal hp and over rose again. By 1912 the total amount raised by taxes on automobiles exceeded that from horse vehicles.

Safety regulations also appeared. In 1897 every motor vehicle had to have a plate bearing the owner's name and address. Starting in 1899, cars had to have two separate braking systems and all control levers within reach of the driver. A driving permit was required of all drivers and maximum speeds were set at 20 kph in urban areas and 30 kph in the country.

NEW PRODUCERS

As demand rose for cars new producers entered the business. De Dion-Bouton first offered small four-wheeled gasoline cars in 1899 and produced about 1,200 in 1900. Several bicycle makers also shifted to automobiles when the bicycle boom collapsed. These included Alexandre Darracq, Adolphe Clément, Georges Richard, and the firm of Chenard and Walcker.

Louis Renault, the 21-year-old son of a textile businessman, entered the trade in Paris late in 1898 with financial aid from his two older brothers. He converted a De Dion-Bouton tricycle into a small, four-wheeled machine with direct drive, which in top gear coupled the engine's crankshaft directly to the drive shaft and through a universal joint to the differential and live rear axle. This capital improvement increased the efficiency of the drive train, but, until tough special steels became available, shaft rather than chain drive was suitable only for relatively light cars.

Another Paris auto firm, Mors, almost collapsed after 1903 due to weak and unstable management, but in 1907 André Citroën was brought in to save it. This young man, a graduate of the elite Paris engineering school, the Ecole Polytechnique, operated a shop cutting gears with an innovative design. Citroën improved the factory organization at Mors and expanded output but did not turn the company into a money-maker.

ELECTRIC AND STEAM POWER

The French concentrated early on gasoline engines for their automobiles rather than on electricity or steam. The poor showing of steam and electric cars in the demonstrations and races of the mid-1890s probably accounts for this. Nevertheless, there were further efforts with the two alternatives. Everyone realized that the limited range of electric cars restricted their use to cities, but some businessmen in New York reasoned that the simplicity, silence, smoothness, and reliability of electric cars made them eminently suitable for cab service. They introduced electric cabs there beginning in 1897 and groups in London, Paris, and Berlin followed suit. At the 1899 auto show in Paris 19 companies displayed electric cars. This excitement quickly faded. With their load of lead batteries and passengers, electric cabs proved too heavy for pneumatic tires, but with solid rubber the batteries suffered too many jolts for long life. Frequent recharging was expensive and inconvenient. Careless drivers sometimes caused serious damage to the motors. By 1900-1901 the electric-cab boom had evaporated in Paris as well as in New York and London, although perhaps not in Berlin. Private electric cars did little better, except in the United States.

Steam cars attracted few in France after the mid-1890s. Steam power was used on tramlines in cities in that decade and more importantly on rural tramways, primarily narrow 60-centimeter gauge lines that were common in France before 1914. By that year over 13,650 miles of local and tram railways operated in France, a tram railway being defined as a line where 70 percent of the route ran along the shoulder of a road.[4] Léon Serpollet, who supplied some of these tram steamers, also made elegant private steam cars, about 100 per year in the period 1900-1903. Their high cost and complex mechanism compared to gasoline cars with equivalent performance led to steam's final decline. Serpollet and two or three other firms also made steam trucks for very heavy loads but never succeeded in uncovering a significant market. In 1914 there were about 700 steam trucks and cars in France. As will be seen, steam wrote a different story in Britain.

PARIS AND THE PROVINCES

In France, unlike Britain, Germany, Italy, or the United States, the country's capital city became the center of its automobile industry. This cannot be attributed to the city's size or to its role as the center of government and finance. Two key factors do explain it. Paris had a large variety of metalworking, carriage building, and bicycle firms that could supply components easily for new automakers, or could go into the new business themselves. These firms also employed much skilled labor and many engineers that the auto companies could draw upon. Second, Paris was the location of several successful early producers – P & L, Mors, De Dion-Bouton, Renault – whose example encouraged others to get into automobiles. Additional factors were that Paris was by far the largest early market for cars and that it was the center of French journalism, which vigorously promoted Paris activities and Paris firms.

Peugeot remained the leading provincial auto firm in France. It abandoned the Daimler engine in 1895 for its own design (as did P & L in 1898) and made about 500 cars per year early in the new century. Other provincial firms included Lorraine-Dietrich of Lunéville in Lorraine, a railway equipment manufacturer looking for a new product, the Delahaye machine shop of Tours, which moved to Paris in 1898, and several firms in Lyon. Entrepreneurs in Lyon, like those in Paris, could begin with a small amount of capital as simple assemblers. A variety of metalworking shops provided components and plenty of skilled labor. Of the several Lyon automakers, one of the two leaders, Rochet-Schneider, began with bicycles and began to shift to motorcars in 1894. The firm remained small until a Marseille financier, Demetrius Zafiropulo, began investing in it and pushed it toward large and elaborate machines. The other prominent Lyonnais company grew from the stubborn persistence of an impecunious mechanic, Marius Berliet. His first car dates from 1894. After years of gradual expansion and thrifty investment he made about 100 of his 1901 model. In 1905 Berliet took the step crucial to his later success, selling for $100,000 a license to the American Locomotive Company to manufacture Berliet cars in the United States. Although these Alco cars did not meet with widespread success in North America, the sudden infusion of capital allowed Berliet to buy new machine tools from the United States, England, and Germany, to increase his labor force to about 800, and produce over 1,000 cars in 1907.

Of the French automakers mentioned, only one, Lorraine-Dietrich, came from the manufacture of heavy equipment. Ultimately, several firms from that sector did enter the new industry, such as the boiler maker Delaunay-Belleville, which made heavy and elegant touring cars, and the armaments firm Schneider, whch produced some trucks and several hundred motor buses for Paris. The large engineering companies in France usually did not do well in auto manufacturing, nor did those in other countries. The design, manufacture, and selling of complex consumer goods like passenger cars was quite different from locomotives, heavy electrical equipment, steam engines, or shipbuilding. The character of operations was so unlike what these firms had been doing that few chose to enter the new business.

SOURCES OF CAPITAL

In general, the accumulation of investment capital was not a major problem for early automakers, for they did not require large amounts. Firms already in metalworking such as P & L, Peugeot, Darracq, and Delaunay-Belleville gradually shifted resources to the new line. The founders of new companies like Renault, De Dion-Bouton, or Delage would obtain $20,000 or $40,000 from family or friends, lease a small workshop, install a few used machine tools, and buy some components on credit. The one-third down payment usually required of customers when they ordered a car provided additional working capital and banks often were willing to make short term advances on the basis of firm orders for cars. Further growth could come from retained earnings, but a faster way was to convert the company to a corporation and sell shares. Banks or investment houses, often small ones, assisted in these public offerings. Even more capital would have allowed some of the more successful firms to expand more rapidly, but in general it appears that the auto companies' cautious marketing strategies slowed down growth more than did capital starvation.

An interesting pattern in the French automobile industry in this period was the refinancing of French firms on the London market, which reached a peak in the years 1903-1906. This began with the successful conversion of the Darracq company into Darracq Ltd. in 1903, with Alexandre Darracq remaining in charge at Suresnes. The company prospered until 1912, when, after making several costly errors, Darracq was forced out and a British engineer took over. In this case most shares of Darracq were held by British investors. Such was not the case for Rochet-Schneider or Delahaye. Rochet-Schneider was floated on the London market in 1905, with most of the new shares placed in France and Italy. It failed in the 1908 recession but reappeared in the following year as a French company. In 1906 Delahaye was reorganized in London and again most of the new shares went to French investors. Its French management remained in charge and guided it successfully into trucks as well as large cars. During the First World War Delahaye reconverted to a French concern. A handful of other French motor companies also went through a refinancing in London. It appears that after the Darracq reorganization most of these conversions occurred as a way for the French owners and English company promoters to make a quick profit. That the rules for new stock issues were less restrictive in London than Paris probably explains most of these cases.

COMPONENTS

When French automobile production expanded in the late 1890s it drew into the business a variety of component manufacturers. These concerns, usually in Paris, supplied axles, wheels, radiators, acetylene headlights, magnetos, carburetors, transmissions, water pumps, and other parts. The Arbel company of Douai made chassis frames; Michelin, Bergougnan, and Torrilhon produced rubber tires. From 1896 to 1913 employment in the French rubber industry rose about fourfold to nearly 25,000 persons, an expansion owing primarily to the automobile trade. Although some automakers produced their own open bodies, especially for small models, in most cases carriage makers converted themselves into auto body suppliers. The customer selected a body style at the time of purchase, and it was delivered and attached at the car factory.

Just as the automobile industry gave a great boost to the rubber business, it also provided a new market for aluminum, used for some body and mechanical parts. More important was the auto industry's demand for special steels, originally developed in the 1860s for cutting tools and for naval armament. P & L and De Dion-Bouton pioneered in the use of special steels in their engines and gears.

FOREIGN TRADE

Although France remained the leading European automobile producer before 1914, Great Britain provided by far the largest European market for the new machines. The early French intercity races attracted great attention in Britain and aroused a strong demand there among well-to-do sportsmen. Shortly after the 1895 Bordeaux race the son of René Panhard (of P & L) wrote to his father, "We receive visitors [at the P & L works in Paris] from morning to night, always English, in a never-ending stream. And every day we receive at least ten letters from England."[5] At first productive capacity fell far short of this demand, but beginning in 1898, when French output began to climb rapidly, a large proportion was exported. Britain was the leading buyer and remained

TABLE 2.2 FOREIGN TRADE IN AUTOMOBILES AND PARTS (IN MILLIONS OF $)

	Exports		Imports	
	1907	1913	1907	1913
France	27.9	43.9	1.7	3.8
Britain	6.5	21.1	20.1	31.7
Germany	3.4	20.7	4.3	3.4
Italy	3.9	7.5*	1.6	2.2*
Belgium	1.9	6.1*	0.85	1.9*
U.S.	5.5	32.8	4.8	2.0

* 1912

Source: J. Laux, *In First Gear* (Montreal: McGill-Queen's University Press, 1976), 209.

so until the First World War. At first this was a consequence of the hesitation of British firms to enter the new business; then by 1905, when British production was well under way, French cars had earned a good reputation and their makers had developed fruitful commercial relations with British dealers. In 1907 French automotive exports to Britain amounted to $11.7 million and all French automotive exports $27.9 million.[6]

Belgium, Germany, and the United States also bought sizable amounts of these products. Cars and parts had become the most important French export among metal goods, but at 2.6 percent of total French exports, they still trailed silk cloth, other textiles, clothing, and wines. In later years French automotive exports continued to climb, although at a lower rate as producers elsewhere began to offer more competition, especially on their home ground. As France's share of the British, German, and Italian markets declined, its sales to less developed countries expanded, especially to Algeria, Argentina, Brazil, Spain, and Russia. The rapid rise of American auto exports (see Table 2.2) reflects the success of the Ford and other low- and medium-priced cars in world markets after 1910. Nevertheless, France's head start allowed it to maintain the lead in exports until the war. Throughout the period to 1914, French automotive exports usually amounted to about half of total production.

As Table 2.2 suggests, French dominance of the European automobile industry began to lose its luster in the three or four years before the First World War. Automobile technology had developed in industrial centers all over Europe from indigenous sources, from the international trade in cars and parts, and from the movement of engineers. When businessmen elsewhere realized that there was a real market for these machines, they plunged in and competed vigorously with the French producers.

SMALLER CARS

The mild economic recession of late 1907 and 1908 halted the expansion of the French auto industry, as it did elsewhere in Europe, but growth resumed in 1909. These years, 1907-1909, mark a turning point in the European automobile industry. The sales slump warned automakers that the market might not expand continually and that they should look more closely at their consumers and try to win them by adapting their products to the public's perceived needs.[7] In consequence, a growing segmentation of the market appeared: more small and inexpensive cars, and more specialized commercial vehicles. Producers devoted more attention to making cars easier to start and to drive, culminating in the adoption of the reliable electric self-starter introduced from the United States in 1912. Just as European producers offered more cars at lower prices, American auto firms were demonstrating that profits could be made with smaller cars. In France the major companies that expanded their output the most from 1910 to 1913 were Peugeot, Berliet, Darracq, and Unic. Peugeot's sales growth came especially from its "Baby," a very small four-cylinder model at a low price, and the other three offered robust machines in the lower half of the middle-price range. Unic began as the Georges Richard Company in 1904 with a policy of making one model only. This strategy did not last long, but the firm succeeded in selling its cars as taxicabs in London.

Shortly after Unic cabs entered service in London in 1906, cabs made by Renault also appeared there. This company's early success had been with small cars employing direct drive. Participation in races had publicized its products and earnings had been reinvested in more productive facilities so that by 1905 it had its own foundry and body shop. Its largest seller starting in 1905 was a two-cylinder taxicab, of which three to four thousand plied the streets of Paris by 1914. Renault also sold cabs in London (over 1,100), Mexico City, Melbourne, and other major cities of the world. These mundane vehicles were the foundation of its pre-1914 success. Darracq, De Dion-Bouton, Delahaye, and Clément also provided taxicabs.

Several other French companies offered small cars in these years. Two in the Paris region were Sizaire-Naudin beginning in 1906 and Zèbre beginning in 1910. Neither appears to have produced over 1,000 in a year. As French automakers began to pay more attention to the low and medium price range, they sold more cars with standard bodies to reduce the total price to customers. They made these bodies in their own shops, or bought body-making companies, or contracted with independent body firms to supply several standard designs. The same trend toward standardization occurred elsewhere in Europe.

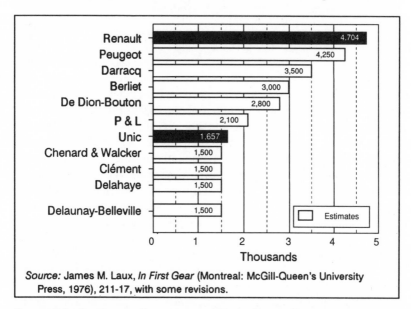

Source: James M. Laux, *In First Gear* (Montreal: McGill-Queen's University Press, 1976), 211-17, with some revisions.

FIGURE 2.1 AUTOMOBILE PRODUCTION BY MAJOR FRENCH FIRMS, 1913

Although the Americans were demonstrating after 1908 that small, four-cylinder cars at a price under $1,000 would dominate the market, most French producers refused to accept this. Only about 6,000 of the 45,000 automobiles built in 1913 fell into this range. Just before the war a very small complete one-cylinder car could be had for about $600 and a small four-cylinder model for $800. The Ford model T – larger and more reliable than these types – gained only a modest success in France. In 1914, 978 were sold there, at prices ranging from $800 to $1,050, a much less impressive showing than in Britain. Ford's impact in France was primarily indirect, through his very large British sales, which cut into the French market share there, and especially through his demonstration in Detroit of mass-production methods, epitomized by the moving assembly lines introduced in 1914. Nevertheless, French carmakers tended to disbelieve in a mass market for automobiles in their own country. Average incomes were lower than in the United States and they doubted that production costs could be cut sharply enough to offer reliable cars at prices comparable to Ford, Willys-Overland, and Maxwell in America. Several actually began to diversify out of cars after 1908, moving into aircraft engines (Renault, Clément), and trucks (Renault, Berliet, Delahaye, and Peugeot).

COMMERCIAL VEHICLES

Some 125,000 motor vehicles circulated in France by 1914, about one for every 318 inhabitants (excluding about 34,000 motor bicycles and motorcycles). Motorcars, then, did not yet affect very many French people through personal ownership. Bicycles had a greater significance, for the 3.5 million bicycles in 1914 amounted to one for every 11 persons, or one for every four males over 12 years of age. Still, many city dwellers who did not possess a car did have an opportunity to ride in a taxicab or rental car (there were close to 10,000 rental cars in Paris and much smaller numbers in other French cities) and many more, at least in Paris, rode on motor buses.

Gasoline buses were the first type of large commercial vehicle to find wide acceptance in Europe. To be sure, since the late 1890s fashionable department stores, postal services, and other enterprises that wanted speedy urban delivery of high-value items sometimes tried electric or gasoline vans, but these efforts were relatively insignificant next to the hundreds of gasoline buses that began to appear on the streets of London and Paris from 1905 on. Motor buses replaced horse-drawn omnibuses because they were faster, and their high-value "cargo" could load and unload itself quickly. Their speed allowed them to cover more distance per day, carry more passengers, and earn more revenue than the horse carriages.

By 1905 engines and drive trains were powerful and reliable enough for this heavy work. In 1906 the Paris Omnibus Company began replacing its horse-drawn omnibuses with motor buses. Residents could also choose to ride electric tramways that appeared in the late 1890s, or the subway (the first Métro line opened in 1900). By 1913 Paris was served by over 1,000 Schneider-built motor buses, using solid rubber tires, and 200 to 300 supplied by De Dion-Bouton. The last horse-drawn omnibus line in Paris ceased operations in January 1913. The omnibus company's inventory of horses had decreased from 17,500 in 1900 to 628. Provincial cities preferred the electric tram to motor buses, but there was a small market for buses to link small towns without rail or tramline service to large cities. The Berliet company made small buses for this purpose beginning in 1906 and in 1908 produced 200 chassis for buses and trucks.

Early trucks did not compete with railways but with horses, as they performed pickup and delivery service in cities and carried goods to and from railway stations. High prices for trucks – upwards of $2,500 – limited sales, but Germany in 1908 showed a way to expand the market with a subsidy arrangement by which the government assisted the buyer of an authorized truck by paying part of the cost plus an annual sum for maintenance. In return, the army could requisition the truck for its own use in wartime. The French imitated this system in 1910. The Berliet and Delahaye companies in particular took advantage of the military subsidy and also became specialists in service vehicles: postal vans, fire engines, street cleaners, and so forth. The truck market remained very small in France and in the rest of Europe, however; its great expansion would come in the First World War.

By 1914 the French automobile industry employed about 36,000 workers directly (some 70 percent of them in the Paris region), perhaps 10,000 in the rubber trade, and another 10,000 in other components. If we add to this the service employment related to the industry – chauffeurs (over 20,000), taxi and bus drivers, salespeople, and repair mechanics, the total must have approached 100,000. The industry had become the largest segment of the metalworking sector of the economy and was expanding more rapidly than any other major industrial branch in France. We must conclude that the auto industry was instrumental in France's 3.7 percent annual rate of industrial growth from

1900 to 1913. This was not quite as strong as Germany's 4.2 percent rate, but well ahead of Britain's 2.2 percent.

3

THE INDUSTRY BEGINS ELSEWHERE IN EUROPE

In Great Britain, Germany, Italy, and the rest of Europe, no well-established industrial firm (with the exception of Benz) moved into automobile manufacturing until just before the turn of the century. This situation puts into relief the boldness of Peugeot and of Panhard & Levassor in France.

A SLOW START IN GREAT BRITAIN

There were about two dozen motor vehicles for passengers in Britain by the end of 1895, half of them imported from France and Germany, and the rest put together by individual experimenters.[1] But only one (Herbert Austin) of the early British enthusiasts for motorcars was associated in a managerial position with a metalworking firm. In Germany and especially France, production of automobiles came first, then the market; in Britain the opposite was the case.

Several reasons may be advanced as to why British manufacturers hesitated to enter the new business. From the early 1890s to late 1897 the bicycle trade enjoyed a marvelous boom; there was no need for these firms to diversify into another line—at least not yet. Second, various laws collectively known as Red Flag legislation limited speeds of mechanical road vehicles to 4 mph in the country and 2 mph in populated areas, and during certain years required these machines to be preceded by a person waving a red flag to warn those riding or driving horses. These regulations had some merit, for an estimated 8,000 steam traction engines operated in England and Wales in the 1890s.[2] Although only 600 of them had licenses for road haulage, most did use the roads occasionally and the sight of one of these hulking monsters, belching smoke and hissing steam, could and did frighten all

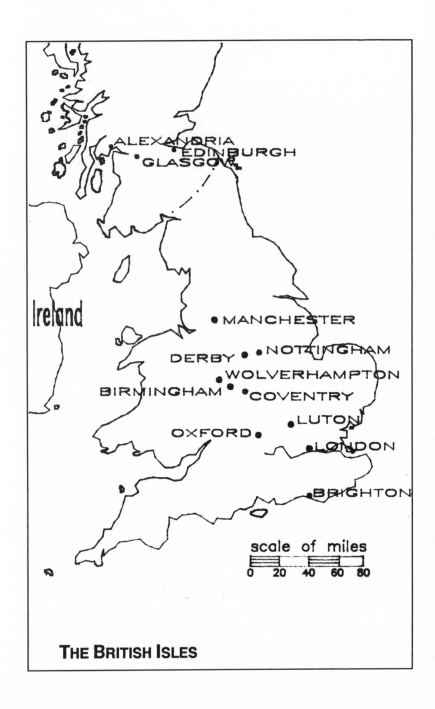

THE BRITISH ISLES

discipline out of normally placid horses. The speed limits may have inhibited some machine-building companies from experimenting with small passenger cars – steam, electricity, or gasoline, and more important, with such restrictions in force it was too risky for a major firm to place substantial resources into car manufacturing.

A third reason was that an unscrupulous company promoter, Harry J. Lawson, jumped into the new auto business and tried to control it to his profit by claiming a monopoly of British rights to key French and German patents.[3] His activities and exaggerated claims may well have discouraged some potential entrants, who feared to become involved in a protracted law suit. Lawson bought the British rights to Gottlieb Daimler's engine patents from Frederick R. Simms, who had held them from 1893 and had imported a small number of Daimler's engines, mainly for marine and stationary purposes. Lawson also obtained a variety of other patent rights and began a grandiose campaign to float stock in new motorcar companies to which he sold licenses to use the patents, for huge sums. Relatively little of the hundreds of thousands of pounds he raised in his motor-promoting activities from 1895 to 1897 actually went into production facilities, but some of the companies he floated finally did begin to produce cars.

As British interest in motorcars began to grow in 1895 and 1896 following reports of races in France and the appearance of a few at home, the Red Flag legislation was soon revised. In August 1896 the law was changed to exempt "light locomotives" (motorcars) weighing less than 3 tons from the earlier restrictions and raise the maximum speed to 14 mph. On the day the new regulations went into effect, 14 November 1896, the flamboyant Harry Lawson arranged for a 52-mile demonstration run of motorcars from London to Brighton. Somewhat over 30 vehicles started the run, including some electric models and gasoline tricycles, two Duryea cars from the United States, and a steam-powered bicycle from Paris. Almost all of the machines were of French and German manufacture. Lawson's publicity machine attracted huge crowds – perhaps 500,000 all told – and he delighted them, driving off in the lead car dressed in a fancy uniform that made him resemble a "Swiss admiral." About 20 cars finished the run, although it was managed in such a slapdash manner that some of them may have done part of it on the train. Despite all the excitement surrounding this affair, British motorcar production continued to develop only very slowly.

Harry Lawson's reputation began to crumble as his companies were slow to produce cars. His Daimler Motor Company, Ltd., had been organized early in 1896, but not until March 1897 did it turn out its first production car and by July it had sold 20. Most of these early British Daimler cars were assembled from French and German components and only around 1900 did they become largely English-made. Lawson receded into the background in 1898, lost an important patent case in 1901, and went to jail for fraud in 1904.

If Lawson's claims were not enough to discourage entry into the motor business, an extensive strike or lockout in the metalworking trades may have done so. This dispute lasted from July 1897 until early 1898. During these months it distracted managements and when it ended many may have been loath to begin a new manufacturing venture, for they were strained financially and eager to fill orders that had been delayed.[4]

DISPERSED LOCATION

Harry Lawson had established his Daimler company in a disused cotton mill in Coventry, the center of British bicycle manufacturing, and so helped determine that this city and the English Midlands generally would become the major center of the automobile industry. The staff of several other Coventry auto firms would include workers who had learned the trade at Daimler. Another Coventry firm, Humber, had begun making bicycles in Beeston, near Nottingham, fell into the hands of Lawson in 1887, and was refinanced in 1895 by Lawson and a more famous company promoter, E. T. Hooley. After Humber's Beeston factory burned down in 1896 it moved its motor operations to Lawson's mill in Coventry where it may have produced a few of the French-designed Léon Bollée gasoline tricycles. After several years Humber began making significant numbers of real cars. Its 1901 model used a De Dion-Bouton engine and the rest of the design resembled this French make.

Other Coventry bicycle firms were cautious about shifting into the new industry, despite the serious depression sustained by the bicycle trade beginning in late 1897. The Swift company, successor to Coventry Machinists, which had begun the bicycle business in Coventry in 1869, moved to motor tricycles in 1900 and then to cars. The Riley, Singer, and Rover companies followed the same route over the next few years.

Two other early car producers in Coventry did not originate in the bicycle trade. Members of the Maudslay family, makers of marine engines, began producing cars under their own name there in 1902, and their cousin Reginald Maudslay, an engineer, started the Standard Motor company in 1903.

Also in the Midlands, two bicycle firms in Wolverhampton entered the motorcar business at the turn of the century, Star and Sunbeam. Both began by imitating the Benz layout and then adopted De Dion-Bouton engines and its drive system. In Birmingham, the large industrial city between Coventry and Wolverhampton, two engineers began experimenting with gasoline cars in the mid-1890s. Frederick Lanchester's unique design came on the market in 1900. Herbert Austin, a farm boy, had gone to Australia in the 1880s and in Melbourne learned machine-shop practice. He returned to England in 1893 where he managed production for the Wolseley Sheep Shearing Machine Company of Birmingham. Austin had the factory make other products too, including steam engines and bicycle parts. Meanwhile, he put together several experimental cars, but when his own company did not wish to finance their production, he persuaded Vickers, the large armaments firm, to buy out the Wolseley automobile activities and set up a separate Wolseley Tool and Motorcar Company in 1901, with Austin in charge. This operation prospered, making 50 cars in 1901 and 804 in 1904, to lead the country. But Austin and the Vickers people disagreed and Austin left Wolseley to establish the Austin Motorcar Company nearby in December 1905, with financial help from a businessman friend.[5]

A second center of automobile production, after the Midlands, was Glasgow, the heart of metalworking in Scotland. There, George Johnston, an engineer with a locomotive company, built a prototype in 1895, attracted some financial backers, and began selling his Arrol-Johnston car in 1897. His operations moved to nearby Paisley in 1902. Two of Johnston's associates left to begin the Albion company in Glasgow in 1900, which eventually became a significant force in the truck business. The third of the important Glasgow producers, Argyll, was the creation of Alexander Govan. This young mechanic learned engineering design in night school in Glasgow. An early effort to manufacture bicycles failed, and he went south to work in the bicycle trade in the Midlands. Returning to Glasgow in 1895, Govan established a machine shop and car repair business in an idle factory owned by a financial backer. In 1899 he began importing Renault and De Dion-Bouton cars, then imported their parts and assembled them. Gradually he increased the share of locally made parts and began to call his car the Argyll.

Govan reorganized his shop as the Hozier Engineering Company in 1900 with £15,000 ($72,900) capital. Production expanded with a variety of engines available, French or British. By 1904 this company may have turned out 400 cars, the third largest in Britain after Wolseley and Daimler. After trips to the Continent and the United States to view the auto industry there, Govan reorganized his company as Argyll Motors, Ltd., in 1905, with the large capital of £500,000 ($2.43 million). He had an immense factory built at Alexandria, a small town 16 miles northwest of Glasgow. Govan opened his new works in July 1906 with the expectation of employing 3,000 workers and making 2,500 cars per year. Argyll did not reach these figures, for Govan died suddenly at age 38 in May 1907, succumbing to food poisoning after eating lunch at a well-known Glasgow restaurant. This "almost Mozartian death" deprived the Scottish motor industry of its most promising entrepreneur. After the recession late in 1907 and 1908 reduced demand for Argyll cars, the company struggled on, but it never recovered the élan imparted by its founder.

Although London was by far the largest market for automobiles in Britain, as it had almost one-fourth of the registrations in 1905, it did not become more than a secondary center for their manufacture. Of the many firms that began production there, two deserve mention. Napier, a veteran machine and hardware maker, began offering cars in 1900, luxury types at first, and then it added a successful taxicab in 1908. Vauxhall, a producer of small steam engines for river and marine work, turned to motorcars in 1903. Making almost all of the components itself, it turned out 120 cars in two years and then moved its auto manufacturing to Luton, some 30 miles north of London, in 1905. There it gradually expanded, producing 197 in 1909.

Other British automobile firms began to operate successfully in a variety of cities, a pattern of dispersal quite unlike the French centralization in Paris, but similar to the German experience. In Manchester the Marshall bicycle company adapted a French design in the late 1890s. By 1901 it was calling its cars Belsize; some used French-made engines. More renown went to the Rolls-Royce. Henry Royce, who operated a shop making electrical equipment in Manchester, tinkered with several cars in 1903-1904, all on French lines. Charles S. Rolls, a young sportsman and aristocrat who ran a motorcar dealership in London selling high-quality French and Belgian cars, tested one of Royce's machines, found the excellence he was seeking, and contracted to sell them under the name Rolls-Royce. Over the next two years Royce made about 100 expensive cars in five different models ranging from two to eight cylinders. In 1907 he introduced his masterpiece, the six-cylinder Silver Ghost, and the firm settled on a one-model policy. Now incorporated as Rolls-Royce, Ltd., in 1908 it moved into a new factory in Derby, 35 miles northeast of Birmingham, where it made several hundred cars annually. Rolls-Royce competed in the high-quality, high-price market, where it was outsold by Delaunay-Belleville and the German Daimler's Mercedes in the pre-1914 years. But Charles Rolls had left the scene. Ever the sportsman, after a fling with hot-air ballooning he took up heavier-than-air aviation in its pioneer days and crashed to his death in a Wright aircraft in 1910, the first Briton to die in an aviation accident.

PUBLICITY

As the founding dates mentioned for these various firms suggest, many British entrepreneurs began to take cars seriously about 1900. By this time it was clear that gasoline would be the preferred power source and that the demand for cars would be permanent. These points received a solid endorsement in the Thousand Miles Reliability Run of spring 1900, sponsored by the Automobile Club of Great Britain and Ireland. This demonstration extended from London to Edinburgh and back, visiting many cities along the way. About half of the 65 starters finished, just a few of them British-made, but including Herbert Austin in his Wolseley, a Napier, a Lanchester, and some Daimlers, largely of continental manufacture. This run served the same purpose as the over-the-road racing in France, to publicize the cars and to allow potential buyers and investors to distinguish among them. Like the French, the British also publicized cars by auto shows and through journalism.

CAPITAL AND COMPONENTS

There was no dearth of capital for investment in the industry. Existing firms shifted resources to motorcars and when newcomers had demonstrated their seriousness they often expanded by means of public share offerings. The flood of publicity about the new industry attracted many investors.

Components makers appeared more slowly in Britain than they had in France. Until about 1905 many of the British firms used engines from De Dion-Bouton or Aster, a French firm with a licensee near London. Other French parts also found a good market in Britain. Alexander Govan of Argyll testified in 1905 that his company obtained its cylinder blocks from France because British castings were unsuitable. In the following year a British technical journal complained, "Most English [car] makers prefer to obtain springs and axles from French manufacturers."[6] The French head start and the British free-trade policy do much to explain this preference. Ultimately, specialists did appear in Britain: White and Poppe of Coventry for engines, Lucas of Birmingham for electrical equipment, and Sankey of Bilston for pressed-steel body parts and wheels. As on the Continent, auto bodies usually were produced by specialist companies.

TAXES, EXPANSION, AND NEW COMPETITORS

After the recession of 1908, British auto production expanded more rapidly and several companies began to turn out over a thousand cars per year. As this occurred, Parliament finally in 1909 approved a tax on motorcars, after France (1898), Italy (1906), and Germany (1906). As in other countries, the tax was based on fiscal horsepower. The annual rate ranged from $10.22 for a small model under 6.5 fiscal hp to $20.44 for a medium-powered 12-16 fiscal hp, to much larger amounts for high-powered prestige and racing cars. Motorcycles paid $4.87, and most taxicabs $13.87.[7] Also in 1909 Britain began to impose a tax on gasoline, 3 pence per gallon. Income from both taxes was designated for highway improvements.

Another symptom of the increasing motorization of Britain was the burgeoning number of automobile fatalities. In 1909 motorcars were involved in 373 fatal accidents; in 1914 the number rose to 1,329, more than those attributed to horse-drawn vehicles.[8] Earlier, in a House of Lords debate of 1903 on a bill to regulate motorcar speeds, Lord Wemyss had warned about motorists "in goggles and a ghastly sort of headgear too horrible to behold. It was clear that when they put on that dress they meant to break the [speed] law."[9] As experience would show, the noble lord's fears were not unfounded.

One of the newer entrants to the expanding industry was the large armaments firm, Armstrong-Whitworth, which took over a failing London carmaker in 1904, moved production to its plant in Newcastle, and gradually expanded output to about 750 chassis in 1913, at very high prices. The primary aim was to keep the company's skilled work force occupied; when the war broke out the firm's auto production ended.[10] Armstrong's major competitor in the military field, Vickers, did better with its subsidiary, Wolseley, which made some 3,000 cars in 1913.

The Ford situation was unique in Britain. This American firm began exporting cars to England late in 1903 and experienced only mediocre results until its small four-cylinder Model N arrived in 1907. The Model T, a larger and better machine first displayed in London in November 1908, sold quite well and Ford established a branch in London under the direction of Percival Perry. At this point the manufacturer shipped the cars unassembled and the branch put them together; they sold 1,023 in the two years beginning October 1909. Anticipating a boom in sales, Perry, at Ford's direction, opened a larger assembly operation in Manchester in October 1911. Some locally made parts were gradually incorporated. Selling at £125 ($600) and up, Ford sales led the country in 1912 at 3,187, then rose to 7,310 in 1913 and 8,352 in 1914, making English Ford the largest producer in Britain and Europe and demonstrating the existence of a large market for low-priced cars.[11]

Some British companies fought back against this new factor on the British market. Singer offered a small four-cylinder model at $950. Another Coventry firm, Hillman, sold a comparable machine at $975, and from France the Baby Peugeot sold in Britain for $825, but all of these were smaller in size and power than the Ford.

The Ford competitor who ultimately would win considerable success was William R. Morris.[12] He grew up on a farm near Oxford and entered the bicycle business in that city in the 1890s. After 1900 he moved into motorcycles, car repair and rental, and car sales. By 1912 he employed some 25 workers in four small shops. In 1910 Morris began planning to manufacture automobiles. Like Renault and Ford, Morris started as an assembler, leaving the cost of designing, developing, and machining components to his suppliers, who by now were numerous in Britain. The capital requirements were therefore minimal: $19,450 from a wealthy friend, Morris's own slender cash reserves, and his good reputation as a businessman were sufficient. Assembling the parts in the buildings of a former school, Morris began production in April 1913 and had completed 1,300 of his light, four-cylinder Oxford model by August 1914. They sold at a base price of $850. Meanwhile, anticipating a higher rate of production in the future, Morris sailed to the United

States twice in early 1914 to order the major components for his somewhat larger Cowley model, scheduled for 1915. He found he could get
the quantities he wanted at much lower prices in Detroit than at home.
These parts began to arrive after the war broke out and Morris assembled another 1,350 cars.

   With the Fords marketed by Perry and the inexpensive cars offered
by other British firms, the British automobile market began in 1912 to
shift toward the low end of the price range. It has been estimated that
some 11,800 low-priced cars (under £200 or $975) were sold in 1913,
perhaps 20 percent of the total and probably about the same proportion
as in France during that year.[13]

TAXICABS

Although electric cabs misfired in London at the turn of the century,
once gasoline cabs began to circulate there in 1906 they soon took over
this business. At the end of 1906, 10,324 horse cabs operated in London
and only 96 gasoline machines.[14] Most of the latter were French, made
by the Georges Richard (Unic) company. In that year French capitalists
formed the General Motor Cab Company to put large numbers of
French cabs on the streets of London. Their initial batch of 70 Renault
two-cylinder cabs, provided with taximeters to calculate fares accurately, appeared in March 1907. The firm added more Renault cabs as
quickly as they could be delivered. The same financial group also took
part in launching the United Motor Cab Company in 1907. It used Unic
and Darracq machines. In 1908 these two cab firms merged to form the
London General Cab Company. (The same financial group also began
the New York Motor Cab Company in 1907, using 600 Darracq cabs.)
The French near-monopoly on London cabs was challenged by the Fiat
Motor Cab Company, which introduced 400 of its own cabs, and in
1909 by the W. & G. du Cros firm. This company was operated by sons
of Harvey du Cros of the Dunlop company and employed Napier and
Panhard & Levassor vehicles. Within a few years Unic cabs became the
most numerous in London, but British makes including Napier,
Wolseley, Belsize, and Austin began to appear more frequently. At the
end of 1910 the 6,397 motor cabs outnumbered horse cabs, and by the
end of 1913 only 1,933 horse cabs remained, compared with 8,397
motor cabs.

COMMERCIAL VEHICLES

The French leadership in passenger cars did not repeat in buses and trucks. The British took to these vehicles more quickly and probably made more of them before 1914. One reason for this may have been their familiarity with steam-powered road haulers. In addition, Britain had a smaller mileage of competing rural tram railways than did France.

After the speed limit went up in 1896, lighter and faster steam wagons, buses, and traction engines came into service, heating their boilers with coke, oil, or kerosene. Steam wagons carried up to six tons on their platforms and several more tons on a trailer. They moved at 8 to 12 mph. Among the more successful producers were Clarkson (with buses), Foden, Leyland, Sentinel, and Thorneycroft. The Fowler company of Leeds specialized in steam road tractors, pulling, among other things, wagons of home furniture and very large loads of industrial equipment, too big for the railways.[15] Precise figures for production and sales of these road steamers are not available, but perhaps 3,000 were in use in 1913.

The Thomas Tilling company introduced gasoline buses to London in 1904. The number rose quickly to exceed 1,000 in 1908 and reached 3,400 by the end of 1913.[16] At first foreign manufacturers supplied many of these vehicles: De Dion-Bouton from France and from Germany Daimler and Büssing. The London General Omnibus Company began to manufacture its own buses in 1909. Its B model of 1910 with double deck and worm drive experienced great success. Management reorganized this operation as a subsidiary under the name Associated Equipment Company in 1912. Making one standard model, it became the largest bus builder in Britain, furnishing some 2,500 through 1913, and then, during the First World War, produced a large share of the British trucks.

Motor bus services outside London began about 1903 when several of the major railways introduced them to serve thinly populated regions. Local entrepreneurs did the same with independent bus lines. Later, in large cities such as Birmingham, motor buses were adopted to supplement electric streetcar networks.[17]

The market for gasoline trucks grew more slowly than for buses. Some producers, such as Halley, Leyland, and Thorneycroft, came from the steam wagon business. Others, like Albion and Dennis, shifted partially or entirely from passenger cars to trucks. Commer and Karrier entered truck making without a background in vehicles. Most of these trucks engaged in pickup and delivery of high value merchandise in cities, especially London, but they hardly dented the market. In 1913 88 percent of goods vehicles in London were still horse powered. At this time there may have been 20,000 to 40,000 gasoline trucks operating in the country, with production in 1913 amounting to about 5,000. Britain also had a military truck subsidy scheme like those of the continental powers but on a very small scale.

MOTORCYCLES

At the other extreme, the motorcycle side of the industry raced ahead in Britain. Significant production of these machines began on the Continent in the 1890s with Hildebrand & Wolfmuller of Munich and Werner Brothers of Paris. Eventually many English bicycle firms entered this business, with Triumph of Coventry the most successful. All sorts of variants were attempted, including a four-cylinder engine as early as 1896 and sidecars in 1903. About 1910 the trade began to expand at a rapid pace, responding to a powerful demand from young men who could not afford a car. At the 1911 Motor Cycle Show 55 separate British makers exhibited machines. Prices began at about $125 for a lightweight model. By 1914, 124,000 motorcycles were registered in Britain, far ahead of France at about 33,750 and Germany with 22,500. The British number hinted at a large potential market for small cars.

FOREIGN TRADE

Britain continued to import large numbers of cars and parts through 1913 (see Table 2.2). The French share of these imports, although remaining the largest, declined before the onslaught of cheaper cars from the United States from 1910 on. Britain's free-trade policy explains in part its large numbers of automotive imports. One analysis has found that a high tariff would have encouraged the growth of the British automobile industry before 1914.[18] Other European producers had modest duties on automotive imports, 3 percent of the value for Germany, 5 percent for Italy, 10 percent for France, and 12 percent for Belgium. Exports from Britain climbed steeply starting in 1910, with Australia the leading market, followed by New Zealand, India, South Africa, Argentina, and Russia.

By 1914 heavy imports and growing home production had made Britain the most motorized of the major European countries. The number of registered motorcars and trucks in that year was 210,000 (one estimate is as high as 265,000), compared with 125,000 in France, 70,515 in Germany, and 23,924 in Italy.[19]

GERMANY

In Germany a wide variety of firms began experimenting with automobile production from 1898 on (see Table 3.1). One reason was the obvious success of Benz, whose production rose from 181 in 1896 to 603 in 1900, and the sale of a greater share of these cars at home (43 percent in 1900). Also, as the bicycle market dried up late in 1897 many of the bicycle makers considered a new line of products, either motorizing their machines or moving to full-sized cars. Publicity about French achievements with automobiles reinforced these considerations. It is no surprise that many entrants to the new industry came from firms producing bicycles and sewing machines. More than in France and Britain, many carriage and wagon builders also experimented with automobiles, as did general machine shops.

Because the metalworking industry was widely spread in Germany, early auto producers appeared all over the country. Although most of them left the auto business within a few years, enough remained to result in a very dispersed geographic pattern as the industry matured. The German situation thus contrasts with France and its centralization in Paris, and with Britain and its concentration of component firms in the Birmingham-Coventry area. This dispersal–from Stuttgart in the southwest, then in various locations on or near the Rhine northward to Cologne and Aachen, to a broad band eastward ranging from Bremen and Zwickau to Berlin and Stettin–probably had the effect of slowing the growth of the German car industry. The lack of centralization tended to delay the appearance of component manufacturers, for they were not able to supply several auto firms in the same locality and so take advantage of long production runs and the consequent economies of scale. The rarity of component makers in turn made it harder in the very early days for the single entrepreneur to assemble cars on a financial shoestring, so frequent in France and Britain. In addition, craft traditions in Germany retained more power than to the west, and it was

TABLE 3.1 MOTOR VEHICLES PRODUCED BY SOME GERMAN FIRMS, 1898-1914

Year	Benz	Daimler	Opel
1898	435	57	–
1899	572	108	11
1900	603	96	24
1901	385	144	30
1902	226	197	64
1903	172	232	178
1904	?	698	252
1905	?	863	358
1906	?	546	518
1907	?	149	478
1908	646	231	500
1909	1,215	829	845
1910	1,721	1,305	1,615
1911	2,706	1,781	2,251
1912	3,664	2,183	3,202
1913	3,327	1,925	3,081
1914	3,164	1,972	3,519

Sources:

Benz: W. Oswald, *Mercedes-Benz Personenwagen, 1886-1986* (Stuttgart: Motorbuch Verlag, 1986), 16-17, except for 1909, supplied by Dr. Otto Nübel, archivist at Daimler-Benz AG.

Daimler: W. Oswald, *Mercedes-Benz Personenwagen,* 72.

Opel: K. Ludvigsen, *Opel: Wheels to the World* (Princeton, N.J.: Automobile Quarterly, 1975), 96.

judged positive for an auto firm to have as many parts as possible made by skilled craftsmen in its own shops. There were two main exceptions to this practice of in-house manufacturing: many German auto companies began operations by importing finished engines from De Dion-Bouton or other French makers, and many used magnetos and other electrical equipment from Bosch of Stuttgart.

BOSCH

The Bosch story is one – like those of Benz and Horch – where a skilled craftsman through pluck and persistence builds a successful firm

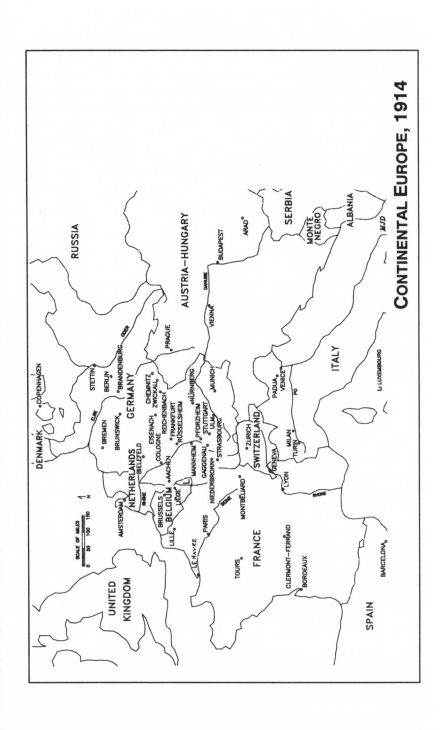

CONTINENTAL EUROPE, 1914

against great odds. Born in 1861, Robert Bosch grew up near and in the city of Ulm in southern Germany.[20] He learned the trade of precision-instrument making and came to specialize in electrical devices. In the mid-1880s he worked in New York City for a time, even meeting Thomas Edison, and then at a Siemens Brothers factory in England. Back in Germany he opened a shop in Stuttgart in 1886 to make electrical equipment. A major problem for gasoline engines in this period was ignition. On early cars neither the hot tube system nor electrical ignition using dry batteries operated reliably. In 1887 Bosch began to make magnetos to provide ignition for stationary gasoline engines. The magneto is a small electric generator that employs the flux from a permanent magnet to produce a current. Bosch gradually improved their performance in the course of the 1890s and delivered his one thousandth in 1896, almost all for stationary engines. As auto production began to increase in Europe, Bosch sold magnetos for cars and developed a type for the fast-running De Dion-Bouton engine. The famous Mercedes car of 1901, made by the Daimler company, used a Bosch magneto and spread its renown. Even better was the high tension magneto invented by Bosch's engineer Gottlob Honold. Introduced in 1902 to an expanding market, this product brought soaring growth to Bosch in the twentieth century. From 45 workers in 1901, the company expanded to 4,500 by 1912, dominating the German and world markets. In 1912 Bosch sold its one millionth magneto, and two years later turned out 6,000 per day.

Meanwhile, in the United States Charles F. Kettering developed an entirely new electrical arrangement for cars. In 1911 he united starting, lighting, and ignition into one system, using a lead-acid storage battery and a generator driven by the engine. To start the car this generator acted as an electric motor, powered by the 24-volt battery. When running, switches converted the starter motor to a generator with 6 volts potential. It supplied ignition current and charged the battery that operated the lights.[21] Previously, night lighting had been provided by burning acetylene gas in the headlights. Introduced first on the 1912 Cadillac car, the generator-battery system ultimately conquered the world automobile industry. Bosch did not suffer, however. Most European automakers continued to use magnetos well into the 1920s and they were necessary for aircraft engines. Bosch adopted its own variant of the Kettering system and branched into other types of automobile parts, most notably fuel injectors for diesel engines.

In 1898 a reported 150 firms manufactured bicycles in Germany, but already international overcapacity had spoiled the market, so some of them tried and found success with automobiles. In Bielefeld, Nikolaus Dürkopp was one of these. Shortly after his birth in 1842 his parents had left him behind when they emigrated to America. Trained as a locksmith, he opened a shop making sewing machines in 1867, later expanding to bicycles and small gasoline engines. Dürkopp offered a car in 1898, on the layout of the heavy Panhard & Levassor machines. Another pioneer, Heinrich Kleyer of Frankfurt am Main, had begun making his Adler (German for "Eagle") bicycles in 1886. Kleyer had a technical education and had spent a brief period working in the United States. He opened a store selling bicycles in Frankfurt in 1880. Soon he began manufacturing bicycles, then typewriters in 1896 and motor bicycles in 1898. His first car appeared in 1900, using a De Dion-Bouton engine. Near Frankfurt, in Rüsselsheim, the Opel works[22] had become a major factor in German sewing machines (1898 production, 25,000) and bicycles (1898 production, 15,000). Its 1,200 workers used 700 machine tools. Operated by the founder's widow and five sons, Opel began in cars in 1899 by producing a few imitation Benz types. When this design fell out of date the company in 1902 began importing Darracq chassis and engines, with bodies supplied by its own shops. Successful with this venture, Opel began to install more of its own parts on these vehicles. In 1903 it produced 178 cars. Far to the east in Stettin, the Stoewer machine shop went from bicycle parts to motorcycles and then to cars in 1899, using De Dion-Bouton engines. This firm soon became independent of outside suppliers and made most of its own components for a wide variety of models.

Less common in Germany than in France or Britain was the individual entrepreneur setting up his own automobile firm. Daimler did start his own company, of course, and with much delay began producing cars; another example was August Horch, a craftsman who spent his early years working in machine shops all over Germany and to the southeast as far as Bulgaria.[23] He joined Benz in 1896 and rose to become head of auto production by 1899. At this point Horch left to establish his own auto repair shop near Cologne. He operated his first prototype car in

1901 and a year later moved his modest operation 235 miles eastward
to Reichenbach, a small town in the heavily populated metalworking
area of upper Saxony. In 1904 he moved again, a short distance to the
larger city of Zwickau. Before long other motorcar companies appeared in this region.

In the Thuringian town of Eisenach, Heinrich Ehrhardt had a factory making horse-drawn military vehicles. In 1898 he began producing
a light car called the Wartburg, after a nearby castle made famous by
Martin Luther. Its design was licensed from the French firm,
Decauville. The company built 197 cars in the six years through 1903,
one of the country's larger producers in this period. When Ehrhardt left
the scene in 1903, the factory's cars were baptized with the name Dixi, a
colloquial expression meaning "the last word." Robust and reliable,
Dixi cars sold well in prewar Germany.

Two huge Berlin firms had moderate success at the beginning of
the industry. The AEG (General Electric Company, with no connection
to the American, British, or French firms of the same name) was a
major producer of electric power and electrical equipment. In 1902 it
bought two small Berlin shops that had made a few cars, AAG and
Külstein, and merged them under the name NAG (New Automobile
Company). Berlin wits said the initials stood for "Nie Automobil
Gewesen" ("Never will be a car"). Nevertheless, the engineer Rudolf
Diesel bought a custom-made NAG for about $5,000.[24] Supported by
its parent's large financial resources, this firm produced a great variety
of reliable cars and buses. The Siemens group, which by 1914 employed
some 82,000 worldwide and was the major rival of AEG in the German
electrical industry, in 1906 began making a few electric and gasoline-
electric (with a gasoline engine generating current for electric-drive
motors) vehicles in Berlin. It bought the small Protos company of
Alfred Sternberg in 1908 and phased out the electric models. Like
NAG, Protos cars were considered high quality. Another large firm,
North German-Lloyd, a leading shipping and shipbuilding company of
Bremen, established the NAMAG (North German Automobile and
Motor Company) in 1906. It began with electric cars built on a license
from the Paris firm of Kriéger but also shifted to gasoline models by
1908. This company's Lloyd cars did not sell widely. As was almost
always the case, cars made as a minor diversification by a large concern
did not become a major factor in the industry.

In the first few years of the twentieth century none of the firms just mentioned played as significant a role as Benz and Daimler. After reaching a peak of 603 cars manufactured in 1900, Benz plunged into an eclipse. Its old fashioned designs, together with growing competition from other German cars and imports from France severely hurt its business. Production fell to 172 in 1903. Carl Benz reacted slowly so his associates brought in a French expert, Marius Barbarou, to design a racing car and they put other engineers to work preparing new models of production cars incorporating recent innovations. Agitated and irritated by all these changes, Carl Benz left the active management of the firm. Because his racers failed to win, Barbarou returned to Paris, but Benz's sales began to climb again in 1905.

Expanding steadily along with the German auto industry as a whole, Benz in 1907 bought a small producer in Gaggenau and built a large new factory in suburban Mannheim in 1908. To its cars in the middle- and high-price ranges, Benz added an 8-fiscal-hp low-priced model late in 1911. This car became Benz's sales leader in the prewar years. Friedrich Nallinger, director of the company, wanted to reduce its range of models from eight to two, but the supervisory board vetoed this. Benz also produced 450 to 650 trucks annually in the Gaggenau works during 1911-13. In the last years before the war Benz was Germany's largest producer, with some 6,000 workers making 3,327 vehicles in 1913.[25]

The Daimler company had begun to work on cars seriously in 1897. Wilhelm Maybach and Paul Daimler (Gottlieb Daimler's son) designed them, following the Panhard & Levassor layout with the engine in front, transmission behind, and chain drive operating the rear wheels, using engines with two, four, and five cylinders. Gradually Maybach increased the power of these cars, especially on the urging of Emil Jellinek. This man, son of a prominent rabbi in Vienna, had made a fortune in insurance. He now lived in Nice, on the French Riviera, and by 1898 was selling German Daimler cars to his wealthy friends there.[26] In fact, Jellinek was the major outlet for the small number produced. He kept hectoring the company to modernize its design and increase the power. As Jellinek's star rose in the company, Gottlieb Daimler's fell and the engineer died in 1900.

The careers of Carl Benz and Gottlieb Daimler, who never met even though they worked less than 70 miles apart, present a curious parallel. Both men preferred not to modernize their designs or to engage in racing, but when their companies passed into other hands these things were done, with great success.

Early in 1901 Maybach and Paul Daimler began delivering a new model, named Mercedes after Jellinek's daughter. The Mercedes performed very well in some races and established a high standard for luxury cars. It popularized some new devices including a honeycomb radiator and pressed steel (in place of wood) chassis frames. For the first time in Europe a car that was not French set the style for automobile design. The Daimler company, with a winner on its hands, began to expand. In 1902 it bought a small producer in Berlin operated by one of its directors that sold cars under the name Daimler. It concentrated manufacture of commercial vehicles there. The main establishment moved into a new factory in the Stuttgart suburb of Untertürkheim in 1904. Production climbed from 96 in 1900 to 863 in 1905, and prices rose also. In 1898 a Daimler catalog listed cars ranging from 3,800 to 7,000 marks ($905 to $1,667), but strong demand for the Mercedes a few years later allowed the company to ask well over 10,000 marks ($2,381) for them. For all their fame, Daimler's Mercedes cars, as well as its trucks and buses, did not sell well in Germany. Of 2,685 vehicles produced from 1902 through 1907 nearly 80 percent were exported, and only 576 went to domestic buyers. Daimler concentrated on the high end of the market and was slow to modernize its production methods, so its output did not grow rapidly after 1904 and its market share declined as other companies entered the business. By 1909 Daimler's production of 671 passenger cars ranked third in Germany behind Opel (845) and Benz (781).[27]

PUBLICITY AND SMALL CARS

The demonstration runs and races in France and Britain had their echo in Germany with the annual Herkomer runs from 1905 through 1907. These reliability contests, continued by the Prince Henry tours from 1908 on, effectively publicized cars outside the major cities. Gasoline taxicabs appeared also. By 1914 there were 2,459 taxis in Berlin but only 327 in Hamburg, out of a national total of 7,451.[28]

The German government introduced more thorough regulations on cars and driving than did the Western countries and in 1906 began to collect a tax based on fiscal horsepower. Determined by the engine's cylinder displacement, the annual tax climbed as the engine's fiscal horsepower rose. It ranged from about 1 percent to 3 percent of the original cost of a car, and so provided a modest incentive to buyers of small cars. The German auto tax was slightly higher than the French and Italian taxes, and the British levy of 1909.

As in France and Britain, small cars began to take a larger share of the growing German market after 1910. Since 1904 Opel always had offered one or two small models called doctor's cars. In 1905 the bicyclemaker NSU in Neckarsulm, halfway between Stuttgart and Mannheim, began producing a few small and inexpensive cars. (Benz's successful venture into small cars from 1911 on has already been mentioned.)

In German Alsace there emerged two quite different examples of small cars, both of which involved Ettore Bugatti.[29] This young Italian from an artistic family of Milan first encountered automobiles when he learned to drive and race a local imitation of the De Dion-Bouton tricycle in 1898. Then, without any engineering training, he began to design cars. In 1901 one of these managed to win one of the 10 prizes in a race near Milan and this publicity, along with Bugatti's charm and self-confidence, earned him a position as an automobile designer for De Dietrich, a railway equipment firm in Niederbron, German Alsace, whose head was a cousin of the De Dietrich of the Lorraine-Dietrich company in Lunéville, France. Bugatti's undistinguished work there led to his dismissal in 1905. During this period he also designed some models for a large Strasbourg car dealer, Emile Mathis, but they also failed. Nevertheless, Bugatti caught on with the Deutz concern of Cologne, the company that had first developed the Otto four-cycle gasoline engine in the 1870s. Bugatti's cars failed again and Deutz showed him the door in 1909. By now the Italian had learned something of his craft and late in 1909 he established his own firm in Molsheim near Strasbourg with financial aid from a banker friend. Here he began to manufacture a small sports car that in fact owed a great deal to the design of a small Isotta Fraschini car prepared for this Milanese firm by its reclusive genius G. G. Stefanini. As Bugatti's production rose from five in 1910 to 175 in 1913, he also prepared the plans for a very small car and sold them to Peugeot, which marketed this machine very successfully as the Baby. In Strasbourg, Mathis then brought on the market a copy of the Peugeot, called the Babylette.

To the east a new producer, Brennabor, located in the small city of Brandenburg, 40 miles west of Berlin, had begun with baby carriages and bicycles, then offered motorcycles in 1902, and finally presented cars in 1908. This concern concentrated on the low- and middle-price range (from $850 up) and sold several thousand cars per year by 1912-13. Not far to the south in Schonau, a suburb of Chemnitz, the Wanderer works followed a similar evolution, moving from bicycles into typewriters, motorcycles, and then small cars in 1911.

Accurate production figures for most German automobile firms in these years are not available, but a rough estimate would be 25 to 30 percent of the 1913 production was 8 hp or less, led by Brennabor, Benz, Wanderer, and Opel. The trend to smaller cars in Germany then, paralleled that in the Western countries.

Daimler remained aloof from the small car, and so did August Horch. In 1909 Horch left the company he had begun in Zwickau, but a court ruled that he had to leave his name with it. So for his new auto company nearby he used the name Audi (Horch means "listen" in German and in Latin it translates to "audi"). Neither the Audi nor Horch companies adopted the small-car strategy.

BUSES AND TRUCKS

Like France and Britain, Germany produced only a few gasoline trucks in the early years of the twentieth century. There was a slightly larger market for buses, especially in England where Daimler and Büssing sold some around 1905. In Germany, however, the bus business never developed as in the Western countries. At the beginning of 1914 the entire German Empire employed only 907 buses, of which 290 were in Berlin and only two small ones in Hamburg. The electric streetcar was well entrenched. Truck use began to grow more rapidly in 1907. In the seven years from that date until 1914 the number of trucks registered rose 10-fold, from 957 to 9,639.[30] A small share of this growth came from the military subsidy system that went into effect in 1908. By 1912, 825 trucks had qualified for the subsidy, about one-tenth of those in service. The leading truck producers included Benz, Daimler, Büssing, NAG, and Mannesmann-Mulag of Aachen. A unique story lay behind the Büssing company. Its founder, Heinrich Büssing of Brunswick, had trained as a blacksmith and then helped establish a firm making railway signal boxes in 1873. After a very successful career, Büssing left the active management of this enterprise at age 60 and set up a company in 1903 to make trucks and buses.[31] Its business was very slow at first, as it disposed of only thirty trucks through 1907 along with 133 buses. Its sturdy machines made Büssing a leading subsidy truck maker but less significant than Benz, which produced 2,773 trucks and buses from 1908 through 1913, and Daimler, which turned out 1,445 over the same period. These two firms, with their powerful engines and heavy chassis for cars, could easily make commercial vehicles. Nevertheless, German truck making was quite a small factor in 1914, less so than in Britain or France, a situation that would have consequences during the war that began in that year.

FOREIGN TRADE

As in Britain, the German auto industry as a whole grew rapidly from 1909, and, as Table 2.2 shows, began to take a larger share of the international market. By 1913 Russia had become the leading buyer of German automotive products, followed by Austria-Hungary, Great Britain, and Argentina. The Germans too were moving into the less-developed countries.

ITALY

Automobile production and sales in Italy trailed well behind the three more highly industrialized countries just examined. Around 1900 most of the cars sold there were French chassis with locally manufactured bodies. A handful of firms began to make the chassis themselves, and by 1905 Italy produced more cars than it imported (see Table 3.2). The domestic market was small, as average income was low, so most Italian automakers at first aimed primarily at the export market with large luxury and sports models. Several succeeded and from 1907 on exports surpassed imports.

The northern cities of Turin and Milan quickly became the centers of the industry. Each had a foundation of small machine shops, railway equipment builders, and carriage makers, along with the skilled metalworkers employed in these establishments. As it was the most economically developed part of the country, northern Italy also was the center of the domestic market for cars.

In Milan the Bianchi bicycle works made a few cars in the late 1890s and in 1899 the Isotta Fraschini company began importing small Renault machines from France. The candlemaker Michele Lanza of Turin began making a handful of cars in 1895. Also in Turin two bicycle

TABLE 3.2 MOTOR VEHICLES PRODUCED BY SOME ITALIAN FIRMS, 1901-1914

Year	Fiat	Year	Fiat	Alfa	Isotta Fraschini
1901	78	1908	1,311		
1902	107	1909	1,848		215
1903	135	1910	1,780	20	125
1904	268	1911	2,631	80	306
1905	461	1912	3,398	150	497
1906	1,149	1913	3,251	205	308
1907	1,420	1914	4,644	272	125

Sources:
Fiat and Alfa: Duccio Bigazzi, "Management Strategies in the Italian Car Industry,
    1906-1945: Fiat and Alfa Romeo," in *The Automobile Industry and Its Workers*, ed.
    E. Tolliday and J. Zeitlin (New York: St. Martin's, 1987), 77.
Isotta Fraschini: Compiled from Angelo T. Anselmi, *Isotta Fraschini* (Milan: Editoriale
    Milani, 1977), 252-358.

mechanics, Giovanni and Matteo Ceirano, started producing a few automobiles designed by Aristide Faccioli in 1898. Such tinkering did not
lead to success, however. Rather, it was a group of wealthy young men
of Turin – Roberto Biscaretti di Ruffia, Emanuele Cacherana di
Bricherasio, Giovanni Agnelli, and others – who in July 1899 established
the Fabbrica Italiana di Automobili di Torino, or Fiat. This company's
first cars followed a prototype of Faccioli's and were made by two local
machine shops until Fiat's new factory on the Corso Dante could be
built and equipped in 1900. Some organizational problems typical of
early auto firms bedeviled Fiat at first: design and experimentation
work was not separated from production, and repair activities interrupted factory routines. Then in 1901 former cavalry officer Giovanni
Agnelli took charge. He insisted on clear lines of authority, with production as the first priority. He began cost accounting and installed
piecework in the shop, with incentive premiums for foremen. He
adopted the best foreign practice, buying parts from France if needed
and offering cars based on Mercedes lines.[32]

In 1903 Fiat's output reached 135 cars. Over the next three years
the company enjoyed a boom and had to enlarge its plant several times.

It aimed to appeal to foreign buyers by entering its cars in races all over Europe and North America and then selling powerful and expensive vehicles to those attracted. Many were. In 1906 its output of 1,149 cars exceeded the largest German producers and probably the British as well. Fiat's best-seller by far was a model with four large cylinders displacing 7.36 liters.

Agnelli followed policies of vertical integration and product diversification. Fiat took control or influence over a steelworks, a foundry, makers of ball bearings and other small parts, a machine-tool producer, woodworking and body shops, a sales agency with a national network, and some public transportation companies. In a country where metalworking on a large scale was much less developed than it was north of the Alps, Fiat was expanding its own industrial infrastructure. It also began to make commercial vehicles in 1903, aircraft engines in 1908, and marine engines, including diesel types in 1909.

The growth of the automobile industry in France and Fiat's success inspired other Italian entrepreneurs. In Turin the Ceirano brothers reappeared; Matteo founded the Itala firm in 1903 and the Spa company in 1906. Giovanni Ceirano was involved with the Rapid and Junior companies begun in 1905 and the Scat in 1906. A former Fiat tester and racing driver Vincenzo Lancia set up the Lancia company in Turin in 1906. Diatto-Clement began assembling the French Clément cars there in 1907.

In Milan, Isotta Fraschini began making its own large models in 1902 and soon entered races to build a reputation. From France, Peugeot established an assembly plant, and Darracq set up a branch. Several Italian investors in the Darracq branch came from southern Italy and wanted to locate the factory in Naples, but Alexandre Darracq and his English ownership group insisted on Milan as close to the market and to an adequate pool of skilled labor.[33] Piacenza, Brescia, Florence, and Genoa also housed small producers in these years.

The Pirelli rubber company of Milan took part in the new industry. It was founded in the 1870s by a former member of Garibaldi's Red Shirts, a revolutionary guerrilla force. It began manufacturing auto tires in 1899 and was the first Italian manufacturing firm to establish a foreign branch – in Spain in 1902. Pirelli dominated the tire business in Italy as did Michelin in France, Dunlop in Britain, and Continental in Germany.

Although the number of motorcars registered in Italy in 1905 barely exceeded 2,000, the government established an annual tax on them and on bicycles, effective at the beginning of 1906. It varied according to the engine's horsepower as determined by cylinder displacement, as elsewhere in Europe. The assessment on a bicycle was $1.93; a motorcycle, $4.63; a small car under 6 hp, $13.61; 6-12 hp, $19.31; 12-16 hp, $23.17; etc. Taxis paid $6.95, most buses $19.31, and trucks various rates. The amount of tax was similar to the French rate for Paris and the British rate of 1909 but less than the 1906 German rate.

The surge to launch Italian automobile companies during 1904-1906 was accompanied by a speculative frenzy in their shares of capital stock, Fiat especially. Through a series of stock splits and intense demand, in 1906 one 25-lire Fiat share reached a price equivalent to 4,625 lire. Such a level could not be maintained, and Fiat stock began to fall late in 1906. Then the recession of 1907 contracted the market for large cars, and they could be sold only by deep price discounting. Some of the new Italian firms disappeared, others scaled back their operations. Fiat, after declaring huge profits in 1905 and 1906, revealed an even greater loss in 1907. This led to official charges of financial manipulation, forcing Agnelli and the board of directors to resign in August 1908. Ultimately, Agnelli was found innocent in 1912 and 1913; in the meantime, however, he continued to dominate the firm, rejoining the board in April 1909. About this time a leading financial institution, the Banca Commerciale Italiana, began to develop close ties with Fiat. Earlier, this and other banks had limited their exposure in the young and risky industry.

In Milan, Isotta Fraschini was saved from failure only when the French Lorraine-Dietrich company bought control in 1907 and advanced large sums to keep it operating. Not until 1911 did Italian interests regain ownership of IF. This company offered about 10 different models every year, selling a handful or a few dozen of each. Its best period was 1911-13 (producing a record 497 in 1912) and in each of these years its best-sellers were the least expensive types, cars in the midrange in power, priced at about 10,000 lire or $1,900.[34] The Darracq branch in Milan had been very slow to begin operations and its cars sold poorly in 1908-1909. In 1910 the Darracq interests reduced their control of the firm, whose name was changed to Anonima Lombarda Fabbrica Automobili, or Alfa, and it began production of locally designed models. Output rose to just 272 in 1914, surpassing IF's modest 125 in that year. Bianchi was the other major producer in Milan, making several hundred large, conventional cars.

In Turin, Itala and Lancia continued to make powerful and expensive cars. Fiat did the same there, and even established an American manufacturing branch in Poughkeepsie, New York, in 1910 to maintain its presence in the United States. Agnelli visited America several times in these years, seeing the Ford plant in 1912, before the introduction of assembly lines there. He tried to reduce Fiat's wide gamut of models and to standardize components among them. Fiat began to sell medium-powered cars of 3- and 2-liter displacement starting in 1906 and did well with them, sometimes as taxicabs. They became Fiat's bread-and-butter passenger cars. Italy, like the other European countries, was moving toward smaller cars. Accurate production figures from 1911 on show that Fiat produced about half of Italy's vehicles in these years. Its jump in output to 4,644 in 1914 made it, along with Renault, the largest motor firm in Europe after Ford of England.

Fiat began making trucks and buses in 1903. The first year of substantial production was 1906, when Fiat produced 52 such vehicles. Output rose slowly to 82 in 1910 but then reached 624 in 1912 and 1,408 in 1914. These numbers show Fiat to be not only Europe's largest truck maker but the only one with a considerable output in Italy, for in 1914 only 1,380 nonmilitary trucks and buses operated in that country. The Italian army's interest in trucks lay behind Fiat's growth in this area. The army's 1911 maneuvers and then the outbreak of the Italo-Turkish War in that year brought Fiat some large orders for 1.5-ton trucks. The war with Turkey was fought in Libya, where Fiat trucks were the only mechanical means of transport. Fiat also received some prewar military truck orders from the Russian government. By 1914 it had some proven truck designs and had made enough of them to have prepared a production system suitable for really large-scale output.[35]

Italy remained the smallest of the four leading automobile-producing countries of Europe by 1914, and without Fiat, Italy's production would have been negligible.

BELGIUM AND OTHER COUNTRIES

Automobile production got under way in Belgium earlier than in Italy but failed to achieve major significance. Bicycle and other metalworking concerns quickly switched to car making, at least 10 of them before 1901. Among the more important were Vivinus of Brussels in 1899 and FN, made by the National Armament Factory in Liège, also in 1899. Germain and Minerva produced large, elegant machines. By 1904 these and other Belgian producers turned out about 1,500 cars per year, supplying most of the domestic market and exporting luxury models.

Automobiles were produced in many of the other countries of Europe, in cities with metalworking traditions such as Barcelona, Geneva, Zurich, Vienna, Prague, Budapest, Amsterdam, and Copenhagen. Although the roads in rural Spain did not encourage automobile travel – an American in 1906 warned drivers "to consider the matter prayerfully before entering upon what is likely to be an unpleasantly unforgettable experience"[36] – the Hispano-Suiza company of Barcelona did make a mark in the business. A Swiss engineer, Marc Birkigt, established the firm in 1904. Hispano-Suiza sold many of its sports-luxury cars in France and Britain and in 1911 set up a branch factory near Paris. Another international movement occurred when the French branch of the Westinghouse company gave up a small auto-making operation in its factory in Le Havre. In 1909 it shipped all its automobile manufacturing equipment to a new firm in Arad, Hungary (now in western Romania). This establishment made a few dozen vehicles and in 1911 was taken over by the Austro-Daimler company.

Russia, despite its wretched roads, became a sizable market for trucks and heavy cars, but manufacturing hardly began before the war. In 1914 about 10,000 motor vehicles of all types operated in the country and one concern, the Russo-Baltic Company, an important railway car producer located in Riga, had assembled some 450 vehicles over several years from components imported from Germany and Belgium.[37]

Automobile manufacturing had become an important industry in Western and Central Europe, employing over 100,000 directly and even more in ancillary positions. Europeans had invented the gasoline car and demonstrated great technical prowess in its development. They had not really developed a mass market for it, however. To do this the producers had to learn to make cars more cheaply, something the Americans were pioneering in the years just before the First World War.

4
MANUFACTURING

When automobile manufacturing began in Europe, cars were assembled in batches, from five to one hundred, as was done in the United States. A few workers would start by bolting wooden or steel frames together on sawhorses at separate stations in a large hall. Then they would add engines, transmissions, wheels, and other components brought to the workstation in carts or by overhead cranes. The assemblers, usually skilled workers, had to adjust ill-fitting parts that rarely were interchangeable. They used files and hammers, working on small benches and at forges nearby. Assembly, then, tended to be slow work. The parts were turned out in the auto firm's own shops or purchased from specialists. Foremen tried to manage production in each shop, controlling, in principle, methods, speed, and coordination of tasks. Academically trained engineers had little to do with production; they rarely went beyond design and experimentation.

Workers, at least in localities with other metalworking shops, were not hard to find. European auto firms did not expand their output so rapidly as to require huge increases in their work forces. They drew the skilled people they needed from bicycle- or machine-building firms, and they had no difficulty attracting teenagers as unskilled helpers.

When the companies began to produce more than a handful of cars per week and price competition became a factor, management began to seek production methods that might simplify and speed output and reduce costs. One approach was to use heavy presses to stamp metal parts into the appropriate shapes rather than cutting them on lathes or milling machines. Stamping produced pieces much faster, made them interchangeable, and required less skilled labor. As the big presses and their dies were quite expensive, this method was suitable only for long production runs. European component manufacturers such as Krupp in Germany, Arbel in France, and Sankey and Rubery Owen in Britain began to stamp auto parts long before the auto firms themselves did.

Another major step was to abandon the customary practice of marking and cutting each piece individually and instead adapting machine tools to make identical parts by providing them with jigs and fixtures that limited the movement of cutting tools. The operator did little more than insert raw stock and remove the finished part. With such arrangements one person might even work two or three machines at the same time. Both the standard machine tools that were altered to single-purpose machines and, later, machines specifically designed to perform a complex task, such as drilling several holes in a cylinder block at the same time, speeded production and could be manned by semiskilled or "specialized" labor.

To increase labor productivity, management sometimes put pressure on foremen to supervise closely or to "drive" their workers. The amount of effort skilled workers put forth was a matter of custom. Everyone realized that it was much less than the possible maximum. Workers enforced this restrictionism with informal social pressure in the shops, and most foremen did not try to confront it vigorously. This situation was much more prevalent in Europe than in the United States.[1] "Driving" fostered strong resentment by workers irritated at a challenge to their custom, and their skilled status made them difficult to discipline. Shops that practiced driving usually had a high rate of labor turnover. So managements in auto factories all over Europe tended to prefer piecework systems. These usually provided for a minimum daily wage plus a bonus for each piece or each job finished above a standard number. The theory was that discipline would come not from a foreman but would be internalized by rewarding workers for the quantity of their output.

Piecework was not new. It had been used for decades in small sectors of European industry but until the twentieth century affected only a minority of workers. Piecework rates usually were set so that workers on this system earned more than day workers. More intensive work brought a greater reward. It brought conflicts too, as workers and management might disagree over the rates, especially upon the introduction of new machines and new methods. The addition of a new fixture to a machine tool might double its output. In what proportion should the productivity gain be shared between the worker and the company? Then too, as a worker gained experience with a job his output might increase with the same effort. If management then cut the pay per piece conflict might develop. In general, it appears that workers, especially skilled ones, learned to adjust their speed to take advantage of piecework bonuses but not to work so fast as to bring a readjustment of the rate. Social pressure from their fellows usually restrained workers from exceeding this optimum speed. The result was that workers maintained most of their control over what happened on the shop floor.[2] In some cases managements recognized what was happening and countered with complex premium bonus systems. These amended standard piecework so as to cut the rate without appearing to do so. Generally, then, piecework did bring somewhat greater output per person, while continuing to allow workers to determine their expenditure of effort and to control the shop. It meant relatively light supervision of labor. If coupled with a rigorous inspection system it did not lead to low-quality work.

Piecework might apply to small teams as well as to individuals. Two or more workers might agree to assemble a given number of chassis per week, or several workers might receive a bonus for assembly of each one over a standard number.

In France a large majority of workers in auto chassis factories were on piecework by 1908. One observer, Etienne Riché, reported 80 percent of workers doing piecework in some Paris factories at this date. Toolmakers and test drivers remained on daily pay, however, for here the output could not be standardized.[3] Autoworkers generally did not oppose the principle of piecework. On the contrary, a majority preferred it, for this system paid them prime wages, higher than those paid to day workers, although there were frequent disagreements over setting the rates. More workers tended to oppose piecework in French body shops than in the chassis factories. Most of the body firms were former carriage makers and had a long tradition of paying their skilled craftsmen by the day. In March 1905, 15,000 of 20,000 body workers in Paris went on strike against piecework, against *marchandage* (management contracting with an individual or a team to complete a given task in a specified time), and for a 60-hour week. After a month the workers won some of their points – a five-day week, special payment for overtime, *marchandage* and piecework to end in 90 days – but *la commandite* would remain (this was *marchandage* by a team rather than a single worker).[4] In reality, it appears that piecework did remain in many body shops. Almost all European auto factories used some kind of piecework by 1905.

These factories usually were arranged like general machine shops, doing a variety of short-run jobs. Machines of the same type would be grouped together and an auto part would move back and forth among several departments as different operations were performed on it. This system had several advantages. The transmission of power to machines by the overhead shaft and belt arrangement was much simpler and cheaper if all the machines in an area were the same type. It was considered very difficult for a foreman to oversee work on different kinds of machines. It provided flexibility in working on different jobs in a shop at the same time. Once a firm decided to produce hundreds of the same model car, however, the flow production principle offered significant advantages. This arrangement provided for raw materials and purchased components to enter at one end of the factory and be routed along one path to final assembly. Machines would be moved to their logical place on this path; different types, therefore, would be intermixed. Individual electric motors would power each machine or small group of them. The flow system permitted greater speed of production and lower inventories of work-in-process; it allowed a more intensive division of labor; and it sharply reduced the time and labor required to move parts and materials. Its advantages increased with greater product standardization.

American automobile factories adopted the flow production arrangement early, and it began to appear in European plants after the 1907-1908 recession encouraged automakers to reduce costs and broaden their market by making larger batches of lower-priced cars. Henry Ford's success with flow production in his new factory in Highland Park, Michigan, opened in 1910, brought many visitors from Europe, and many more read about it.

Another American, Frederick W. Taylor, also began to influence European motorcar production during this period. "Taylorism" aimed to increase labor productivity by thorough preparation, measurement, and inspection of work in factories. Taylor insisted that management carefully determine the best way to do specific jobs and that workers follow management's instructions without any deviation. In return, they would receive significantly higher wages. Taylor did not have mass production in mind but aimed to increase productivity in a typical machine shop or small factory. The Taylor system examined each task performed by a man or a machine and tried to increase the output. The Ford system ("Fordism") went farther: it tried to change or eliminate the task itself by mechanization, thereby reducing the labor input sharply, especially skilled labor.[5]

One aspect of Taylor's proposals that management in many European factories seized upon was time-and-motion study, an allegedly scientific way to determine how to perform a task and how long it should take. This, they believed, might be a way to resolve disagreements over rates for piecework. Management would use time and motion study to determine the best way to do a job, instruct the workers, their output would increase, and both sides would share the benefit. The time-study man with a stopwatch symbolized this method, but, to the dismay of many managements, it often brought bitter struggles with labor. Skilled workers felt ill-used. They saw it as a frontal attack on their craft, on their autonomy, and on their power in the shop. Management was investigating and discovering the secrets of craftwork. This challenged the power of the skilled workers and threatened to replace them with narrowly specialized workers with little training or craft knowledge. As the skilled workers saw it, time study was one more step in the degradation of their skill and authority, more threatening than the principle of piecework, and present was a human object to personify their fears. In automobile factories in much of Europe in 1912 and 1913, strikes occurred in which time study was a major factor.

In France, Berliet and Renault experienced such strikes, with management winning out. In Germany, a strike at Bosch in 1913 climaxed a series of changes by management to raise productivity. These changes included the introduction of machine tools, often imported from the United States, that operated automatically and were more precise; centralization of work instructions; and the elimination of workers from the process of determining piece rates. These and other issues brought on a strike of several weeks that resulted in a complete victory for management.[6] There were many disputes in Italy over setting piecework rates and some major strikes in Turin in 1912-13. In these, management won more control over factory operations in return for concessions on hours and wages.[7] British management had less confidence in scientific rate setting and did not push it as hard as continental firms did.

European auto factories also began moving toward the flow production system. An unusually early instance was a new Lorraine-Dietrich factory erected in 1906 in Argenteuil near Paris. Machines were placed according to their role in the manufacturing sequence and powered by individual electric motors. Cars were assembled in a stationary line, supplied by four separate stores of parts. But output was not large, and there is no indication that interchangeable parts were used. Berliet in Lyon reached a similar stage by 1911. There each of the major components was added to the chassis frame by a team of specialists moving along the stationary line of frames, doing the same job at each station and pushing wheeled workbenches along with them. Berliet made vehicles in large batches, five models of cars and two truck chassis, for a total of about 3,000 by 2,000 workers in 1913.[8]

At Peugeot the initiative for moving toward greater managerial control over production came from the engineer Ernest Mattern, whose career the scholar Yves Cohen has drawn out of obscurity.[9] Mattern began as a design engineer at several small auto companies. In 1906 he decided to move into production engineering and took a position with the Westinghouse company in Le Havre. This factory made electrical equipment and a small number of automobiles. There Mattern learned production-cost analysis from the firm's Swiss-American manager, Albert Schmid. After a few months, Mattern joined Peugeot at its branch factory in Lille and rose to become production manager. In 1912 Peugeot promoted him to manage its larger plant in Audincourt near Montbéliard. In both Peugeot factories Mattern followed the same policies. He instituted piecework, but his generous treatment of the workers fended off any overt opposition. He standardized parts and installed jigs and fixtures on machine tools to make these parts interchangeable. He centralized stores and established routes for parts. He divided the assembly process into tasks and had teams of workers move along the workstations, performing the same job on each chassis. He established a general production plan including cost analyses of supplies and production. Mattern's innovations included something of both Taylorism and Fordism, but more of the former. These policies did cut costs at Lille where production did not exceed two cars per day and at the Audincourt factory, where production rose to four cars per day in 1914. They also prepared the way for mass production using specialized or unskilled workers to make munitions during the 1914-18 war.

In Great Britain more progress toward flow production occurred than has been realized. Wayne Lewchuk has found that some bicycle firms moved toward interchangeable parts and flow production in the late 1890s and automobile firms began the same progression around 1905.[10] Jigs and fixtures were attached to machine tools operated by semiskilled workers. The Sunbeam factory in Wolverhampton introduced an advanced system, assembling chassis by having a crane carry them from one group of fitters to the next. But Sunbeam only produced about 1,700 cars in 1913. Cautious policies of making small batches of different models prevented the British firms from taking much advantage of these methods. The Ford assembly plant in Manchester was the most advanced. In September 1914 the chassis assembly line began to move under mechanical power, but the body and final assembly lines remained hand powered. All the major components came from North America except the locally made bodies.[11]

German automakers traveled in the same direction, but some rather reluctantly. Daimler's self-image was that of a producer of luxury automobiles for the "better situated classes."[12] It decried the "cheap and nasty" vehicles from America and argued the benefits of careful hand work on its cars. It failed to recognize (at least publicly) that greater precision was required to make interchangeable parts for mass-produced cars than for its handmade models. In fact, Daimler did use American machine tools because of their greater precision and the factory did begin to change from a confederation of almost independent shops ruled by their foremen to a more centrally managed concern. In 1909 management began using job cards that accompanied parts through the shops and allowed a central office to track them. It soon issued a catalog of piecework rates that superseded the authority of foremen to set these rates. Daimler's final assembly system by 1914 resembled Berliet's, with specialist teams doing one job on a series of stationary chassis.[13] But the firm's policy of product diversification – over a dozen car models and four truck types in the years before the war – worked against large scale production. On the other hand, Benz took a step toward standardization by reducing its range of models, as did Opel.

At Opel there was always much more central control over the production process than at Daimler.[14] Beginning in at least 1906 it had a central production office that coordinated operations to fit a general plan. It determined the sequence of operations for each part in such a way as to try to keep every machine tool working full time. Although Opel usually grouped machine tools by type, it organized the engine department on the flow principle, presumably because there was more standardization and therefore longer production runs for engines than chassis. Opel also used wage books to set piecework rates and job cards for each operation. That Opel was somewhat ahead of other German

concerns in adopting new methods is suggested by a big strike that occurred there as early as 1907 over a reduction in piece rates. As Ernest
Mattern promoted new methods at Peugeot, the engineer Wilhelm
Wenske worked to this end at Opel, consciously following American
examples and the teachings of Taylor.

In 1911 a great fire burned most of the Opel factory. Rebuilding
provided an opportunity to introduce new machines and a simplification
of vehicle types, but production methods did not change sharply and
there is no indication of any further conversion to the flow production
principle. In 1911, 2,640 workers produced 2,251 cars, and in 1913,
2,950 workers made 3,081. These numbers show productivity growth,
but we know nothing about a possible change in the share of parts purchased from subcontractors that would affect these numbers, nor how
many workers were assigned to bicycle or sewing machine production.
In 1912 the proportion of skilled workers at Opel stood at 71 per-

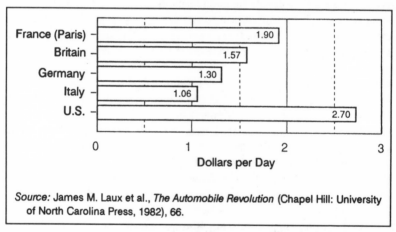

Source: James M. Laux et al., The Automobile Revolution (Chapel Hill: University
of North Carolina Press, 1982), 66.

FIGURE 4.1   ESTIMATED AVERAGE DAILY WAGE OF AUTOWORKERS, CA. 1910

cent, hardly changed from 1906, and similar to the figure at Daimler.
This suggests little change in production methods, but it is probable
that many of those rated as skilled worked at tasks that could have been
performed by those with less training.

In Chemnitz, the Wanderer company erected a large new factory
building in 1913. It did not dedicate this building to one product only,
but divided the machines by type so as to make in the same shop parts

for bicycles and typewriters as well as for automobiles. It placed the stamping presses in the basement, automatic machines making parts for various products on the ground floor, and at stations on the next two floors workers assembled cars and other items. The factory generated its own electric power but used it to turn shafts that drove belts to power the machines. This new factory already lagged behind the state of the art when it opened.[15]

There is no question that Fiat led the way in adopting the newer manufacturing methods in Italy, especially from 1911 on. This is shown by rising output per worker, in turn brought by the increasing use of American machine tools as well as gauges and fixtures to make parts faster and more accurately. At Fiat in 1911-12, 347 workers operated machines and 496 worked as fitters in the assembly shops. This 70 percent ratio of machinists to fitters contrasts with 22.7 percent at Itala, 38.9 percent at Spa and similar numbers at other Italian auto firms.[16] That Fiat required relatively fewer fitters suggests that its parts were made more precisely and required less adjustment in the course of assembly. Labor union complaints over these years that many more parts and vehicles were made with about the same number of workers also attest to rising productivity. Agnelli's visits to United States auto firms in 1906 and 1912 probably encouraged these changes as well as the techniques learned by the Italian engineers associated with Fiat's branch in Poughkeepsie, New York. In 1914 Fiat opened a new five-floor building where stamping presses occupied the ground floor and body making the upper floors. There is little evidence of flow production at Fiat, but the moves toward fewer types of vehicles and interchangeable parts were significant steps on the way to it. The other Italian firms finished only a few hundred cars per year and made no major changes in their production processes.[17]

Working conditions in European auto factories tended to be slightly better than in other metalworking establishments. Usually the working day lasted from 9 to 11 hours, five and one-half or six days a week. In the dozen years up to 1914, weekly hours tended to decline and wages to rise. Workers at Bosch in Stuttgart had one of the best arrangements, for the eight-hour day was standard, and weekly pay exceeded that at nearby Daimler.[18]

Frequent causes of labor disputes were the assignment of unskilled workers to machines (Britain), time study and piecework rates (France), compulsory overtime and piecework rates (Germany), and shop discipline, hours, and piecework rates (Italy). Nevertheless, labor disputes were not the norm in the motorcar industry. More striking to contemporaries were the new product and its manufacture as a symbol of modernity: orderly and precise, clean and tidy. In 1910 a journalist visiting the Peugeot assembly plant in Turin wrote with enthusiasm, "It is not a seething crater vomiting smoke, a black and gloomy place, but a busy and clean factory, powerful and wisely organized, above all, orderly. This is the great magic word that brings well-being and strength."[19]

By 1914, then, some European automakers had begun to make the transition from machine shop to large-scale production. None of them (except Ford in England) had installed a moving assembly line with components flowing to it on conveyors. Their marketing efforts did not generate sufficient demand to require mass production. The First World War, with its great hunger for identical vehicles and other mechanisms, would pull the industry farther along in this transition.

5
AUTOMOBILES IN THE GREAT WAR

"The war was a huge glutton whose favorite dish was motor vehicles." So commented the head of the German Daimler company.[1] But it feasted not only on vehicles. When it became clear that the conflict would last more than a few months, armies began ordering great amounts of conventional munitions – artillery shells, machine guns, and other weaponry – from automobile firms. Then, as motor vehicles proved their value in moving supplies, troops, and artillery, orders for trucks, buses, and tractors mounted. When the military in 1915-16 recognized how the airplane had become a valuable weapon, motorcar companies expanded or launched into aircraft engine manufacture, and some even made airframes. Finally, a few of these companies produced an even newer weapon, the tank. The war therefore brought a great expansion of the European motorcar industry and millions of people became much more familiar with automobiles.

That European automakers had not yet committed themselves to rigid programs producing large numbers of one standardized product (Fordism) proved an advantage during the war. Many companies demonstrated great flexibility in shifting their output to a wide variety of products as demanded by their war ministries. Then, by 1917 and sometimes earlier, the military officials decided that standardization would work for them too, and they strived for more concentration on a limited range of trucks, aircraft engines, and munitions.

MILITARY PRODUCTION BY THE FRENCH
AUTOMOBILE INDUSTRY

In the French case the automobile industry played a prominent role in the war. Few of its factories were in the area occupied by German forces in the north, although the output of the important group of foundries along the Belgian frontier was lost and the Peugeot shops around Montbéliard were threatened but never overrun.

Early in the war most of the companies began to make artillery shells, but André Citroën registered the most spectacular success. Desperate for more shells, the army gave him a large contract in February 1915. Citroën, hitherto head of the small Mors auto company, quickly built a large factory in Paris and began production in mid-1915. He planned the facility for mass production, along the lines of the Ford and other American auto plants he had visited in 1912. He installed lifts and automatic metal-cutting machines, and transported parts with electric carts. Citroën's extensive mechanization and assembly lines for sections of the process allowed him, like Ford, to pursue an extreme division of labor and thereby utilize many unskilled workers, especially women. In November 1915 one-fifth of his 3,500 wage earners was female; at the Armistice this proportion had risen to one-half of 11,700.[2] Citroën's 26 million shells, his flair for publicity, his factory's location in Paris, and his innovations in production and labor policy brought him much favorable attention. He became a national hero and he decided to adapt his factory to mass produce cars after the war.

Unlike Citroën, Louis Renault produced a great variety of military goods.[3] His company made shells, of course, over 8.5 million of them, but also much more. It produced 9,320 various types of trucks; 1,360 artillery tractors, including 350 of the track-laying type; 12,510 aviation engines of its own V-8 and V-12 designs; 1,160 aircraft; and 1,760 light tanks designed primarily by one of the firm's engineers, Rodolphe Ernst Metzmaier. To assemble the tanks Renault put the chassis on carts that ran on railway tracks inside the factory.[4] Renault put these products together in its own shops, which at the war's end employed some 22,500, but more and more of the parts for them came from subcontractors. Renault-designed aircraft engines and tanks were made by outside firms including Peugeot and Berliet. Government pressure forced the auto and other metalworking firms to work together in groups to make complex items. This arrangement of military product groups worked well and helps explain how the French outproduced the British and Germans in automotive equipment such as trucks and aviation engines.

Peugeot also produced a variety of war materiel, including some 6,000 trucks, 6,500 aircraft engines (mostly Hispano-Suizas), and some 1,400 engines for Renault tanks (enough for nearly half of those delivered during the war), but this firm did not expand nearly as fast as Renault or Berliet.[5]

In Lyon Berliet produced millions of shells but concentrated more on vehicle manufacturing, ultimately producing 25,000 4-ton trucks, as the French authorities moved further toward standardization in trucks than the British, Germans, or Americans. Before the war Berliet had organized final assembly so that special teams of workers mounted subassemblies on the stationary chassis as they walked from one workstation to the next. It expanded this arrangement as the military orders poured in.

Early in the war Marius Berliet decided to fulfill his dream and build an immense new factory. On a large tract of land southeast of Lyon at Vénissieux, buildings began rising in 1915, including a forge, stamping shop, and truck assembly hall. When finished, the complex had one very large building fronting the highway and behind it stretched several long parallel buildings 100 feet apart. Like Henry Ford's contemporary River Rouge works just outside Detroit, an integrated complex, including a steel mill purchased from the United States, was Berliet's goal. Insisting on the latest methods, Berliet threw out the shaft and belt system and powered each machine with its own electric motor. Electric cranes and hoists moved materials. At the war's end Berliet employed about 10,000, half at Vénissieux, where there were assembly lines for trucks and tanks. It is not clear if either of these lines moved. Berliet did assemble 800 of the Renault light tanks at Vénissieux.[6]

One of the outstanding wartime manufacturing achievements in France was the production of nearly 90,000 aircraft engines, more than twice the total of either Britain or Germany. When the war began the two leading types were the Gnôme and Rhône (G & R) air-cooled rotary, in which the cylinders rotated around a fixed crankshaft, and the more conventional Renault air-cooled V-8. When the G&R rotary design proved unsuitable for engines producing over 150 hp, the authorities ordered more Renault air- and water-cooled engines, some fixed radial types, and also adopted the design of Marc Birkigt, head of the Hispano-Suiza automobile company. His engine was a water-cooled V-8 with aluminum block and steel cylinder sleeves. H-S engines went into service in September 1916 and quickly became the backbone of the French fighter squadrons. Hispano-Suiza had only a small factory near Paris and it made only 3,813 of the 25,741 of its engines delivered by

November 1918.[7] Fourteen other French firms, including the automakers Peugeot, Brasier, Chenard et Walcker, De Dion-Bouton, Delaunay-Belleville, and DFP also manufactured H-S engines, as well as British and American companies. Unfortunately, parts on these engines produced by different firms usually were not interchangeable. Altogether, some 20 prewar French automobile makers engaged in aircraft engine production during the war.[8]

WARTIME PRODUCTION IN GREAT BRITAIN

The British automobile industry did not expand as much as the French, nor did it exhibit as much flexibility. English Ford continued to assemble vehicles shipped from North America, some as cars but many adapted to serve as ambulances or light trucks. The 33.3 percent McKenna tariff slapped on imported cars and parts (reduced to 22.2 percent for Canada and the rest of the British Empire) in 1915 led to considerably more manufacture of parts by English Ford. Late in the war Henry Ford bought a site near Cork, Ireland, for a factory to make small tractors. This factory did not go into production before the Armistice, so Ford shipped 6,000 of these Fordson tractors from Detroit to the Britain, half of which were assembled at Manchester.[9] The Austin company made primarily nonautomotive war materiel: 8 million shells, 650 artillery guns, and over 2,000 aircraft, along with some ambulances, trucks, and armored cars. Most of this came from two large factory buildings constructed and equipped by the Ministry of Munitions.[10] Austin employed a maximum of 20,000 during the war.

Most of the truck makers expanded their output and a dozen or more made between 1,000 and 5,000 during the war. Leyland produced 5,932, Thorneycroft made 5,000, but the Associated Equipment Company (AEC) supplied the largest number of trucks, about 10,000. It was the first British-owned motor vehicle firm to set up a moving assembly line.[11] This came in 1917, when it was making 50 chassis per week. Ten chassis were placed on a moving platform 265 feet long. This arrangement did not lead to increased output but did simplify movement of the heavy chassis through the plant. AEC employed many women on this assembly line and in some of the machining departments.

The government entrusted tank manufacturing primarily to a railway-car firm, the Metropolitan Carriage Wagon Company, which assembled 70 percent of the 2,600 produced, along with a steam-tractor firm, Foster. The English Daimler company supplied most of the tank engines.

British production of aircraft engines expanded very slowly. Before the war G & R engines from France dominated British aviation and there had been little domestic development. The unavailability of imported Bosch magnetos also delayed the industry's growth. Several automobile companies did design and produce aircraft engines, Rolls-Royce most successfully with the Eagle and Falcon, water-cooled V-12 designs. Only 4,500 of these types were made because of the complexity of their manufacture and Rolls-Royce's refusal to permit licensed production by other concerns, although it finally agreed to some subcontracting of parts.[12] The Humber company produced 4,000 rotary engines that had been adapted by the automobile engineer W. O. Bentley from a French design. English Daimler made some 4,500 G & R engines and Wolseley produced Hispano-Suizas. The Sunbeam company made several types designed by French-trained Louis Coatalen, but their performance was disappointing. So most British aircraft engines were either purchased from French makers or made on license from French designs.

ITALIAN AND RUSSIAN MILITARY OUTPUT

The Italian army took advantage of nine months of neutrality to continue its motorization before it entered the war. By May 1915 it possessed 3,500 trucks and ambulances, mostly Fiats.[13] This company's 1.5- and 3.5-ton machines found almost unlimited markets both at home and for its allies. Fiat produced about 45,650 trucks during the war, by far the largest total in the world.[14] It sold 17,500 to the French and British armies and an unknown number to the Russians. Its peak production came in October 1917, when it turned out 2,023 vehicles, and on the last day of 1917, when it produced 176.[15] In addition to these standard truck models Fiat made a great variety of other military supplies, including buses, about 650 artillery tractors, and 25,000 machine guns. It also built some 15,000 aircraft engines and even 1,400 airframes. Fiat itself produced almost all the parts used in these vehicles and engines. It did not have a moving assembly line but did continue its prewar evolution toward making interchangeable parts on single-purpose machines operated by unskilled labor. By the end of 1918, Fiat's many factories employed some 40,000 (compared to the prewar 4,000) and a substantial share of these were women and boys, perhaps 10,000.[16]

Early in the war, Giovanni Agnelli decided to build an entirely new factory in Turin, incorporating the latest techniques from America, the same strategy followed by Berliet in Lyon, although not as grandiose. Fiat designed the new five-floor plant, Lingotto, for flow production and ultimately a moving assembly line, unlike the confusion of separate buildings on the original Corso Dante site. The ground floor was finished in 1917 in time for stamping presses to begin work in May. Completion of the Lingotto building came in 1919, but the transfer of machines and production took several more years.[17]

The other Italian auto firms made much smaller numbers of vehicles during the war, in particular trucks for specialized purposes. Isotta Fraschini produced a considerable number of powerful aircraft engines that earned a good reputation, as did those of Fiat. Allied observers in 1917 found the engines of these two firms reliable and standardized with interchangeable parts.[18]

The Russian automobile industry had barely begun before the war. Its only significant concern, the Russo Baltic company of Riga, was overrun by the Germans in 1915. Renault opened a factory in St. Petersburg in 1914 to assemble trucks and also to make shell fuses. In 1916 Renault began building another plant in Rybinsk to make auto and aircraft parts, but it did not reach production. With government financial assistance, several additional auto factories were constructed. Early in 1917 Moscow's AMO company began manufacture and assembly of Fiat 1.5-ton trucks with machinery obtained from the United States and France. Russo Baltic built a new factory in Moscow but manufactured little. Another plant was erected in Yaroslavl but never began production.

Slow decisions, lack of machinery, and lack of time ruined the possibilities of Russian auto manufacturing in the war years before the 1917 revolutions. However, some 40,000 motor vehicles were imported during 1914-17, primarily from the United States.[19]

TABLE 5.1 MILITARY VEHICLE PRODUCTION DURING THE FIRST WORLD WAR

	Britain	France	Germany	Italy
Total vehicles produced for military service	58,149	65,592	*60,000*	*55,000*
Military verhicles in service in 1918	86,837	90,535	*56,000*	36,000
Trucks and tractors in service in 1918	56,659	69,104	*28,000*	*27,000*

Figures exclude tanks and motorcycles.

Italicized estimates should be within 5 percent accuracy.

Source: J. Laux, "Trucks in the West during the First World War," *Journal of Transport History*, 3d ser., 6, no. 2 (September 1985): 68.

THE CENTRAL POWERS AND THEIR AUTOMOBILE INDUSTRIES

The German motor-vehicle industry engaged heavily in military production but showed less adaptability than the French or Italian. Trucks and aircraft engines were the main products. The largest firm, Benz, cut back on passenger-car production to as low as 213 in 1918, but truck output did not expand, remaining steady at 1,100 to 1,300 per year. In 1915 the Prussian War Ministry persuaded Benz to take financial control of the Aviatik aircraft factory in Leipzig, but this connection did not seem to have much effect on the motor firm's Mannheim activities. At Mannheim it produced 11,360 aircraft engines during the war, but Benz engines were not among the best. Benz also received orders for submarine diesel engines and became a major supplier of them. Over the course of the war its employment rose from 7,700 to 16,000.

Similar developments occurred at Daimler, where passenger-car output dropped to 108 in 1918 and truck production rose to nearly 1,000 in that year. Daimler's primary wartime achievement came with aviation engines. It had designed and produced a small number of them starting in 1911 and was the country's leading producer throughout the war. Its Mercedes engines, water-cooled, six-cylinder, in-line types, were heavier than French engines but more reliable, durable, and simpler to maintain. Daimler delivered 19,876 of the estimated 41,200 aircraft engines made in wartime Germany. Its production reached a peak of 735 in January 1918, or about 170 per week, but it usually made about 105 per week.[20] These numbers are large, but the term *mass production* is not appropriate for output on this scale.

In 1915 Daimler began building a factory in Sindelfingen, 12 miles south of Stuttgart, to make aircraft, on the urging of the Prussian War Ministry. This venture failed. Daimler produced only 271 aircraft in this facility, and in July 1917 it decided to make aircraft engines here also. Shortages of skilled labor and equipment, and probably poor management, slowed progress so much that this plant delivered no engines during the war, although it had 5,450 workers by November 1918.[21] Peak employment in the main factory in Untertürkheim reached 16,000, and at the heavy-vehicle operation in Berlin-Marienfelde, 3,700. The total of over 25,000 surpassed wartime employment at Renault, France's largest automotive employer, but was well below Fiat's. Factory organization changed little at Daimler during the war, although the concentration on just a few types of aircraft engines at Untertürkheim permitted more single-purpose machines and the greater use of unskilled men and women. At this plant 17 percent of the labor force was female at the end of the war.[22]

A scandal erupted at Daimler early in 1918. In February the director, Ernest Berge, an inflexible and self-righteous man, wrote the War Ministry that unless Daimler received higher prices for its engines because of higher labor and material costs, night work and overtime would have to end and output would fall. The company, however, refused to submit detailed calculations to support its claims. This letter became known to the Reichstag and to the public within a few days. At about the same time a clerk at Daimler claimed that a year earlier, in March 1917, he had been ordered to prepare grossly exaggerated cost figures for engine production, for possible presentation to a Reichstag committee. The angry military authorities reacted in March 1918 by placing Daimler under military supervision, and they ejected Berge from the firm. The political Left made much of this affair, suggesting that treason had occurred, and the War Ministry's calculations of Daimler's wartime profits, published only in September 1919, did show numbers much larger than the firm's official figures.

Even after the army took control, troubles continued at Daimler. The company's shortage of certain gears and engine cylinders led the military authorities to demand that these parts be subcontracted.

Daimler officials refused and only after a two-month delay and the threat of prison did they relent. The company's position was that they could not guarantee the quality of parts made by outside concerns. Director Berge was allowed to return to the firm in October 1918 and after the revolution of that November the new republican government ended the investigation of the cost clerk's charges of fraud.[23]

Opel became a major German truck builder during the war, turning out 4,400, most of which were a standard 3-ton-capacity model. This concern also made aircraft engines, first a design of the small Argus company and then the exceptionally good BMW on license. BMW (Bayerische Motoren Werke) of Munich had made motorcycles, but it presented a fine aircraft engine in the middle of the war, 250 hp with the conventional German layout, six cylinders in-line. It made 734 of these engines, and Opel made 2,260 more. Other German auto firms also made a few thousand trucks during the war, but none produced them in really large numbers as did Fiat and Berliet. The War Ministry could not seem to act on the idea of making one or two standard models by the tens of thousands.

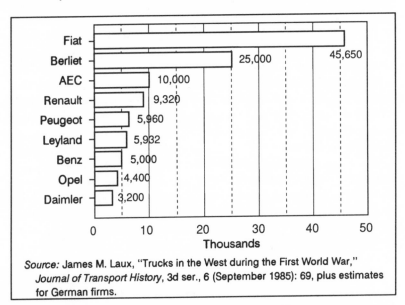

Source: James M. Laux, "Trucks in the West during the First World War," *Journal of Transport History*, 3d ser., 6 (September 1985): 69, plus estimates for German firms.

FIGURE 5.1 ESTIMATED TRUCK PRODUCTION BY LEADING EUROPEAN MANUFACTURERS DURING THE FIRST WORLD WAR

The British first used tanks in battle in September 1916. Although they were less than successful in this episode, the German authorities asked for some prototypes in November 1916. In the middle of 1917 they ordered 100 of a design presented by the experienced automobile engineer Joseph Vollmer. Weighing 32 tons, it was powered by two 100-hp Daimler engines. Chassis of up to 80 of these machines were completed and used as tractors to pull artillery, and 20 more were armored and used in combat in 1918. In April four German tanks encountered three British ones. The Germans came out ahead, but their large and heavy machines with a crew of 16 and six machine guns, were not effective on rough ground. Ludendorff, the German military commander, wrote after the war that tanks could be effective only in mass attacks and that German industry did not have the capacity to produce them in large numbers. He probably was right.[24] Nevertheless, in June 1918 the War Ministry ordered 580 tanks of a lighter design by Vollmer; none could be delivered before the Armistice.[25] The fully completed heavy tanks were assembled by Daimler, Büssing, and Lang of Mannheim with components supplied by many firms including the caterpillar treads from the Holt branch in Budapest, armor plate by Krupp, and transmissions by Adler.[26]

The difficulties the German army experienced in using trucks early in the war – the inevitable breakdowns of the subsidy trucks and of the 3,000 or 4,000 others requisitioned in 1914 – emphasized the immense problems with providing spare part and repairs for all these different models. The Prussian War Ministry reacted in 1915 by establishing norms for automobile parts: bolts, pins, rivets, gear wheels, and more complex items such as rubber tires, carburetor parts, clutches, brakes, and radiators. It also provided specifications for a standard 3-ton truck.[27] These beginning moves toward standardization allowed simpler production methods and more use of less-skilled labor. Such dilution of labor did occur, but apparently to a lesser degree than was the case in the Allied countries. It is not clear why the German automobile firms did not make trucks in larger numbers: Because the government did not order them? Because the companies believed they lacked capacity due to the higher priority given to submarines and aircraft? Because the companies failed to move very far toward American-style mass production methods? Or was it due to raw-material shortages? After the war an expert American journalist visited many German auto plants and concluded, "It is obvious that during the war, the German automobile factories did not learn the lessons of quantity production to the same degree as the Allied nations."[28]

In Austria-Hungary about a dozen automakers built trucks and innovative artillery tractors, but not in large numbers. In Austria an annual output of 2,000 trucks may have been attained during the war.[29] The Czech and Hungarian production reached a smaller total.

MILITARY TRUCKS IN ACTION

When the war broke out in 1914, military officials believed that railways and horse-drawn wagons would provide the vast bulk of transport during the conflict. They expected to use trucks in special situations, as the Germans did when they employed several hundred for ammunition supply in their advance through Belgium and northern France in August. These trucks were not handled well, however, and 60 percent broke down before the Battle of the Marne began in early September.[30]

When military operations settled down to trench warfare, the armies found that horse-drawn wagons were insufficient to link the railheads with the trenches and artillery batteries 5 to 25 miles forward. So they began to build light railways, usually 60-cm gauge, to help. Trucks also were pressed into this service; motor buses and ambulances moved men.

The larger British and French, and then later Italian, supply of these vehicles gave those armies an advantage. The impromptu use of Paris taxicabs to move French soldiers to the battle of the Marne became famous. More significant was the French employment of motor vehicles at the Battle of Verdun in 1916. For several months French forces in the fortress town could be supplied only by a limited-capacity steam tramway and by a gravel road that wound 35 miles to the nearest railhead. The French Automobile Service threw 3,500 trucks into the supply effort along this "Sacred Road," which also was used by thousands of other motor vehicles – ambulances, buses, staff cars, and specialized vehicles for the artillery and air force. It controlled all this traffic rigidly, adapting principles of railway traffic management to the highway. The French success at holding Verdun with truck transportation gave these vehicles a high military reputation and encouraged even more use by the Allied powers. The French, with more trucks than any other belligerent, also worked out a system of repair depots to handle the one in ten that broke down on any day of heavy service.

Trucks and tractors also replaced horses in moving light and heavy artillery. The Austrians and Germans developed four-wheel-drive machines for this purpose from 1905 on, but they never had very many of them. The French and British also made some of this type but imported more from the United States. In 1904 the Holt Tractor Company of Stockton, California, and Peoria, Illinois, had introduced caterpillar tractors, and some of them were sold in Europe. These proved effective in moving artillery over rough ground. Holt sold many of these tractors to the Allied armies, while the Germans and Austro-Hungarians copied them. The caterpillar tracks, of course, lay behind the development of tanks.

By 1918 the Allied forces on the western front had a four-to-one advantage over the Germans in trucks, which had a significant effect on military operations. In the spring of 1918 several German offensives began well but slowed down after a few days without breakthroughs. Important reasons for this were the German lack of transport to bring up supplies and reserves, and on the Allied side the effective use of trucks to shift hundreds of thousands of troops quickly to weak points.

It is clear, then, that the larger prewar motor industries in France and Britain gave them an unexpected advantage over Germany in the war. France alone outproduced Germany in trucks, tanks, and aircraft engines. With the addition of production from the British, Italian, and American auto industries, the margin was overwhelming.

6

EUROPE AND THE AMERICAN MODEL IN THE 1920S

In the dozen years through 1920, the American automobile industry scored some huge gains. Output of cars and trucks rose from 65,000 in 1908 to 2.227 million in 1920, and the number of motor vehicles in service multiplied from 198,400 to 9.24 million over the same period. Production innovations lay behind this soaring growth, for without the sharply lower cost of manufacturing and massive use of lower-skilled workers, car prices could not have been cut nor enough cars produced to bring millions of farmers, small-town residents, and urban middle-class buyers into the market.

During the First World War, American car production boomed although raw-material shortages required a cutback in 1918. More and more U.S. vehicles were exported – trucks to Europe and cars, especially Fords, there and to the other continents. The United States dominated the auto business by 1920; its production was about 19 times larger than that of still-recovering Europe in that year.

In the 1920s most developments in the European motor-vehicle industry had some relationship to this American leadership. Before the threat of American conquest of the European auto industry – by flooding the area with good-quality but cheap cars, by assembly in Europe of American-made parts, and by manufacture in Europe by American firms – the European manufacturers followed positive and negative policies.[1] Positively, they adopted many American production methods (Fordism) and imported American machine tools to raise output and cut costs. To sell their expanded output of cars they also adapted American marketing techniques such as exclusive and closely inspected dealerships, installment sales, widespread advertising, and sales campaigns. Negatively, they lobbied their governments to discriminate against American cars by taxing motor vehicles on the basis of cylinder capacity and gradually won higher tariffs. The ubiquitous American as-

TABLE 6.1 MOTOR-VEHICLE PRODUCTION, 1921-1929*

	France			Britain			Germany			Italy		
	PC	CV	Total	PC	CV	Total	PC	CV	Total	PC	CV	Total
1921	41	14	55									15.5
1922	49	26	75									16.4
1923	72	38	110	71	24	95						22.8
1924	97	48	145	117	30	147						37.5
1925	121	56	177	132	35	167	48	21	69	46	3.6	49.6
1926	159	33	192	154	44	198	36	15	51	61	3.3	64.3
1927	145	46	191	165	47	212	91	33	124	51	3.6	54.6
1928	187	36	223	165	47	212	108	40	148	54	3.7	57.7
1929	212	42	254	182	57	239	96	38	134	52	3.2	55.2

* in thousands

PC = private cars

CV = commercial vehicles

Sources:

B. R. Mitchell, *European Historical Statistics, 1750-1970* (New York: Columbia University Press, 1975), 467-68.

For Germany: *Statistisches Jahrbuch*, various years.

sembly plants established in Europe in the 1920s were countered by raising tariffs on automobile parts. Ultimately the Americans set up a few manufacturing plants in Europe, most of them in the 1930s. By this time some European producers came close to competing in price and quality.

Labor relations in the European auto industry did diverge somewhat from the American model. All over Europe the labor movement reached a peak of activity, influence, and radicalism from 1919 to 1921. It won some gains, including the eight-hour day, but everywhere its power soon waned in the face of internal divisions, management counterattacks, and the onset of the postwar recession of 1920-21. Labor unions thereafter played a small role in the industry until the Second World War, except in France from 1936 on. The European manufacturers did not follow Ford's policy on workers' pay. They believed that Ford's system – high hourly wages to compensate for higher labor effort as enforced by close supervision and machine pacing – would not work in their firms. They assumed that the high wages and additional "unproductive" supervisors would cost too much and that this part of Fordism would bring rapid labor turnover and strikes. So they maintained piecework pay systems, even though workers quickly learned to manipulate these to their own advantage. Management tried to accommodate piecework to flow production, where the individual has less control over the pace of work by establishing group bonus arrangements and other complicated systems. One important advantage of Ford's hourly pay was that it made it easy to change methods and machines; under piecework such changes might bring conflicts over the new rates. Piecework also required that some persons, either from management or labor, coordinate production so that parts or components were always available on which the pieceworkers could perform their tasks. This was not easy to do.

In labor policy then, the Europeans did not slavishly imitate all features of the American industry. In product policy they moved away from American-style cars. As the U.S. models grew larger, more powerful, and more luxurious, the Europeans produced smaller and less expensive cars, following the center of gravity of their car market as it shifted downward in the economic scale.

TABLE 6.2 MOTORCYCLES IN EUROPE IN THE 1920S

	1924		1929	
	Registrations	Persons/cycle	Registrations	Persons/cycle
Britain	477,500	94.3	741,700	61.6
Germany	130,000	477.7	650,000	99.5
France	102,000	398.1	405,500	104.1

Source: Great Britain, Papers by Command, Cmd. 3841, 128-31.

GROWTH AND CONCENTRATION IN FRANCE

France and Britain shared the leadership of the European industry in the 1920s, each producing about 250,000 motor vehicles in 1929. The French market, weaker than Britain's before the war, strengthened and absorbed more than the British. The national economy generally was prosperous, and car prices, in real terms, fell some 40 percent from 1921 to 1930. The waxing domestic demand, which compensated for a decline in exports after 1925, was strongest in the countryside and small towns, where the lack of much public transport made personal cars especially useful. Motorcycles in France, as well as Britain and Germany, enjoyed a great boom in the 1920s, suggesting a large potential market for low-priced used and new automobiles (see Table 6.2). Imported cars did not play an important role in France as the tariff now reached 45 percent. The annual tax on cars continued to discriminate against those with large engines – that is, those from America – and now also covered trucks and buses.

THE BIG THREE: CITROEN, RENAULT, AND PEUGEOT

The most vivid, even theatrical, performance in France came from André Citroën. He moved quickly, because he chose his postwar course as early as 1917, because he held full control of his firm, and because impetuousness was his personal style. He wanted to make cars the way Detroit did, and decided upon a low-priced people's car. He had Jules Salomon design the first model that would bear the Citroën name. Salomon had fathered the small Zèbre car before the war. The new model, "A," had four small cylinders displacing 1,300 cc. Salomon made it easy to manufacture and repair and Citroën sold it complete with open body, electric lights and starter, even a spare tire. Citroën excited public interest as early as May 1919 by advertising a four-door, open-body car for about $475. But he could not hold this price and his first clients, in July, had to pay $660. His former shell factory on the Quai Javel in Paris was far from ready for large-scale production. It needed thorough reorganization and new equipment. Citroën wanted to mass produce cars using up-to-date machinery (largely American) and assembly lines, but he never took the time to be precise about the details of manufacturing and especially its cost. Throughout his period of leadership the firm was characterized by improvisation. The 1919-20 arrangement for producing cars involved making parts in a variety of buildings and then assembly in several stages, the last of which put the cars, already supplied with wheels and drive train, on a wooden track about one foot off the floor and pushed by hand from one workstation to the next. In 1920 Citroën's work force of some 4,500 produced 12,244 cars, surpassing the best prewar output of any French automaker by more then 2.5 times.[2] Even so, Renault made almost 19,000 cars in the same year.

In 1921 Citroën introduced a new car and thereafter usually had two or three models available in various body styles, including six-cylinder types from 1928 on. The firm sold an even smaller car in 1922-26, named the 5 CV because it was rated at 5 fiscal hp. It had an engine of only 856 cc and two or three seats. This model usually came with a yellow body, a play on Citroën's name, close to the French word for lemon – *citron*. Nearly 81,000 of this model were sold at prices from $700 to $900.[3] Peugeot and Renault had similar small cars, as did Austin with the "Seven" in England, Opel in Germany, and Fiat in Italy.

By 1924 Quai Javel had a mechanically operated assembly line. Already in 1921 Citroën had begun expanding his productive plant, buying the Clément-Bayard auto firm in Levallois, a Paris suburb. He established a stamping factory in the northern suburb of Saint-Ouen in 1924. There Citroën pioneered all-steel body making on license from the American Budd company. Considering his short production runs compared with American standards, the tooling for these bodies was extremely expensive. In addition, the process worked only with imported American sheet steel. He built a very large forge and foundry plant in

Clichy, near Saint-Ouen, in 1926. These two establishments were designed and equipped on modern lines, with guidance by the engineer Ernest Mattern who had come to Citroën from Peugeot in 1922. Citroën brushed aside suggestions that locating these and other plants on the periphery of Paris was expensive in cost of construction, labor, and transportation. In fact, parts from the Levallois plant had to be trucked to Quai Javel on the Champs-Elysées. All this expensive equipment, usually American, permitted Citroën to assemble 95,067 cars in 1929 plus 7,824 exported as subassemblies, the total well above that of any other European maker. Employment that year was about 30,000.

In 1926 Citroën moved to expand exports, establishing small assembly plants in Britain, Italy, Germany, and Belgium. Foreign assembly rather than export of the complete car had several advantages: shipping costs were less, parts sometimes paid a lower tariff, no tariff would be paid on the labor cost of assembly and any parts that could be purchased locally, and local tastes might be met by slight design changes, especially in the body work.

Citroën's publicity was bold, in the European context. In 1927 he opened the Quai Javel factory to tours. For ƒ10 one could enter and walk five miles along the production lines. From 1925 to 1934 he rented space on the Eiffel Tower and installed his name in lights. He spent large sums to develop half-track vehicles and to experiment with them in the Sahara. Then he sent a group of them on the highly publicized "Yellow Expedition," from Beirut, Lebanon, to Peking in 1931-32, hoping to demonstrate their reliability to the French Army. Citroën built many branch sales agencies in France and the rest of Europe, often extravagantly large and luxurious.

Analysis of the company's finances shows that its earnings were enough to pay for its capital investments but that it frequently lacked working capital, especially in periods of slack sales. The large French commercial banks refused to extend short-term credit to Citroën. Finally, a major investment bank, Lazard, became its financier in 1927 and exerted some financial discipline on operations. When Lazard and Citroën parted company in 1930 the automobile firm again became vulnerable to the banks' hesitation to extend short-term loans.[4]

Louis Renault was the tortoise to André Citroën's hare. Renault's firm emerged from the war with greatly expanded capacity. Its floor space nearly tripled from 1914 to 1920, and its stock of machine tools rose almost 2.5 times.[5] Renault worked to expand production and cut costs with a policy of vertical integration. He established or gained control over a wide variety of parts and raw material suppliers, not so much to build a personal empire in imitation of Henry Ford but to ensure high quality and reliable deliveries at lower cost. The newer assembly methods demanded parts with more precise tolerances – that is, interchangeability – and regular deliveries to avoid large inventories. He led a group of steel consumers in operating a former German steelworks in Lorraine and established his own electric steel mill in the Alps. To further exports, Renault followed Citroën and established small assembly plants in Belgium (1926) and England (1927). He created his own finance company to service consumer installment loans. He retained a diversified output: several models of cars and trucks, agricultural tractors, military tanks, aircraft engines, and gasoline-powered (later diesel) railcars to serve lines with light traffic. Renault moved gradually to up-date his manufacturing methods. A final assembly line appeared in 1922, but at this stage it did not move continually. Given Louis Renault's cautious policy of diversifying output and consequent short production runs, his hesitation to adopt highly mechanized assembly was justified, especially when he could keep the prices of his cars competitive with Citroën and other French makes.

From 1921 through the rest of the decade Renault was always second in motor-vehicle production to Citroën, but from 1928 until 1931 the company registered losses on automobiles, which forced Louis Renault to undertake a major modernization in 1929-30. On Seguin Island in the Seine he built two large assembly buildings adjacent to the Billancourt works. These housed new chassis and body assembly lines; meanwhile, the older buildings were renovated and reequipped. Renault now was ready to confront archrival Citroën even more vigorously, but the major challenge would come from elsewhere – the business cycle.

Of the automakers that would become the French Big Three, Peugeot had the most trouble getting cars out the door in the immediate postwar years.[6] Its production system included several factories dispersed about the Montbéliard region, along with some shops in the Paris area and Lille. At first it tried to produce an extended range of models, along with bicycles, motorcycles, and trucks. Coordinating all this was difficult, especially when management seemed indecisive, until 1923-24. After enduring severe difficulties in the 1920-21 recession, the firm revived. It gradually reduced the number of models and concen-

trated on small cars. This evolution did not come fast enough for
Ernest Mattern, who left for Citroën in 1922. Peugeot's "cyclecar," or
Quadrilette with an engine of just 667 cc, replaced the prewar Baby in
1921 and was followed by a series of variants through the decade totaling 95,000 vehicles. Most of the larger types fell by the wayside. Peugeot
introduced a new small car in 1929, a 6 CV with 1122 cc. This model
became a best-seller in 1930-32 as Citroën and Renault had difficulties.
Figure 6.1 compares the growth of the three firms.

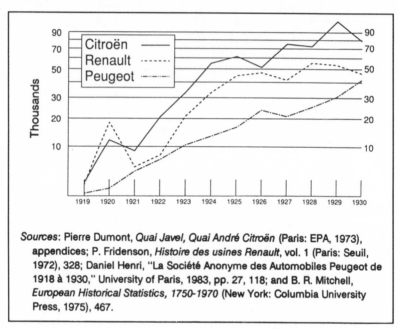

Sources: Pierre Dumont, *Quai Javel, Quai André Citroën* (Paris: EPA, 1973),
appendices; P. Fridenson, *Histoire des usines Renault*, vol. 1 (Paris: Seuil,
1972), 328; Daniel Henri, "La Société Anonyme des Automobiles Peugeot de
1918 à 1930," University of Paris, 1983, pp. 27, 118; and B. R. Mitchell,
European Historical Statistics, 1750-1970 (New York: Columbia University
Press, 1975), 467.

FIGURE 6.1 THE FRENCH BIG THREE: 1919-1930 MOTOR-VEHICLE PRODUCTION

   In the later 1920s Peugeot concentrated its operations at its
Sochaux site near Montbéliard, establishing a new body plant with
moving assembly there in 1926, then a stamping plant, foundries, and
expansion of the machine shops. This process was finished in 1931. The
unneeded older facilities, including the bicycle and motorcycle operations, Peugeot sold to other firms owned by the Peugeot family. A major difficulty facing the firm was finding labor in its thinly populated
area and the dearth of housing for workers who might consider relo-

cating there. The company built dormitories and apartment buildings, and it used buses to bring workers in from neighboring towns. The day of workers commuting long distances in their own cars had begun in the United States but lay well in the future in Europe.

Peugeot's effort at exports bore little fruit, but its domestic marketing was effective. In 1928 it established its own consumer credit company, which extended the loan period to 24 months in 1929. In France, cars bought on credit rose to 23 percent of the total in 1930, compared with 58 percent in the United States in 1928.

As early as 1923 the French Big Three made over half the country's motor vehicles, and in 1929 their share reached 74 percent. The concentration typical of the auto industry was proceding apace.

THE SMALL FIRMS IN DECLINE

The First World War marked a great triumph for the Berliet firm of Lyon. Its achievement in truck output was startling and demonstrated what could be done by standardizing vehicle production. It certainly convinced Marius Berliet, who planned to make one model car (based on the American Dodge) and one model truck in his huge new Vénissieux factory and become a major player in the world automobile industry.

It did not happen. Severe blows rained down on Marius Berliet. The steel he made from French iron had less strength than the American steel that went into the American Dodge, so his new car based on the Dodge dimensions suffered many breakdowns, costly repairs, and a poor reputation. Sales of his trucks, and new trucks generally in France, almost stopped for several years as military surplus trucks (French and American) were sold at bargain prices. Marius Berliet also had to bear unusual financial pressure as he had paid too much for his American equipment during the war and war profits taxes came due. At the end of his rope, Berliet in April 1921 asked for a receivership. This provided that he pay 20 percent of his current debt and convert the rest to 6 percent bonds. Bankers were brought into the firm to protect the bondholders and Marius Berliet's managerial authority was restricted. Gradually the concern began to recover, making a variety of cars and trucks far from the single-model policy. By 1929 the company and Marius Berliet personally had repurchased all the bonds and he regained full control of his firm. His difficulties showed the dangers of standardization when not supported by thorough engineering and a correct analysis of the market. The great potential of 1918 had been followed by disappointing results.

The other French automakers in the 1920s took only a small part of the business. Some (Hispano-Suiza, Delage, Delaunay-Belleville, Panhard & Levassor, Hotchkiss, Talbot, Voisin, and Salmson) aimed at the luxury end of the business; others tried to compete with the large companies in the low- and middle-price ranges (Mathis and Chenard & Walcker); and still others (Delahaye, Unic, and Rochet-Schneider) gradually shifted to trucks and special-purpose vehicles. Some of these firms and many others left the market entirely in the 1920s and early 1930s, pushed to the wall by competition from the major companies and their lack of resources to modernize production. Ettore Bugatti had left Alsace for France during the First World War. In Paris he designed an aircraft engine that was purchased by the United States, but production models of this failed. Back in Molsheim between the wars, he made small numbers of luxury cars and racers. He managed to survive the depression of the 1930s in part by installing his larger engines in powered railcars, competing with Renault, Michelin, and others, as these machines began to replace the light steam locomotives on lines with light traffic.

Ford tried to play a larger role in France in the 1920s. Before the war, fewer than 2,000 Model T cars had been sold in France. During the conflict the number rose to about 15,000, assembled in Bordeaux from parts shipped from Detroit or Manchester. After rejecting a bid from André Citroën in June 1919 for a joint venture in France, Ford sold a relatively small number of cars there and then established a new assembly plant in Asnières, near Paris, in 1926. Saddled with poor local leadership, Ford continued to show only mediocre results.[7] Henry Ford's influence in France was important. It did not come from selling his cars on the French market, however, but from the adoption of his ideas by French automakers and engineers.

BRITISH CARS

British developments in the 1920s resembled those of France: expansion of the automobile market and dominance of it by a small number of producers who gradually adopted flow production methods and assembly lines. Car prices dropped, falling more than 30 percent from 1924 to 1930.

Britain gave up its role as a large market for other major producers' exports. The McKenna tariff of 1915 (33.3 percent) on passenger cars and parts usually had a protective effect. This was not so in 1919 and 1920, when domestic manufacturers made few cars, or again in 1924-25, when the tariff was briefly rescinded. But the share of imports in total domestic sales of passenger cars trended downward, reaching 12.8 percent in 1929. The United States and Canada (whose cars paid a 22.2 percent tariff) were the major suppliers. For commercial vehicles the proportion of imports tended to be larger, especially in 1929, when they accounted for an unusually high 24 percent of sales. Almost all of these were Ford and General Motors chassis for light trucks, but in the 1930s the American firms manufactured these trucks at their British branches. Exports of motor vehicles from Britain exceeded imports from 1926 on. Australia, the Irish Free State, and New Zealand were the largest customers.

ENGLISH FORD

A major difference between Britain and France was the role the Ford company played in the British Isles, especially in the first half of the decade. Ford took advantage of the strong demand for cars when the war ended, demand that British firms could not satisfy for two years owing to problems in converting back to automobile production. Ford rushed parts to Manchester and assembled 12,000 cars there in 1919, and 46,000 in the 15 months ending December 1920. Ford accounted for about two-thirds of total British production of about 60,000 in 1920. Other circumstances conspired handsomely to aid the American firm. Its Manchester factory had continued to assemble cars throughout the war and did not have to be converted. Its American-made parts were so low-priced that, even after paying the McKenna tariff duty, Ford could deeply undersell domestic cars. British firms did cut their prices sharply in 1921 and thereafter, but they never got down to the level of the T.

But Henry Ford and his managers made errors in the British case and frittered away their opportunity. Percival Perry was forced out as head of the British operation in 1919 and was succeeded by a series of mediocre American executives. These leaders had to follow policies determined in the Dearborn, Michigan, headquarters, with little or no consideration given to the unique features of the British market. For example, Dearborn insisted that Ford sell left-hand-drive cars in Britain, even though the Americans had already agreed to right-hand drive for its English Fords before the war. Ford dealers were forced to give up their representation of other makes of cars and to take delivery of cars they had not ordered. Most important, Ford refused to alter the Model T's engine to take account of the revised horsepower tax, raised in 1921 to £1 ($3.85) per hp. This boosted the annual tax from $24.26 to $88.55, or about 10 percent of the basic price of a Ford in 1921. The tax on lower-powered British cars in the bottom half of the price range varied from $27 to $54 per year. Although the tax on gasoline was eliminated from 1921 to 1928, the higher annual tax on the Ford was a significant negative.

Ford did make or buy more of its parts in England to reduce the tariff problem and also shipped engines, transmissions, and rear axles from the Ford factory in Cork, Ireland, to Manchester. Parts from Ireland paid no tariff until April 1923 and 22 percent thereafter. By 1927, 92 percent of the materials and labor for the Manchester-assembled cars was British and Irish.[8] The Cork plant also made tractors from 1919 through 1922, and again from 1929 to 1932. Ford relented and did move to right-hand drive for its vehicles in 1923, but its output did not increase over the 1920 and 1921 level for the rest of the decade. The 1-ton TT truck accounted for an increasing share of Ford's production, for it was more popular than the car from 1925 on.

In the United States as well, Henry Ford's rigidity weakened sales. He finally bowed to the evidence and halted production of the Model T in May 1927. Overseas, production stopped when the supply of parts ran out. Deliveries of the new Model A (24 fiscal hp) began in Britain in May 1928, and, as a bow to the horsepower tax, it could be supplied with a smaller engine (15 fiscal hp). The light truck version, the AA, was more sought after than the car, and the company made 35,000 of them during 1928-31, compared with 15,000 cars.[9] Still, Ford sales remained below Morris and Austin, which had overtaken Ford in 1924 and 1926, respectively. In 1929 Ford car sales were fourth on the British market, with less than a 4 percent share.

Unlike most of the British firms, Ford did not use the piecework pay system. It transferred its philosophy of high-pay/high-labor-effort to Britain. In 1928 Ford paid its workers from 66 to 91 percent more per week than did the average British auto factory.[10] In return, workers had to accept close supervision and eschew trade unions.

Henry Ford came to England in 1928 and decided to expand operations there. He authorized construction of a large integrated works at Dagenham, on the north bank of the Thames, downriver from London. It was to be a scaled-down River Rouge plant, with a capacity of 200,000 cars, many of which were to be exported elsewhere in Europe. He changed the firm's name to Ford Motor Company, Ltd., and, finally, rehired Percival Perry to run the British operations.[11]

Ford aimed its cars at the low end of the market. So did those who made cyclecars, small and low-slung machines with two seats in tandem, powered by small air-cooled engines, obviously aimed at the motorcycle market. The Rover company, a maker of mid-range cars and motorcycles, went after the cyclecar buyers with its Model Eight, introduced in 1920. This was a very small car with a two-cylinder air-cooled engine of 998 cc. It sold well at first at $1,050, and sales rose when the price was cut to $850 in March 1921. In its best year, 1922, sales amounted to 4,900. Its price never dropped to that of the much larger Ford Model T, and by 1923 it met a powerful contender in the small Austin Seven, a better car, inspired in part by Rover's success.[12] Rover never seriously challenged for the lead in the British industry, but Morris did.

MORRIS MOTORS

Quite unpredictable was the rapid rise of William Morris's automobile empire to leadership in the 1920s. Morris had done well as an assembler of small cars just before the war, but his firm had not played a prominent part in munitions production from 1914 to 1918. He had seen that the market was moving toward small cars before the war and afterward he stuck to this approach. He resumed assembly of his prewar models with few changes and avoided expensive investment and consequent indebtedness. Morris showed great skill in finding and bargaining with suppliers, but sometimes they failed to meet his standards. Eventually and reluctantly he began to make some parts himself to assure quality and delivery times. By 1923 he had his own radiator and body shops and in that year bought an engine factory in Coventry from the French firm Hotchkiss. He financed this gradual investment in expensive facilities with current earnings and so protected himself from the heavy debt burdens carried by Citroën and Berliet in France and Austin in England in these years. Morris continued to make just two models of relatively small cars using the same engine. When the postwar recession arrived late in 1920 sales fell off, but he soon cut his prices. With this bold strategy he conquered the sales leadership in Britain by 1924.

Morris followed American precedents by standardizing output, cutting prices, expanding his sales network (by 1927 he had in Britain 1,750 dealers, who each sold an average of 30 to 35 Morris cars that year), vigorously advertising and promoting, instituting installment sales, offering repair warranties, and standardizing repair rates. He did not limit his innovations to sales. In 1920 he reorganized production, placing final assembly in a line, with the cars pushed manually between workstations. This arrangement persisted until 1934. With Morris's approval, Frank Woollard reorganized the former Hotchkiss engine plant on flow-production lines, with conveyors bringing parts to the engine block. He quadrupled output in a few months. To machine engine blocks, he arranged a transfer line where workers moved the blocks between machines on conveyors and hand loaded them into machines.[13] This was not an automatic transfer line as sometimes reported.

As Morris's financial resources grew he began to invest in a variety of automotive enterprises. In 1924 he bought a failing auto-parts factory in Birmingham and concentrated his expanding commercial vehicle operations there, making taxicabs, buses, and trucks of all sizes. The M.G. (Morris Garage) car began in 1923 as a sports variety of a standard model with a modified engine. This evolved by 1930 into an entirely separate car made in its own factory. In 1924 Herbert Austin proposed a merger of his own company, the financially ailing Wolseley concern, and Morris. William Morris declined the offer but in 1926 bought Wolseley as a personal investment and kept it operating largely independent of Morris Motors. In 1925 Morris purchased the Léon Bollée auto factory in Le Mans, France, as a way to break into the French market. This venture failed, and he sold it in 1931. Morris also promoted the establishment of the Pressed Steel Company in Oxford in 1927, using the Budd system for making all-steel bodies. As for Citroën in France, this business was more expensive than Morris had expected, and he sold out his share in 1930.

In Britain in the 1920s the market was still in the phase of initial demand where most sales went to reasonably well-off buyers. Morris stopped cutting his prices in 1925, when his Cowley model was at about $965, compared with Ford's $580. Morris's sales remained on a plateau in the second half of the decade, ranging between 48,000 and 63,500 per year. He needed new models and lower prices to win a large increase in sales.

AUSTIN SURMOUNTS ITS DIFFICULTIES

Although the Austin company with its extensive manufacturing facilities appeared to have an advantage over most other British motorcar firms in the postwar years, there were unsuspected problems. Herbert Austin did not make large profits from his war production, so to purchase the government-built factories in his industrial complex he incurred a large debt. Then he misjudged the nature of the postwar market. He decided to make two vehicles only–an expensive 20-hp sedan and a 1.5-ton truck. The standardization made sense, but like Marius Berliet, who followed a similar strategy, Austin found that after an initial boom sales fell off for his motorcar and were very poor for the truck in the face of 60,000 war-surplus trucks thrown on the market by the British government. By 1921 it was clear that the 20-hp car did not appeal to a wide enough market, so Austin prepared a smaller version, the 12 hp. It appeared in September 1921 and enjoyed good sales, but already in April the firm had been placed in the hands of a receiver. This circumstance brought new people into the company's management–Carl Engelbach as production manager and Ernest Payton as financial director, both of whom continued to play leading roles in the firm. The company emerged from receivership in April 1922 but found solid financial footing only in 1927.

In 1921 Herbert Austin decided to enter the market for very small cars. He and a very young draftsman, Stanley Edge, began to design a miniature car at Austin's home. Inspired by the Rover Eight and Peugeot Quadrilette,[14] it had a very small four-cylinder engine of 747 cc. He introduced this Austin Seven, or Baby, in July 1922 at a price of $995, slightly above that of the Ford Model T. Just 178 Sevens were made in 1922, but this rose to 2,409 in 1923, when the price was cut to $750, and reached 26,540 in 1929 at a price of $607. Although originally aimed at consumers who were buying motorcycles with sidecars, its price never did catch these, for their price fell even faster. The Seven probably drew most of its customers from those who would otherwise have chosen Fords or small models from other British or French producers. The Seven's good performance and low operating costs won them over. The Baby Austin also attracted interest on the Continent, where the Dixi company in Germany made some 14,000 of them on license in the late 1920s, and Lucien Rosengart took a license and made almost as many in Paris during the same period. An effort to sell a variant, the Bantam, in the United States failed, but the American Bantam company went on to design the Jeep, so successful during and after the Second World War. In Japan the company that would become Nissan produced a copy of the Seven and Austin eventually forced it to obtain a license.

The Austin company continued to make a variety of larger cars in addition to the Seven and thoroughly modernized its facilities in the mid-1920s. Single-purpose machines were installed, operated by semiskilled workers; hand-powered moving assembly began for bodies and chassis. But Austin and almost all the other British firms retained a piecework pay system as a way to encourage labor to work efficiently. In this system most of the British firms also depended on shop stewards, who were not part of management, to coordinate production in the shops. In the short run this reduced friction between labor and management, but in the long run it held back possible gains in productivity and would generate major problems when British factories became strongly unionized in the 1950s.[15] Employee productivity at Austin doubled from 1924 to 1927. All this brought profits, and Austin paid off most of its debts. Together, Morris and Austin won from 56 to 60 percent of the car market in Britain from 1928 to 1930. It looked like a two-car race.

OTHER BRITISH PRODUCERS

For a time in the mid-1920s the Clyno company bid to become a major factor in the auto business. Assembling small cars in Wolverhampton, it offered strong competition to the leaders, making over 12,000 in 1926. After investing large sums in a new factory and introducing some poor models, however, Clyno failed in 1929. Rolls-Royce continued to make very high-priced luxury cars and, like Hispano-Suiza in France, maintained production of aircraft engines. The firm also made cars in a branch in Springfield, Massachusetts, but this failed as the company refused to accept any significant alterations in its designs or methods to suit the American market. The Singer company made some good cars but offered too many models to take advantage of long production runs. In 1928-29 the Rootes brothers, very prosperous car dealers, took over the financially troubled Humber and Hillman companies of Coventry, along with a body maker. There followed some, but not enough, rationalization of product policy and manufacturing.

General Motors usually followed behind Ford in moving into overseas markets. In Britain it did offer to buy Austin in 1925. When this fell through, it picked up the Vauxhall company for just $2.6 million later that year. This firm made only about 1,500 high-priced cars a year and it took GM an extended period to decide what to do with it. By 1928 the Americans had installed a moving assembly line for chassis and made the entire body in the plant, using stamping presses extensively. Output of Vauxhall cars remained low at first – 1928 was its best year with 2,560 – but GM moved its assembly of Chevrolet cars and trucks, which had begun in 1924 at Hendon (near London) to the Vauxhall factory. Management saw an opening for the new six-cylinder Chevrolet light truck, a market where only the Ford AA and Morris competed. These sold briskly, and by 1930, 85 percent of the chassis made at Vauxhall were Chevrolet trucks and vans; of these only 20 percent of the value was imported.[16]

Britain was following the American lead in manufacturing and selling cars, except for labor policy. Automobiles were penetrating economic and social life, as indicated by the decline of horses. From 1911 to 1924 the figure for horses employed in British urban areas to move goods or to carry people in cabs or buses fell from 995,000 to 374,000. The number of horses on farms decreased also, but more gradually, from about 1.5 million to 965,000.[17]

GERMANY IN RECOVERY

The auto industry in Germany took longer to recover from the war and postwar dislocations than it did in France and Britain. Many difficulties beset it until 1924-25, and output fluctuated around a low level. A more normal situation then followed, and in 1927-29 the business was bouyant, only to fall into a sharp depression in the early 1930s. The shrinking prices for cars (after the end of the inflation), development of small cars for a broader market, and modernizing of manufacturing facilities came in Germany as elsewhere in Europe. The ownership of the auto companies went through a complicated shuffling that finally led to an outcome with one major producer, six or eight making a few thousand each, and some specialist firms making small quantities.

The industry's major problem in the early 1920s was, on the demand side, that after the war the middle class hesitated to buy cars – for most of them a luxury or discretionary purchase – in the face of uncertainty caused by rapidly rising prices. Prices rose in 1919 and then again in 1921-22, leading into the galloping inflation of 1923. Only at the end of that year was the currency stabilized and by then many Germans had lost their savings. Farm incomes were low, so little demand came from rural and small-town Germany. A 15 percent luxury tax imposed on passenger cars also weakened the market until the tax was finally abolished in 1926. On the other hand, at some points during the inflation period foreign exchange rates were such that German vehicles became bargains for foreigners, and many were exported – for example, thousands of surplus military trucks.

There were difficulties on the supply side also. In 1919 and 1920 traditional labor discipline broke down, a situation triggered by the military defeat and the revolution of 1918, which discredited the ruling elites and authority generally. At the same time came news from Communist Russia where peasants and workers had seized control of land and factories. In this context labor disputes were frequent, often set off by price inflation and by such particular issues as the end of wartime contracts, which required sharp and painful cuts in employment. At Daimler, for example, workers and their leaders engaged in obvious restriction of output as a way to raise piece rates.[18] Raw materials, including coal, which many of the larger firms burned to generate their own electric power, ran short. It took time to rebuild supply and sales networks and to design new models. Almost all car imports were banned for several years – a policy aimed at saving foreign exchange, but one that protected the weak domestic industry from competition as well. It also delayed modernization of design and production.

OPEL SPEEDS TO THE FRONT

In this difficult environment the Opel company survived for a time by making bicycles and motorcycles, but it ended the decade as by far the largest German producer. Its automobiles sales were poor at first, reaching bottom in 1923 when it produced 910 cars of five different models. In the early 1920s the Opel factory stood in the French zone of occupation, cut off from most of the German market. Opel had no protection from foreign competition, so it faced the need to modernize early and began doing so in 1924. It decided to offer one model only – a copy of the 5-hp Citroën, changed only slightly from the French design and rated at 4 fiscal hp by the German calculation. Available in green rather than the Citroën's yellow, Germans called this small car the "Treefrog." Priced at $950, the car was a winner, and Opel made almost 4,600 of them in 1924. In succeeding years Opel increased the size of this car, dropped its price to $645, and added other models. Its best year of the decade, 1928, saw total output at 42,771, well below the largest French and British concerns. The plant was full of conveyors bringing parts to moving assembly lines to construct major components, including bodies, which in turn fed the final assembly lines. Opel had its own foundry in Düsseldorf and bought out its large forgings and electrical equipment. The other parts it made itself, using many single-purpose machines. Employment reached 13,000.[19]

DAIMLER AND BENZ DECLINE AND RISE

Both Daimler and Benz, with their traditions of high-priced vehicles, had serious difficulties in the postwar years. Car sales remained below the best prewar levels, although the truck and bus output of both firms was somewhat better. Benz produced an average 1,630 cars per year from 1919 to 1926, while Daimler's average output reached only 1,145. Occasionally their managements considered a merger, and their bankers pushed hard for this. Finally, Benz, fearing an unfriendly takeover, and Daimler, with financial problems, in 1924 entered a "union of interests" – an arrangement in which they began to eliminate duplication of products and facilities. This led in 1926 to their merging as the Daimler-Benz Company, whose cars and trucks were sold under the name Mercedes-Benz.

In this period the great automobile designer Ferdinand Porsche worked for Daimler. Born to a German-speaking family in the Sudeten area of Bohemia in 1875, he had designed electric and gasoline-electric cars for the Lohner concern of Vienna around the turn of the century, then headed design at Austro-Daimler from 1905 to 1923. He had to leave in 1923, for in a heated discussion at a board of directors' meeting he hurled a spark plug at another director. Porsche arrived at Daimler that same year, but after frequent disagreements he left Daimler-Benz in 1928 and the next year set up his own independent design office in Stuttgart.

In the year of its merger with Benz, the Daimler works introduced a mid-priced touring car, unlovely in appearance but affordable at

$1,860, compared with the $4,500 to $6,000 asked for the usual machine produced by the two predecessor firms. In 1927 the company made 4,788 of this model, and it sold well for several years. Daimler-Benz continued to make a variety of models in the middle-price range and a few very expensive prestige cars. It also engaged vigorously in racing.

Over the decade Daimler had modernized production somewhat more than Benz. It began by making subassemblies in separate shops, using the flow principle, and consequently breaking up the departments that had been organized by the nature of the tool used – lathe, milling machine, and so forth.[20] The Germans called this system group production, and the larger carmakers generally adopted it in the 1920s. At the body works in Sindelfingen the company installed a moving assembly line for bodies in 1925-26, and at Stuttgart-Untertürkheim it established a final moving assembly line for chassis in 1927.

COMPETITION FROM IMPORTS

The modernization or rationalization of production at Opel, Daimler-Benz, and other German auto firms – along with price cutting and the manufacture of smaller cars – were stimulated by the return of international competition to Germany. The embargo on imports was lifted in 1926. A very high tariff replaced it, but the rates were reduced every six months until July 1928. Because the tariff on completely knocked-down auto parts was considerably less than on finished cars or major subassemblies, some 10 foreign carmakers, including General Motors, Ford, Chrysler, Citroën, and Fiat, set up assembly plants in 1926. Cars imported fully assembled or as parts for assembly sold well, amounting to 28 percent of the German market in 1927. Imports at this level frightened the German producers, who urged their government to protect them. They received modest relief in January 1928, when the tariff on imported auto parts was raised to equal the rate for complete cars. Then, in July 1928, the rate for both was cut to about 30 percent, a figure close to the British tariff on imported automobiles and parts. In 1928 sales of imports rose to 39 percent of the domestic market and remained at that level over the next two years. In its Berlin plant General Motors assembled some 18,000 cars and light trucks in 1928, making it the second largest producer in Germany in that year after Opel. A growing share of these parts came from German sources – for example, the best-selling Chevrolet got its chassis frames from Krupp and bodies from a Berlin licensee of Budd, along with locally made glass, headlights, upholstery, and lacquer.[21] In 1929 Chevrolet's new six-cylinder car sold for $950, while a Mercedes-Benz with similar attributes but still using magneto ignition cost three times as much. Ford's sales in Germany were hurt by the transition from the Model T to the Model A, but the company assembled 7,000 of the newer type there in 1929 and 9,900 in 1930. This Ford sold for about 15 percent less than a comparable Adler.

Price alone did not account for the popularity of American cars: they were better than German ones. The years of the First World War and the embargo on imports had isolated German automakers from technical changes elsewhere. It took several years after 1925 for them to make up lost ground. A young auto mechanic who toiled at Frankfurt an der Oder from 1933 to 1936 observed, "A few customers had American automobiles which were – at that time – far superior to our German cars. . . . The Fords, Chevrolets, Buicks, Terraplanes, Essexes, Hudsons, La Salles, and Packards were sturdier, more powerful and very much easier to work on than the great German makes – Mercedes and Horch, Opel, Audi and BMW."[22] Imports declined sharply in 1931 and fell to just 4,600, or 11 percent of new cars registered, in 1932.[23] Part of this decline came because both General Motors and Ford, the two largest importers, began manufacturing automobiles in Germany – GM bought Opel in 1929, and Ford opened a new factory at Cologne in 1931 – and because of the onset of the Great Depression.

WINNERS AND LOSERS

Among the other successful German auto firms in the postwar decade was Hanomag, a former steam-locomotive maker that began selling a very small one-cylinder car in 1925 for under $500, and Adler, which made from 4,000 to 9,000 middle-price cars per year in the later 1920s. The wartime aero-engine builder BMW made automotive engines and motorcycles in the 1920s and then in 1928 bought the Dixi firm of Eisenach. Dixi had begun producing the Austin Seven on license in 1927, and BMW continued making it with variations for a few years and then moved toward larger models.

DKW was another new name on the German automobile scene in this decade. It stood for *Das kleine Wunder* (The Little Wonder), a low-powered motorcycle made by the Danish engineer J. S. Rasmussen in the small Saxon town of Zschopau. By the end of the 1920s DKW was Germany's largest motorcycle maker, using a moving assembly line to turn out up to 450 a day. Meanwhile, Rasmussen bought several other small automotive companies, along with foundries and forges. In 1928 he began manufacturing small cars in Berlin using the DKW name and a two-stroke, water-cooled engine. This car, designed by Rudolf Slaby, had no frame but was held together by a unitized plywood body. A later model of 1930 used front-wheel drive. Despite their many faults, DKWs found a good market. Such was not the case for cars made by the Audi company. In 1928 Rasmussen bought control of this declining firm in which August Horch no longer was active. He had it make two models based on the Rickenbacker car of Detroit. The American flying ace Eddie Rickenbacker had founded this company and made some excellent but not expensive cars. The firm failed nevertheless, and Rasmussen bought its designs, patterns, and equipment and brought them to Germany. Now, in a delicious irony, Audi made Rickenbackers in Zwickau. In the event, they proved too expensive for the Germans, and Audi neared collapse. So did the Horch company, which had priced its automobiles out of the market. The upshot was a merger of Rasmussen's DKW and Audi with Horch in 1932, under the name Auto Union, which in turn bought the Wanderer car operations in Chemnitz in the same year. The Saxon companies had united.

Other firms making expensive cars fell by the wayside. Siemens sold its Protos car operations to NAG in 1926, but then NAG gave up the business in the early 1930s. Brennabor succeeded in the 1920s with quantity production of small cars, but its experiments with large, front-wheel-drive cars did not pay off, and the firm succumbed in 1934.

DIESEL ENGINES

Although the German auto industry ran a poor third to the French and British in the 1920s, it led the way in an important new development, the automotive diesel engine. The engine's father, Rudolf Diesel, was born in Paris to German parents in 1858. He spent his first 12 years there and then studied engineering in Germany. While working as a refrigeration engineer he conceived the idea of igniting the fuel in an internal combustion engine by injecting it directly into a cylinder where the air had been highly compressed and therefore was very hot. He patented this principle in 1892 and then persuaded two important firms – MAN of Augsburg and Krupp of Essen – to support its development. By 1897 Diesel achieved satisfactory results, injecting the fuel with a blast of compressed air. His early engines had a thermal efficiency about 50 percent higher than contemporary gasoline engines, burned about half as much fuel per horsepower, and could use less expensive petroleum products than gasoline. Because these early diesel engines were heavy and slow-running and required an air compressor, they were used as stationary power sources and for marine purposes. Before the First World War the European navies began to install diesel engines in submarines. The MAN company developed a relatively light model used in most German submarines during the war.

After the war MAN and Benz (which had made many of the diesels for submarines) strove to apply diesel engines to automotive use, to replace high-cost gasoline. They succeeded in reducing the weight and struggled with injection systems to eliminate the air compressor. Both placed a few diesel trucks on the market and Daimler joined them. Meanwhile, the Bosch company took up the question of diesel fuel injection in 1922 and by 1926 perfected an improved system that soon was adopted by most makers of automotive diesels, including Daimler-Benz. By the end of the decade some 310 trucks used diesel engines in Germany, and the technology was under development in other parts of Europe.[24]

ITALY

The Italian motorcar industry in the 1920s was a matter of Fiat along with a handful of specialist producers. Its growth stopped after 1926 as a recession set in, average incomes remained low, and none of the manufacturers tried to market a really small and cheap car. Imports that might have been competitive were restricted.

Just after the war Italian industry was marked by considerable labor agitation, which reached a climax in 1920. At the end of March a dispute broke out at Fiat, triggered by some workers' refusal to accept daylight savings time. Behind this issue was a serious price inflation and the question of factory councils. How much power should these worker-elected bodies have over production? The socialist theoretician Antonio Gramsci, by now a Leninist, urged that these councils take control of production in the factories, call themselves soviets, and lead the Italians to a communist revolution. His views came to dominate among the leaders of the councils in Turin, whose members were called commissars. The Fiat strike quickly spread to all of Turin and to hundreds of plants throughout the province of Piedmont. But it faded even more quickly and labor accepted terms on 23 April. The factory councils would continue but with limited authority. Management, once having taken control of the shop floor, would concede almost anything rather than give it back. It was a serious defeat for labor, but the strike committee said its battle for communism would continue.

The second act came in August, when long-running negotiations between the national metalworkers union and management representatives over wages and the recognition of factory councils broke off. The union thereupon ordered workers to engage in a slowdown to hurt the firms but allow the workers to maintain an income. Irritated by this, management at Alfa-Romeo in Milan locked out its workers on 30 August. In reaction the union, which was not led by revolutionaries, ordered workers to occupy metalworking factories in the Milan region, some 280 of them, to forestall other lockouts. This was a defensive tactic and rested on the assumption that it would force the government to intervene in the dispute. The occupation movement quickly spread to metalworking establishments in Genoa, Turin, and elsewhere in Italy, including all the auto factories. In many occupied plants production continued, but only until coal or other raw materials ran out. The occupants could not obtain bank credit and had trouble selling their output, so workers received little or no pay. Radical or communist worker groups frequently tried to take the lead in these occupations, to go much further than the union leadership intended and turn occupations into a seizure of power. Red flags with hammer and sickle flew over factories, portraits of Lenin appeared on their walls, and at Fiat there was talk of shipping cars and trucks to Russia to earn money to pay the workers' wages.

Under Prime Minister Giovanni Giolitti the government maintained a neutral stance and held back those who urged that the army expel the workers by force. Giolitti waited until the radical effervescence subsided, until differences among the workers widened, and then began negotiations on 15 September. These led to an agreement and the workers evacuated the factories between 25 and 30 September, with a wage increase and a promise of significant participation by the factory councils in plant management. As this promise was not kept, the agreement really amounted to a defeat for the radicals and for organized labor generally. The postwar recession already in effect soon led to layoffs and a further weakening of the labor movement.[25] As organized labor waned, authoritarian attitudes waxed in Italy. The fear that labor's actions and rhetoric generated among the middle and wealthy classes in 1919 and 1920 brought support to nationalist and fascist movements. In 1922 the Fascists won out, and Mussolini became prime minister.

FIAT RETAINS ITS DOMINANCE

The Fiat company continued its policies of integration and diversification in the interwar years. The labor upheaval just discussed had no lasting effect on the firm. By 1924 it comprised 20 large plants, including its own steel mills and foundries, employing some 26,000. In addition to cars and trucks, Fiat made aircraft and aircraft engines, diesel engines, agricultural tractors – both wheeled and tracklaying, military tanks, small and medium-size ocean vessels, and railway freight and passenger cars, along with diesel-electric locomotives, ball bearings in large numbers, tools, and firearms.[26] It continued to make trucks in its original Corso Dante location and gradually expanded car production in the new Lingotto factory. For the postwar market Fiat engineers had prepared a very small car in the class of the Peugeot Quadrilette or Austin Seven, but it never went into production.[27] Instead, the firm emphasized its 1.5-liter 501 model, which soon earned a good reputation for reliability. In the middle price range, it sold some 80,000 from 1919 to 1926. A majority of these were exported, with Britain, Switzerland, Australia, and Spain the leading markets. Italy and Fiat took up the role of prewar France, exporting a large share of output, because at the prices asked the domestic Italian market could not absorb anywhere near the firm's productive capacity. In 1925 the 501 model was replaced by the 509, a smaller 1-liter car. It also sold quite well in foreign markets, including Germany in the late 1920s.

At Lingotto, Fiat slowly introduced flow production with conveyors for various subassemblies. In 1925 the final assembly line of the new 509 model shifted from hand to mechanical power. Cars were assembled on the fifth floor and then driven up to a test track on the roof. Piecework was abandoned, and workers were paid on a collective bonus system. In effect, their pace was determined by the speed of the machines. Fiat refused to emulate Ford to the extent of complete standardization of product. Production of a range of different models and variations within them, along with sharp sales fluctuations, meant that Lingotto never produced at its capacity of 300 cars a day. Fiat's Fordist blicy was contradicted by its diversified model policy. ctivity doubled from the early to the late 1920s. In an- t policy, some workers were moved back to piecework in 1926, and then the Bedaux pay system, which required workers to split their piecework bonuses with the firm, was introduced at Lingotto in 1929.[28] The complex nature of Fiat's operations required many variations in its pay systems.

ELSEWHERE IN ITALY

Italy's other automakers competed in the middle and upper ranges of the market at home and abroad. Bianchi and Lancia sold at most a few thousand cars a year, the latter introducing unitary frame and body construction in 1923. Alfa had become Alfa-Romeo in 1915 when the engineer Nicola Romeo bought control. Its cars won many races in the 1920s, but this did not translate to much greater production or sales. Only in 1925 did the firm make more than 1,000 cars. Itala and Isotta Fraschini catered to the maharaja market with small numbers of luxury machines. Ford had begun assembly at a modest rate in Italy in 1922 and purchased land in Livorno for a grander operation. Pressed by Fiat, Mussolini forbade Ford to proceed unless it could operate with 100 percent Italian manufacture. When Ford thereupon tried to form a union with Isotta Fraschini, Mussolini again objected, and Ford backed away, settling for assembly of a few imports – a number that shrank when Italy raised its tariff in response to the higher U.S. tariff of 1930.

THE AUTOSTRADE

Although Italy was the least motorized of the major European automobile producing countries, it was the first to build express highways. This surprising development can be attributed in part to the father of the modern expressway, Piero Puricelli, a civil engineer of Milan who worked for his father's road construction firm. A committee of the Milan-based Touring Club of Italy first proposed the idea in March 1922, suggesting new roads (soon called autostrade) for automobile use only and emphasizing how their construction would help solve a severe unemployment problem. Puricelli's name appeared on this proposal. The scheme quickly hardened, for in 1922 an Autostrade Company was formed to promote the idea. One can find partial precedents for this Italian initiative in the United States, where parkway construction began before the First World War around New York City. These roads sometimes were divided highways, had overpasses to eliminate intersections, and banned commercial vehicles. They were first designed for 35-mph speeds. The Italians preferred to take as their model the ancient Roman roads, especially spokesmen for the Fascist regime that came to power in October 1922.

Puricelli's plan was more innovative than the New York parkways and bore some resemblance to a railway. Its major features were (1) no slow traffic (no horse-drawn vehicles or bicycles); (2) very limited access with no level crossings for railways or other roads and no access by adjoining property owners; (3) one hard-surface highway wide enough for three lanes of traffic and as few curves as possible; and (4) service facilities and special police assigned to the autostrada.[29]

Mussolini's government immediately approved the Milan group's idea, and the private Autostrade Company began construction in March 1923, with Mussolini breaking the first ground for a road from Milan to the lake country northwest of the city. The first 30-mile section was opened in September 1924, and the entire 53-mile project was finished a year later. The project's 90 million lire ($4 million) cost was financed by the company's share capital (50 million) and by bank loans guaranteed by the national and local governments. Seventeen interchanges gave access to the road, on average three miles apart. The company charged tolls to meet its maintenance costs and debt service, but traffic was sparse. In 1926 only 1,155 vehicles used the road on an average day. Nevertheless, many other Italian localities and private companies soon proposed autostrade for their regions. From the national government's point of view, the policy had much to commend it: it increased employment, encouraged an important industry, brought prestige, and was financed by private capital. The only immediate cost was the guarantee of interest payments on the loans.

In 1927 a second expressway opened from Milan 30 miles eastward to Bergamo. A private firm built it with financial arrangements similar to those of the Milan-lake country route. In the following year came still another expressway, a 13-mile route from Naples to Pompeii. This road over difficult terrain cost twice as much to build per mile as those of the flat Po Valley. A decade later autostrade stretched from Turin to Brescia and then, after a long gap, from Padua to Venice and from Florence to Lucca and the sea. The most challenging job was a route from Genoa north through very difficult topography to the Po Valley. The

TABLE 6.3 MAJOR EUROPEAN AUTOMAKERS IN THE LATE 1920S

	Citroën	Morris	Renault	Fiat	Austin	Opel	Peugeot
1928			55,884	47,765	43,638	42,771	
1929	102,891	63,522					30,036

Figures include all motor vehicles except for Morris and Austin,
  where they indicate cars only.

state financed this project, finished in 1935, which included frequent tunnels and bridges.

These autostrade were built well ahead of effective demand, for none of them carried much traffic. In 1937 the busiest was the first one, Milan-lake country, which carried an average 2,166 vehicles per day. The least used was the Brescia-Bergamo segment, traveled by only 496 per day. The net income of all of them after maintenance expenses was just 1.7 percent of the capital invested, so the state and local governments had to subsidize interest payments on the debts. The national governnment had taken over management of several of the autostrade, and all of them were to revert to the state after 50 years. The toll rate for a small car was about 0.5¢ per kilometer, except for the Naples-Pompeii stretch, where cars paid about 2¢ per kilometer. At the end of 1937, 299 miles (482 km) of autostrade were operating, including some difficult-to-build mountainous segments. Although starting later, German expressways by this time surpassed the Italian achievement, as will be seen in Chapter 7, but the Italians had led the way for Europe and the world.

OTHER AREAS OF EUROPE

Domestic automakers in the rest of Europe were of comparatively minor importance. In countries with low tariffs, automakers could not compete with imports; in protectionist countries, however, the market was not large enough for efficient production. Some firms found an answer by manufacturing medium-size and large trucks, where mass production was not feasible because purchasers had special requirements.

A protectionist case is Czechoslovakia, where domestic auto production expanded to about 12,000 or 14,000 a year by the end of the decade. The renowned arms maker Skoda entered the business in 1923, at first making Hispano-Suizas on license and then taking over the Laurin & Klement firm. It made a variety of vehicles based on that company's designs, about 3,000 in 1929. Skoda was the third-largest Czech producer, behind Praga, which by 1929 offered a range from a small, 856-cc model to six- and eight-cylinder touring cars, as well as trucks – about 6,000 vehicles altogether. Tatra was the new Czech name for the Nesselsdorf company from 1923 on. Hans Ledwinka designed its unusual best-seller, a car with a central tubular frame powered by a 1-liter, air-cooled, twin-cylinder engine. Tatra made some 4,500 cars and trucks in 1929. Total Czech motor vehicle registrations reached only 63,000 in that year. Protectionism encouraged these producers to make a wide range of vehicles and kept prices high. Did it serve the country's interest to reduce the availability of low-priced cars for Czech consumers? Belgium's tariff was about 30 percent in the 1920s, but, even so, domestic producers gradually faded before American and French imports.

Spain, Sweden, and the Soviet Union were the largest markets in Europe without significant local producers. The Soviet Union is a special case, treated in the next chapter. Ford, Citroën, Fiat, and Renault supplied most of the vehicles to Spain, where Ford had an assembly plant from 1920. Ford also assembled cars in Denmark (starting in 1919), Belgium (1922), the Netherlands (1932), and Romania (1936).

Sweden maintained a low tariff of 15 percent, and Ford dominated the passenger-car and light-truck market, although Scania-Vabis had made trucks since before 1914. In 1927 Volvo entered the business. Its name – meaning "I roll" – came from a type of ball bearing formerly made by the SKF firm. Founded by Assar Gabrielsson, former sales manager of SKF, and Gustaf Larson, an engineer once associated with SKF, Volvo became a subsidiary of SKF and operated in a Göteborg factory obtained from SKF and with capital loaned by it. Gabrielsson's plan was to take advantage of high-quality Swedish steel and engineering skills, along with low wages to make vehicles sturdy enough for the country's poor roads and rigorous climate. Volvo's engineers designed the vehicles and engines and the company contracted with specialized firms, including the well-known arms maker Bofors, to supply the components for assembly. Gabrielsson consciously used the British firm

Morris as a model. Some of the suppliers, however, were unused to quantity production of interchangeable items, and Volvo had to teach them new methods; in 1930 it took over its engine maker, Pentaverken. Volvo's cars sold poorly, competing not only with Ford but with General Motors, which established an assembly plant in Stockholm in 1928. In that year SKF seriously considered abandoning the enterprise and invited the American expert Charles Nash to visit Sweden to examine it. Gabrielsson fought hard to save Volvo and prevailed, aided by rising sales of trucks. These trucks, of 1.5- and 2-ton capacity, were in between the light Ford and GM models and the heavier Scanias. In 1930 Volvo built 1,256 trucks and about half as many cars, and registered its first profit.[30]

By the end of the 1920s the Europeans had begun to assimilate some of the characteristics of the American motorcar industry. Output and productivity remained considerably less than at the larger U.S. firms, but the greater flexibility of their manufacturing processes allowed the European firms to react more quickly to changes in demand. Tariff protection had slowed both the development of the market for low-priced cars and the introduction of new production methods, but it had not smothered innovation, as seen in the most obvious examples – diesel engines and the expressways – and in front-wheel-drive, just around the corner.

7
NEW DIRECTIONS

The American producers dominated the automobile industry in the 1920s, in 1929 making 5.3 million motor vehicles while output in the four large West European countries was 682,000, just 13 percent of U.S. production. Toward the end of the 1930s the situation had changed. The European total in 1937 had risen to 1.1 million, 23 percent of the American 4.8 million. The American decline was countered by the European growth of 62 percent.[1] A major reason for this European improvement was the Great Depression, which in the United States went deeper and lasted longer than in most of Europe. In Britain the depression did not hit hard, and by 1934 the economy was climbing above its output of the late 1920s. The cycle in Germany was quite different – a very deep depression by 1932 followed by rapid emergence from this crevasse. The French economy slid into the depression in 1931, and although France did not suffer a serious decline, significant expansion came only in 1939. Italy went through a minor contraction and, starting in 1935, experienced growth above the levels of the 1920s.

The advancing prosperity in Britain and Germany, and to a lesser degree in Italy and France, helps explain the expanding automobile output. In technical terms, annually from 1925 through 1938 there was almost a perfect correlation between national product and motor-vehicle production in Germany (0.92, with 1.0 representing a perfect fit) and Britain (also 0.92). In France and Italy the correlation was 0.62 in each case over the years. Also fostering higher output were lower car prices, owing in turn to the adoption of mass-production methods in the later 1920s and to manufacturers' increasing emphasis on small cars. The major European manufacturing countries protected their domestic auto industries from competition from the United States and from each other by tariffs and other restrictions, Britain the least and the others almost completely.

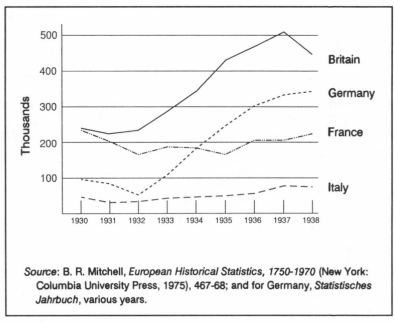

FIGURE 7.1   MOTOR-VEHICLE PRODUCTION, 1930-1938

BRITAIN: EXPANSION WITHOUT CONCENTRATION

During the depression Britain experienced serious unemployment problems in certain locations and some industries, but the economy as a whole did not suffer anything like the economic disasters in Germany or the United States. Car and truck production dropped only 5.4 percent from 1929 to 1931 and then rose regularly, reaching more than double the 1929 level in 1937. British auto output overtook France and led Europe from 1930 on. The continued health of the British economy kept demand for cars strong. Prices for food and other imported products fell, leaving more disposable income for middle-class people, who were the car buyers. The serious unemployment of coal miners and textile workers did not have a direct effect on the car market because these people had not received enough income when employed to purchase many cars. Production costs and car prices continued to decline as imported raw materials cost less and more efficient production methods were introduced. From an index 100 in 1924, car prices fell to

68 in 1930 and 52 in 1934.[2] Exports rose as the pound sterling was devalued and as more countries discriminated against American competition by taxing cars according to cylinder capacity.

It has been observed that when the average annual wage in a country first exceeds the retail price of a popular family car, the country has reached the point of takeoff for a rapid increase in car sales.[3] This does not mean that those who receive the average wage can now afford a car, but that the relationship of incomes and prices is such that a large number of consumers can and do buy cars. This wage-price relationship occurred in 1912 in the United States; in Britain it arrived in 1935. In that year the average annual wage reached £120 from its low of £116.7 in 1933, while the Morris Eight sold for £118 and the Ford Eight (or "Popular") sold at £115 (cut to £100 late in the year).[4] Passenger-car sales in Britain did expand. From 1935 to 1938 they reached a total of 1.423 million, 76 percent more than in the previous four-year period, when the number was 808,000. (The model designation – Eight – refers to the fiscal horsepower, not the number of cylinders.)

The concentration that characterized the auto industry by the end of the 1920s, in which Morris and Austin together held 60 percent of the passenger car market, declined in the 1930s. The two leading firms did sell more cars, but lost market share to four others (Ford, Standard, Rootes, and Vauxhall), so the Big Two of 1929 became the Big Six. This surprising development came as a result of errors by Morris and Austin as well as vigorous competition by the others.

MORRIS AND AUSTIN FAIL TO PREVAIL

William Morris shifted his policy from mass producing just two models to making a proliferation of types, seeking the approval of an allegedly fickle public. In 1928 he introduced a small 8-hp model, the Morris Minor, to compete with the Austin Seven. By 1933 the firm offered nine basic lines of cars, with 26 body styles, but its share of the market dropped and Austin outsold it in 1933 and 1934. Behind this loss of market lay management problems: Morris could no longer control his many enterprises but found it hard to delegate authority to others. He came to recognize the problem and in 1933 promoted Leonard Lord to operating head of the firm while Morris himself devoted more attention to his very important philanthropic activities. Even so, Morris continued to intervene in his firm's policies in a fitful way, often to its disadvantage. There is an interesting parallel to Henry Ford here. Lord thoroughly reorganized the production system at Cowley to install moving final assembly lines fed by conveyors bringing subassemblies and other parts. At the same time, and essential to the system's success, he reduced the number of car models and improved quality. In a bold move, the company stopped the practice of annual model changes that had crept into Britain and returned to the earlier policy of keeping successful types in production for several years. Even though Morris had cut the price of his Minor to £100 in 1931, it did not overcome the popularity of the venerable Austin Seven. In 1934 a new Morris entry in the very small range, the Eight, offered a stronger challenge. Bearing a strong resemblance to the Ford Model Y or Eight, it became the bestseller in Britain for the rest of the decade. The Eight helped Morris regain its sales lead over Austin, although Opel became Europe's top auto producer by the end of the 1930s. For his pains in reviving and rationalizing the various Morris operations, Leonard Lord was forced out of the firm in 1936. Apparently Morris disliked Lord's widening influence. Two years later Lord joined the Austin company and became Herbert Austin's heir apparent.

William Morris began his extraordinary philanthropies in 1926 and continued them until his death in 1963, with the bulk of the funds disbursed between 1936 and 1943. The total amounted to over £30 million or about $136 million, taking account of the changing rate of the pound to the dollar over that period. The major recipients were Oxford University, hospitals and medical science, military charities, and economic development schemes. Much of the money went into endowments so Morris's money continues to benefit British society. Morris's motives for these benefactions were mixed: partly to help those who could not help themselves, partly to escape inheritance taxes, and partly to gain recognition. Honorific recognition did come. He was made a baronet in 1929, elevated to the peerage as Baron Nuffield in 1934, and created Viscount Nuffield in 1938. (The name Nuffield will be used for William Morris from 1934 on.) Nuffield was the only major philanthropist among the British motor pioneers and apparently the most important for all of Europe. As the technical, administrative, and financial aspects of his manufacturing operations became more difficult to understand, Nuffield had to depend on others, a distasteful situation for him, but he could and did retain control of his philanthropy. For some of his benefactions Lord Nuffield gave cash that ultimately meant taking money out of the firm, but the majority involved his transferring stock in Morris Motors to the recipient organizations. To give more value to this stock the company paid high dividends from 1936 on, and thereafter few profits went back into the business until 1950. There was, then, a negative side to the philanthropy. Nuffield's wealth and notoriety brought a kidnapping attempt in 1938, foiled when a confederate of the kidnapper revealed the plot to the police.

The Austin firm also presented a multiplicity of models in the early thirties, then settled down to a smaller gamut and finished second to Morris in car sales during the second half of the decade. In 1939 the famous Seven ended its run, its output since 1922 amounting to 290,946, the largest-selling European car between the wars. When Leonard Lord came on board in 1938, he quickly began making a line of trucks, using an engine closely resembling GM's Bedford six-cylinder. The British forces used over 100,000 Austin trucks during the Second World War.

FORD AND VAUXHALL GAIN SPEED

Ford's English operation rebounded in the early 1930s to vigorously challenge the Morris/Austin leadership. Ford now had the fully integrated Dagenham complex, built in 1929-31 to include steel making, a foundry, and machine shops. The firm closed its Manchester factory, and Cork was limited to assembly for the Irish market; its tractor production moved to Dagenham. Car and light-truck production began slowly at Dagenham in 1931, making Model A's, but these cars never did draw much interest in Britain. Nor did the V-8 model, also made at Dagenham from August 1932. Ford engineers in Dearborn during 1931 designed a new car specifically aimed at the European market, the Model Y or "Popular." Rated at 8 hp, this went into production at Dagenham in 1932 and attracted many buyers. With it Ford quickly became the third largest car producer and held this position for the rest of the decade. In 1935 English Ford's chairman, Percival Perry, cut the price of the Popular to £100 ($490), the lowest ever for a four-seat sedan, and its sales boomed. Throughout the 1930s Ford also made from 16,000 to 20,000 light trucks per year. Its total car and truck sales in 1936-38 moved it into second place in Britain, ahead of Austin, which then made few commercial vehicles. But Dagenham never produced near its capacity (200,000) during the 1930s. The original plan to ship parts made there for assembly in Germany, France, and Italy foundered in the face of protectionism in those countries.

General Motors followed a more cautious policy with its British subsidiary, Vauxhall. In 1930 GM chose an English managing director, Charles Bartlett. His appointment, like that of Perry at Ford, showed that the American managements now would adapt their products to the British market. Bartlett showed respect for the shop workers and enjoyed good labor relations until he retired in 1954. The firm introduced its first car designed under the new management in 1931 and for most of the decade sold 20,000 to 30,000 cars a year in the middle-price range. The company showed more innovation than the British-owned firms, introducing independent front suspension in 1935 and unitary body construction in 1938. More important than its car sales, Vauxhall came to dominate the light-truck market with its Bedford line, derived from Chevrolet vehicles. Bedford sold 22,000 in 1935 and exceeded Vauxhall car sales over the decade.

The Rootes group produced a variety of models of which its Hillman Minx was especially popular. The Standard company also did well in the same midrange market. Captain John Black took over its management in 1934 after the death of the founder, Reginald Maudslay. A former army officer, vain and autocratic, who liked to chat up his workers, Black enjoyed organizing people and machines. By 1939 he had raised output to 55,000 from 8,000 in 1931, with little increase in the work force.

Specialist carmakers all over Europe limped badly or gave up in the 1930s – the French Hispano-Suiza, the Italian Isotta Fraschini, the British Bentley (taken over by Rolls-Royce in 1931). A rare one that grew was S.S. (later Jaguar). Begun in Blackpool, England, as a specialist body maker in the 1920s, its central figure, William Lyons, moved it to Coventry and in 1932 began selling S.S. cars using a special Standard chassis and engine. Other models followed and sales rose, always with Standard engines and in 1936 with the Jaguar name. Lyons's success came from his elegant designs and very careful attention to costs. His "cad's cars" looked quite expensive but cost much less than Rolls or Rolls-Bentleys. Sales in 1939 surpassed 5,000.[5]

British exports expanded somewhat in the 1930s, almost entirely to Commonwealth countries, where they paid a lower tariff than their American or continental competitors. There was a disquieting note: in markets like Sweden, Switzerland, or Latin America where British cars competed on even terms they did not sell well.

Although the British car industry led Europe in this decade, most of its firms' product policies remained cautious. The British firms seemed to lack enough good design and production engineers. Morris and Austin chose to spread their resources over a wide range of models, dissipating the economies of scale and possible lower prices that might have arisen from a more focused product policy. Their failure to fully dominate the low and middle ranges of the market allowed smaller firms such as Standard and Rootes to survive. The shakeout would come after the Second World War. Ford illustrated the other option, producing just four models over the years 1932-37.

COMMERCIAL VEHICLES

British truck and bus production doubled in the 1930s over the 1920s and trucks gradually rose in size and power. Although most of the freight haulage by trucks continued to be to and from railway stations, they did expand their long-distance business. Generally, trucks provided a cheaper and more flexible service than railways. The decrease in British railway freight traffic between the late 1920s and the late 1930s (the tonnage of general merchandise fell 18 percent) despite an expanding economy indicates growing truck competition. From 1930 to 1938 the number of trucks in service rose from 348,000 to 495,000, the majority of which were light delivery vehicles engaged in work done by horses before 1914. Three major passenger-car firms – Vauxhall-Bedford, Ford, and Morris – made most of these light trucks and vans. AEC, Leyland, and Thorneycroft dominated the market for heavy machines, including buses.

In the 1920s motor buses had spread their routes throughout the country and offered greater mobility to people in small towns and rural areas. The introduction of pneumatic tires around 1925 increased their comfort. Regulation came in 1930 with the Road Traffic Act. It established regional commissions that granted a monopoly on a bus route to an operator for several years. On long-distance routes the commissions were obligated to protect railways from bus competition. The number of buses in service remained steady at about 50,000 during the 1930s, but electric streetcars lost about half their traffic to motor buses, trolleybuses (which enjoyed a temporary boom in the decade), and especially passenger cars. Through the end of the 1930s railway passenger traffic outside the London area does not appear to have been reduced by road competition, although it surely would have grown considerably without it.[6]

In 1928 diesel-powered trucks from Daimler-Benz and the Swiss firm Saurer were demonstrated in England, and their success sparked diesel automotive development there. The diesel's attraction lay in the lower price of its fuel, its more economic use of it, especially at less than full power, and the engine's longer life. If a vehicle's annual mileage were high these advantages would outweigh its higher initial cost. AEC developed its own diesel engine for its buses and trucks. It received crucial aid in this effort from the private research organization run by Harry Ricardo, who introduced the "Comet" swirl chamber to promote more complete combustion of the fuel and less smoke and smell. About the same time the Gardner engine company of Manchester began supplying small diesel engines for buses and trucks. The first British diesel bus entered service in Sheffield in March 1930. Buses adopted diesel engines faster than trucks because they tended to operate a greater distance per year. All the British heavy-truck makers offered diesel power from the early 1930s on, either using their own engines or those supplied by Gardner, Dorman, Saurer, or others. Later in the decade the small diesel engines made by the Perkins company began to appear in delivery trucks and taxicabs.

THE GERMAN AUTOMOBILE INDUSTRY AND HITLER

The very rapid expansion of German motor-vehicle production in the 1930s stands out in the history of this industry between the world wars. This rapid growth revived the brief booms of 1910-12 and 1926-28.

At first production fell sharply during the depression, back to the low level of the early 1920s. Then from late 1932 the economy began to revive and the automobile industry rose with it for the rest of the decade. Motor vehicle output actually rose much faster than did industry in general, stimulated by the Hitler regime's motorization policy. Growth also came from investment by General Motors and Ford in their German subsidiaries and their vigorous marketing, from domestic firms' putting to use the modernization of their production facilities undertaken in the late 1920s, and especially from the emphasis manufacturers now put on low- and medium-priced cars, which turned out to have a large market in Germany just as they had in the United States

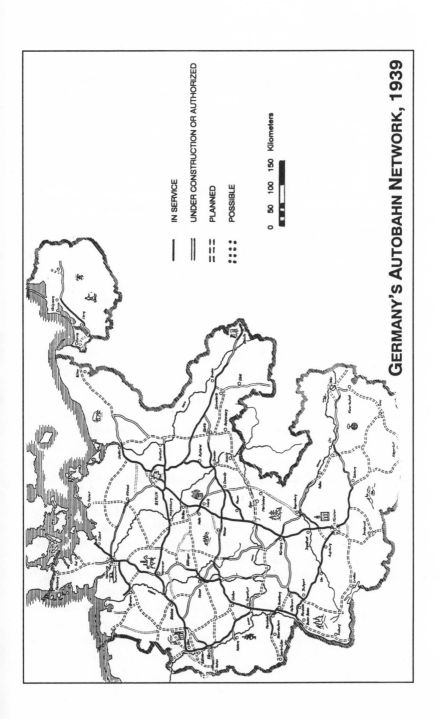

GERMANY'S AUTOBAHN NETWORK, 1939

IN SERVICE

UNDER CONSTRUCTION OR AUTHORIZED

PLANNED

POSSIBLE

0   50   100   150   Kilometers

and Britain. The index of prices for passenger cars shrank from 100 in 1925 to 62 in 1929, and then to 46 in 1936. The average annual wage reached 1,650 marks in 1936, just the level of Opel's low-priced P-4 model.[7]

Economic recovery in Germany began with government public works programs. The Nazi government greatly expanded these when it came to power late in January 1933 with a massive road building and repair program as well as the construction of public buildings. This policy aimed at cutting the very high level of unemployment and it succeeded, as almost a million workers were engaged in road and other transportation construction in 1934.[8] Hitler also began a rearmament program, but this required more planning and more caution in the early years because of its international risk. By 1935 rearmament was well under way and henceforth was the primary force pulling the economy forward. Before that year public works provided a more significant stimulus.

Road building, including the expressways or autobahns, indirectly encouraged the auto industry, but Hitler did more than this. In April 1933 his regime eliminated annual taxes on new motorcars, which reduced the annual expense of operating a car by 10 to 15 percent. Later, industrial firms, farmers, businessmen, and professionals received tax rebates on the purchase of new motor vehicles. Automobile sales had begun to climb late in 1932 and they shot upward in the following year. Employment in the motor-vehicle industry almost tripled from 34,400 in 1932 to 101,000 in 1935,[9] and production of cars and trucks rose almost fivefold in the same period – an expansion that continued until the war.

Although the British and German motor industries were expanding and modernizing in the mid-1930s, they still trailed far behind the United States in labor productivity. In vehicle output per worker, the British and German industries were on a par with each other but lagged behind the United States, with only a quarter of that country's productivity. The proportion of administrative, technical, and clerical staff appeared to be larger in the European firms. Both of these measurements show the clear advantage still held by the Americans, owing to more standardization, mechanization, and economies of scale.[10]

Opel maintained its leadership of the German auto industry throughout the 1930s. Under family ownership in the late 1920s it had sold many cars but failed to make much money. As early as 1926 Opel had invited General Motors to interest itself in the firm, and after considerable study GM bought 80 percent of Opel in March 1929 and the rest in 1931 for $33.36 million. Wilhelm von Opel remained as president, but American executives operated the concern. American-designed models began to appear in 1931 and set a new standard for the German industry.[11] In 1935 Opel's Olympia model employed unitized construction, which made obsolete the traditional chassis frame, an arrangement also used in some small German cars of the late 1920s and in the Citroën front-wheel-drive car of 1934. A smaller version of the Olympia, the Kadett, appeared in 1937 to become a best-seller. Both remained in production until 1940. The firm began to offer medium-sized trucks beginning in 1931 and in 1936 shifted all its truck operations to a new plant in Brandenburg, west of Berlin, from which it filled military orders.

Opel's production peaked in 1938 with over 140,000 cars and trucks made by 26,000 employees. Its 1,750 domestic dealers probably sold an average of 50 cars each. In 1938 Opel exported a quarter of its production as the German government pressured automakers to boost exports in order to accumulate foreign exchange. The regime allocated steel and other raw materials to automakers in accordance with their export performance.

The Ford entry in Germany did less well than Opel. Ford followed its usual practice of building its own company there rather than buying out a local firm. After operating an assembly plant in Berlin for several years, Ford began construction of a plant in Cologne in 1930. The original idea of 1928 was to ship parts made in Dagenham for assembly in Cologne, but limits on imports advised a change to making some parts and buying others in Germany. In fact, government monetary exchange control starting in 1931 and then quotas on imports made it impossible to import many cars or parts. The Cologne factory began operations in May 1931, at first using some British-made parts, but by August 1933 the Ford four-cylinder cars made in Cologne were entirely German, and by 1935 the V-8 models followed suit. The four-cylinder at first was the small Model Y, originally prepared for English Ford and named the Köln in Germany. The Eifel model soon (1935) replaced it, the German version of the English Ten. This car was by far the best-selling German Ford during the 1930s, although not the cheapest car of its size. Ford by 1938 held fourth place among German producers of passenger cars, but it did better with trucks, where it was second behind GM's Opel.[12]

Fiat expanded its operations in Germany in 1930 with an assembly plant in Heilbronn that it bought from the NSU concern. There it produced German versions of its more successful models under the name NSU/Fiat. By 1935 some 90 percent of the value of the parts and labor of these cars was German.

GERMAN-OWNED PRODUCERS

The Auto Union combine, including DKW, Wanderer, Audi, and Horch, prospered once the demand for cars rose. Its management purged the number of basic models and focused each of the constituent firms or divisions on a segment of the market, with each doing considerable design and manufacturing for the others. It was rather like a small General Motors. DKW, at the bottom of the size and price range, sold by far the most cars. In 1931 it introduced a new model with a front-wheel drive developed by the Audi engineering staff and using DKW's standard 584-cc two-stroke, two-cylinder engine, along with unitized steel (instead of plywood) construction. This unusual arrangement and low price appealed to many, and DKW became second only to Opel in car sales in the late 1930s. From 1937 through 1940 one could buy an open-body DKW for $660. Wanderer, Audi, and Horch produced successively larger and more expensive types, with Audi offering both front and rear drive.

The Daimler-Benz concern seized its opportunities in the economic revival of the Hitler period and, among the larger auto companies, probably had the closest ties to the Nazis. Most of its board of directors were at least nominal members of the party, and one of them, Jakob Werlin, was an old friend of Hitler. The führer liked to be driven in a Mercedes-Benz car in parades or on tours, and eventually the firm became a central element in military production for his war. In 1933 Daimler-Benz ranked as Germany's third largest auto firm, behind Opel and Auto Union. In 1936 the firm introduced a new, moderately priced (base $1,500) four-cylinder car. This 170V model became by far the most popular Mercedes-Benz car, aiming for the average middle-class family and hitting the target, for it sold some 95,000 from 1936 through 1942, almost five times better than any other made by this firm or its predecessors. The company also carried the German colors, along with Auto Union, in races during the decade, and both received government subsidies for this prestige activity on which the regime set great store.

Daimler-Benz made an increasing number of diesel trucks and for several years experimented with a diesel car it began to market in 1936. It made just under 2,000 of these through 1940. Starting in 1937 Hanomag offered a smaller diesel car of which it produced some 1,100. Daimler-Benz had retained its interest in aircraft engines since the First World War, and with the Nazi regime came large orders. With the government, it built in 1936 a new factory in Genshagen (about 15 miles south of the center of Berlin) to make these engines. This plant would become the largest such facility in Germany during the Second World War.

In 1938 sales revenue among German automakers, including motorcycle makers, Daimler-Benz ranked fourth, with 9.2 percent of the total, following first-place Opel (30 percent), Auto Union (14.5 percent), and Ford (10.7 percent). Borgward was fifth with 3.9 percent. Karl Borgward had begun as a manufacturer of auto parts in Bremen in the 1920s. In 1931 he bought the bankrupt Hansa-Lloyd firm and thereafter produced cars with the Hansa name along with Borgward trucks.

THE VOLKSWAGEN PROJECT

In the 1920s and early 1930s many types of small German cars were produced, targeting a market currently buying motorcycles or without motor vehicles. The most successful of them were the Hanomag, the Austin Seven made by Dixi and BMW, and the DKW. The cheapest closed DKW in 1933-35 cost $750. Then the Opel P-4 in 1936 came in at 1,650 marks (or $665), but these prices remained too high for the average German.

Adolf Hitler was fascinated by cars and correctly assumed that many Germans shared his interest. Since his imprisonment in 1924 when he read Henry Ford's autobiography, *My Life and Work*, he made mass motorization one of his policies for Germany. Hitler's unofficial advisor on motorcar matters, Jakob Werlin, brought him together with Ferdinand Porsche in 1934.[13] Hitler asked Porsche to analyze the feasibility of producing a people's car (or Volkswagen) to sell at a price under 1,000 marks ($400). Porsche already had designed and built prototypes of two small cars for motorcycle companies that had been unable to finance their production. He considered Hitler's target price utopian but prepared a proposal nonetheless. Hitler went ahead on this basis and asked the German Automobile Manufacturers Association to develop the project with Porsche as designer. With considerable delay Porsche made three prototypes in 1934-36 and visited the United States to examine production methods that might reduce costs closer to the target of 900 marks.

The Manufacturers Association tested Porsche's cars and found them satisfactory but urged that other designs be tested also. Its members feared the proposed people's car as possible serious competition, especially as the regime was likely to subsidize it. They finally realized that Hitler meant what he said and Opel cut the price on its P-4 model to 1,450 marks in 1937, but Hitler could not accept that an American-owned firm would keep his promise to the German people. Seeing that the German auto industry was delaying the project because it opposed it, Hitler in February 1937 assigned the Volkswagen program to the German Labor Front, the Nazi labor organization, with Porsche, Werlin, and Bodo Lafferentz of the Labor Front ordered to prepare for production. Werlin got Daimler-Benz to make 60 more prototypes for further testing and for publicity.

In May 1938 some of these preproduction models of the Volkswagen were revealed to the public and the price set at 990 marks. A small plant was established in Brunswick to begin making parts, and in a rural area east of Hannover the Labor Front began construction of a huge new factory to build VWs as well as a town to house the workers. Meanwhile, the company had purchased many American machines and hired some 20 Americans to help get production started. The final version of the car did not differ much from Porsche's 1933 prototype: a rear-mounted, air-cooled engine with 985 cc, torsion-bar suspension, and seats for four in a streamlined steel body. Some of the details may have owed something to the Czech Hans Ledwinka, with whose ideas Porsche was familiar. To reduce costs and to raise public interest, the government decided that buyers would pay in advance for their Volkswagens by purchasing weekly savings stamps from the Labor Front and pasting them in a book. Ultimately, 337,000 people set up such savings accounts[14] – not very many considering that the factory was initially supposed to turn out 400,000 a year and eventually reach 1 million. When the war broke out in September 1939 construction had not finished on the Volkswagen factory, nor had it made any cars.

German truck manufacturing grew somewhat faster than the private-car business in the 1930s. Opel and Ford dominated the market up to 3 tons, and eight or ten firms shared the medium and heavy types, an expanding segment. In just two years, 1936 to 1938, the number of trucks 3 tons and up almost doubled and rose to 14.8 percent of the total. These trucks began taking over from horses for local delivery work, and a few engaged in intercity freight traffic. (The number of horses in Germany had begun to decline after 1926.) Diesel engines rapidly conquered the heavier end of the truck business, dominating registrations of trucks 3.5 tons capacity and larger in the later 1930s. In 1939, 6,428 of these new trucks used diesel power, and only 336 burned gasoline.[15] Daimler-Benz was the third largest truck maker in these years and especially strong in diesels. Other truck firms included MAN, Büssing, Magirus, Krupp, and Henschel. The German army decided to standardize on gasoline engines for tanks when it rearmed. This was an error; a choice of diesel in the mid-1930s would have saved much fuel and caused few problems.

REARMAMENT?

Was the Nazi regime's motorization policy essentially a veiled program of rearmament? So argue some historians.[16] The evidence does not appear to support this view, however. The German emphasis on low-power small cars in the 1930s does not suggest rearmament. The regime's major direct involvement in the passenger-car industry – the Volkswagen project – had nothing to do with rearmament. The generals disliked the scheme, for it diverted scarce resources from military production, and they foresaw little use for such a low-power, two-wheel-drive machine. The factory was not prepared for war production in 1939 and was only partly utilized to make military equipment during the war. Not until August 1939 did Hitler ask Porsche to design a military version of the VW, about one year prior to the development of the Jeep military vehicle in the United States. As for the rest of the industry, the German army in the 1930s was interested in trucks, but not too many of them. From 1934 through 1937 it acquired 28,840 trucks; in the next two years it bought 55,350 more. The total was 20 to 30 percent of all German trucks manufactured in these years.[17] The 84,000 trucks is an unimpressive number if the German army really contemplated a motorized war. Of course, the military planned not for motorization but for a railroad war, as in 1870 and 1914. Army leaders realized, even if some historians have forgotten, that Germany lacked the petroleum to operate a largely motorized military force. There was a government effort to reduce the models of trucks and cars so as to come closer to standardization, but this began only in 1939 and achieved little. If it is held that motorization in the 1930s aimed at developing a large motor industry that could be converted to military production, then it remains to be explained why there was little planning for this conversion and why it was done so inefficiently when the time came.

The autobahn construction program also has been characterized as a military policy.[18] Again, the evidence points in the other direction. Several pressure groups in Germany in the late 1920s urged the construction of express highways, inspired by the Italian example and the need for more efficient passenger-car traffic. Intercity freight movement by truck was not on their agenda, for it was handled by an efficient system of railways and canals. Among those with an expressway program in the 1920s was a highway engineer and Nazi since 1922, Fritz Todt. Hitler proposed the autobahn program immediately after coming to power, primarily as an employment scheme, and he placed Todt in charge. It was also a monument to himself, characteristic of grandiose construction projects so often favored by autocratic rulers.

The autobahns were more elaborate than the Italian autostrade. The German system had dual roadways in most cases, with two lanes in each direction. A concrete surface covered nine-tenths of the mileage, with an interchange about every six miles. Government financed, with no tolls, traffic was heavier than in the Italian case although still far from dense. For example, in 1937 the Berlin-Stettin section counted an average of 2,054 vehicles per day and the Cologne-Oberhausen section 4,840 per day.[19] Evidence has not appeared that the routes were laid out for strategic reasons or that construction began on those with the most significant military use. The first long stretch finished ran from Berlin to Munich, which had less military importance than the one from Berlin to the Ruhr, still incomplete in 1939. An American expert who examined the system several times in the 1930s considered that it had primarily civilian rather than military aims, pointing out that some stretches of road and viaducts were built to be as spectacular as possible, not hidden as a military road would be. The only possible strategic influence he suspected was the location of the Rhine route on the east side of the river rather than the more populous west bank.[20] When the war began in September 1939, just 1,908 miles of the planned network of 8,680 were finished. Only some 200 additional miles were opened to traffic by 1942, when construction came to a final halt. Perhaps the most revealing decision was that of 1943 that banned all repairs and maintenance on the autobahns. Clearly the military authorities saw little value in the system. They considered it, like the VW, a competitor for scarce resources. Late in the war autobahn tunnels and narrow cuts were used to shelter military production facilities and to house war prisoners.

The wartime economy did not employ the autobahns very much. Such trucks as were not assigned to military units in Western Europe, Russia, or North Africa engaged in short hauls between railway stations and factories. In fact, long-distance freight movement by truck was banned early in the war. The reason for this ban was also the reason that autobahns were neither conceived nor heavily used for military or war production purposes: the German shortage of petroleum fuel.

In 1938 Germany consumed about 7 million metric tons of petroleum. Its oil fields produced only 0.6 million, with Austria's producing 0.9 million. The rest came from imports, 3.9 million, and from synthetic production from coal, 1.6 million. The Nazi regime had promoted the synthetic oil program. In case of war or other emergency that might threaten imports, about 4 million tons were in storage, only a six-month supply.[21] Fuelwise, Germany was ill-prepared for a motorized war, and any policy that shifted freight or passengers away from coal-burning railways to petroleum-fueled vehicles increased the country's military vulnerability.

THE FRENCH AUTOMOBILE INDUSTRY IN THE 1930S

France's automobile industry in the 1930s took quite a different route from Britain's or Germany's. Its output did decline during the depression, although not sharply, to 1932. It revived thereafter but never supassed its 1929 production before the Second World War. This evolution paralleled the movement of the national economy, and the primary

TABLE 7.1   MAJOR EUROPEAN AUTOMAKERS, 1937 AND 1938

	No. vehicles	Year
Opel	140,580*	1938
Ford, England	94,165*	1937
Morris	*90,000*	1937
Austin	89,745*	1937
Citroën	66,723	1938
Fiat	64,157*	1937
Renault	58,396*	1938
Peugeot	47,213	1938

* Includes trucks
Italicized numbers are estimates.
Sources:
Opel: Karl Ludvigsen, *Opel: Wheels to the World* (Princeton, N.J.: Automobile Quarterly, 1975), 96.
Ford: Mira Wilkins and F. E. Hill, *American Business Abroad: Ford on Six Continents* (Detroit: Wayne State University Press, 1964), 437.
Morris: R. J. Overy, *William Morris: Viscount Nuffield* (London: Europa, 1976), 128.
Austin: Roy Church, *Herbert Austin* (London: Europa, 1979), 114.
Citroën: P. Dumont, *Quai Javel, Quai André Citroën* (Paris: EPA, 1973), appendix.
Fiat: Duccio Bigazzi, "Management Strategies in the Italian Car Industry, 1906-1945: Fiat and Alfa Romeo," in *The Automobile Industry and Its Workers*, ed. S. Tolliday and J. Zeitlin (New York: St. Martin's, 1987), 77.
Renault: P. Fridenson, *Histoire des usines Renault*, vol. 1 (Paris: Seuil, 1972), 328.
Peugeot: Jean-Louis Loubet, *Les Automobiles Peugeot* (Paris: Economica, 1990), 83.

reason for the stagnation of the industry's output must be ascribed to weakness on the demand side. The industry's resilience was further weakened by a failure of the major firms to play the card of the very small car in this decade. The French Big Three offered no such car, and historian Patrick Fridenson has discovered why.[22] Each of them by 1935 had designed a very small model with 5 fiscal hp. But Citroën and Peugeot doubted the wisdom of introducing these cars and persuaded Renault to abandon its efforts also. Early in 1935 Citroën was skating close to outright bankruptcy. The Michelin rubber company was trying to rescue it and take it over, so this was not the time to assume a major new risk.

Negative arguments also came from the marketing side, where it was feared that new small models in large numbers would strain the finances of the firms' dealers, who would have to expand their facilities but would receive only a small commission. It was suggested that such small cars would perform more poorly than the French were used to, so those with low incomes would prefer to buy used cars with better performance and comfort but pay even less. (This used-car argument may have been valid in the United States at this time, but it did not operate in Britain, Germany, or Italy in the 1930s and probably was also inaccurate for France.) The only serious danger to this cautious policy was that a foreign producer would jump into this niche in the French market. The high French tariff presumably would defend against this, but in fact Fiat's French affiliate, Simca, did just this in 1936.

In the truck area of the market, French producers had great difficulties. Government budget cuts meant smaller government purchases. Private firms were affected by an economy that discouraged capital investment and by 1934 legislation to reduce truck and bus competition with the railways.

The government authorized the first French expressway in 1935, leading westward from Paris. It proceeded slowly, and only a few miles were finished when the war broke out.

CITROEN

Usually full of surprises, the Citroën company upheld this tradition in the 1930s. In 1933 André Citroën rebuilt and re-equipped his Quai Javel factory at great speed and heavy expense without halting car production there. He introduced state-of-the-art assembly, and customers could wait at the end of the line for their cars amid potted palms and illuminated fountains. In May 1934 Citroën offered a new and remarkable car, the *traction avant* (front-wheel drive). This was in no way the first commercialization of front-wheel-drive cars. Recent predecessors included the Tracta in France (1926), Alvis in England (1928), Cord in the United States (1928), and the more successful DKW (1931) and Adler (1932) in Germany. In addition, the Budd company in the United States presented André Citroën with a prototype front-wheel-drive model in 1931. DKW and Adler may have sold some 25,000 front-wheel-drive cars before Citroën's version appeared. Nevertheless, it was an excellent vehicle with an outstanding engine and brakes. Low to the road, streamlined, bereft of running boards, it had remarkable road-holding qualities owing in part to suspension by torsion bars recently developed in Germany by Ferdinand Porsche. This reputation for maneuverability led a generation of French filmmakers to place their characters in Citroën traction cars for the chase scenes. Like most of this firm's new models, the first ones sold revealed many mechanical difficulties; these required expensive repairs and reduced sales. In fact, the situation brought the Citroën industrial empire to a crisis.

That a relatively small problem like repairing a few thousand faulty cars could force André Citroën up against the wall was because he lacked adequate working capital.[23] He had built and was paying for a productive enterprise that operated at only about half its capacity. Citroën had rebuilt his Quai Javel factory with his usual extravagance, topping it off with a banquet for 6,000 in the halls of the factory itself in October 1933. His cars did not sell well over the 1933-34 winter, in part because rumors circulated of an entirely new and different model coming in 1934. André Citroën assumed that he could surmount a cash shortage for several months – as he had before – by delaying payments to his suppliers and borrowing short term from commercial banks and from his dealers. He did this early in 1934 and persuaded the banks to convert some of the short-term advances into loans of three to five years. Still desperate for revenue, he moved the introduction of the front-wheel-drive car up from October to April. But the car was not ready. Personal rivalries among his engineers had delayed development, but the transmission caused the major problem. Against the advice of his technical people, Citroën had insisted that the car use an automatic type. At the last minute even he recognized its faults so his engineers had to substitute a hastily designed and poorly operating manual transmission. Production of the new car began slowly in April, but many required expensive repairs. Neither production nor sales climbed as rapidly as planned, so the company suffered a severe financial squeeze.

Citroën asked the Michelin company (his largest creditor except for taxes and customs duties owed the government) for help. When Pierre Michelin and Pierre Boulanger arrived in June, Citroën cried, "On these two Pierres [rocks] I shall rebuild my temple."[24] The Michelin executives began inspecting operations and cutting costs. Michelin's aim at this point is unclear. Was it trying to keep an important customer by making Citroën viable as a French firm rather than seeing it become American-owned as Opel had just a few years earlier? Or was

Michelin moving gradually to take over a major industrial enterprise that it believed it could manage better than André Citroën? At first its ambition probably was the first of the two, for we should not assume that the outcome of a complex series of events involving many players can be foreseen by participants several months in advance.

The factory kept pushing out the new traction cars; in fact, some 30,500 were produced in 1934, but the financial circumstances did not improve. On 28 November, Michelin presented a rescue plan that asked suppliers to accept for funds due them longer-term debt instruments that they might discount for cash at commercial banks, and to supply more material on a short-term credit basis. Michelin itself would also advance some cash. At about the same time as this scheme was placed on the table, a small steering-wheel supplier with ties to the Michelin company sued Citroën for payment. One must assume that Michelin could have stopped this action if it had desired. This act brought the commercial court into the picture. On 21 December it admitted the Citroën company into judicial liquidation, a status similar to receivership in that independent liquidators try to devise a way to keep a financially troubled firm operating and satisfy its creditors. Outright bankruptcy would have been much harsher, forcing a sale of the assets. A committee including Pierre Michelin and Paul Frantzen of the Lazard investment bank managed the firm for the liquidators. All but some 2,000 of the 20,000 employees were laid off.

In January 1935 the Michelin rescue plan of the preceding November collapsed. It was now clear that Citroën's creditors would not keep the company afloat by extending their loans unless André Citroën gave up the helm. He had lost their confidence. In these years of financial crises and industrial failures (some 110 French banks failed and many small auto firms closed during the depression) Citroën's extravagant spending on his factories and sales agencies, his flamboyant personal publicity, his notorious gambling in casinos all exasperated his lenders. Michelin, with its legendary financial probity, was quite another matter. So the Michelin people, encouraged by the minister of finance, returned to the task. They now were probably convinced that they might be able to gain control of the largest automobile firm in Europe at a modest cost. This time they won the support of two major investment banks, the Banque de Paris et des Pays-Bas and Lazard Frères. With these solid names as a guarantee, a temporary plan was accepted on 3 February. It involved another consolidation of short-term debts and an advance of ƒ60 million from the Bank of France, Michelin, and a number of other banks and suppliers. Some of this advance was in the form of parts such as tires and castings. André Citroën had to surrender all his authority and he may have sold some or all of his shares in the company to Michelin at this point. Seriously ill with stomach cancer, he retired from the firm and died in July 1935.

André Citroën often was right. He publicized American methods of production and adopted some of them. He Americanized his marketing. For his front-drive car he did not hesitate to adopt new designs. But he was in too great a hurry, always assuming that greater sales tomorrow would pay for today's gambles and extravagances.

Nobody wanted the Citroën company to close its doors. Suppliers, other creditors, employees, and the government all stood to gain if it continued to operate. It did, at a gradually increasing rate. More Michelin personnel came into the management to replace those dismissed. On 21 June 1935 the Citroën creditors accepted a permanent liquidation plan by which they received equal amounts of 30-year bonds and preferred stock for their claims. The common stock capital was written down from ƒ400 million to ƒ75 million on 1 October and on 19 December increased to ƒ210 million by a new issue guaranteed by Michelin and the two investment banks. By mid-1935 faults in the front-wheel-drive car had been eliminated, production increased, and employment revived to 14,000. The Michelin group now called the tune, based on the stock it had obtained either from André Citroën or purchased on the stock exchange at the very low prices prevailing from December 1934. Although the Michelin and Citroën operations were not legally merged, together they probably amounted to the largest industrial group in France.

In 1935 Pierre Boulanger became the de facto head of Citroën, and the official head in 1937 when Pierre Michelin died in an auto crash. Boulanger continued production of the traction car for the rest of the 1930s and after, along with small numbers of rear-wheel-drive vehicles. The firm regained production leadership in France in 1937 and in the next year made 66,723 vehicles, its best performance in the later 1930s. Early in 1936 Boulanger decided to try for the very-small-car market. He asked his engineers to design one that could carry two farmers and 50 kg of potatoes at 60 km/hour and would sell for the price of a motorcycle. They did not rush; only after four years their 2 CV model was ready for the Paris Auto Show of October 1939, but the outbreak of the war cancelled both the show and production of the car at this time.

RENAULT

Renault continued to follow cautious policies in the 1930s, trailing Citroën in automobile output most years and toward the end of the decade even falling into third place behind Peugeot. In 1930 Louis Renault brought his nephew by marriage, François Lehideux, into the firm as heir apparent but did not allow him a free hand. Renault's labor policy was unenlightened and brought some serious problems in the later 1930s. Louis Renault held consistently to his strategy from before 1914: reduce risks by offering a wide range of cars and other products. He continued to produce light and heavy trucks and buses, military tanks, aircraft engines, diesel-powered railcars, and farm tractors. He acquired an aviation firm – Caudron – in 1936. He worked hard to cut his raw material costs, even creating a firm to produce special steels and sheet steel and making his own tires after his chief competitor fell into the grasp of Michelin in 1935. All these activities spread Louis Renault's attention very thin and required considerable capital investment. Automobile production did not receive enough new equipment or innovation in design. Renault cars broke no new paths in this decade. In fact, the small Juvaquatre of 1937 very closely resembled the Opel Kadett. This caution and diversification looked good when André Citroën crashed in 1934, but the new management at Citroën soon regained leadership in passenger cars, following virtually a one-model policy.

PEUGEOT AND OTHER AUTOMAKERS

By the late 1920s Peugeot had settled on a product policy of just a few types of cars and no heavy trucks, made in up-to-date facilities and kept in production with only minor changes for several years. Its small 201 model and 202 successor dominated the 1-liter range through the 1930s. It offered a new 1.5 liter in 1932 and a 2.1 liter in 1933. These machines appealed by their reliability and durability, pulling Peugeot into second place in French passenger-car sales most years after 1935.

Many of the small French carmakers failed in the early 1930s. Some of those that remained tried to get along by adopting the developments of others. For example, after leaving Peugeot management in

1928 Lucien Rosengart made Austin Sevens on license and then introduced a French version of a midsize Adler front-wheel-drive machine. Chenard & Walcker survived by buying instead of manufacturing its major components. In the late 1930s its cars used engines by Citroën or Matford (owned by Ford) and bodies made by the specialist Chausson and identical to those supplied to Matford.

FOREIGN-OWNED FIRMS

The Simca concern mounted the strongest challenge to the French Big Three in this period. Its founder was Henri Pigozzi. From Turin, he had come to France in the 1920s as a buyer of scrap iron for Fiat's steel furnaces. He soon became the French distributor for Fiat cars. As importing became more difficult in the 1930s, he established a manufacturing firm, Simca, in 1934 and with Fiat's help moved into the failed Donnet company's auto factory in the Paris suburb of Nanterre in 1935. There Simca began making Fiat cars for the French market, just as NSU/Fiat was doing in Germany at this time. The Simca 5 of 1936 was Pigozzi's version of the Fiat "Topolino." It entered the market below the smallest Peugeot in size and price (f9,900 or $600). Simca quickly became the fourth largest French carmaker, turning out some 21,000 in the last prewar year.

Ford was the only American firm with a strong presence in France in these years, but its performance there was much poorer than in Britain or Germany. Its cars assembled at Asnières did not sell well in the early 1930s because the tariff, raised in April 1930, kept Ford prices high. Maurice Dollfus, managing director of French Ford, aimed to get around the tariff by making all the parts in France but without a large investment in new facilities. He did this in 1934 by forming a joint venture, Matford, with Emile Mathis, whose auto firm in Strasbourg was struggling. Mathis made the Ford parts formerly imported for assembly in Asnières. Matford offered two sizes of V-8 cars, reaching a peak output of 13,849 in 1937. This figure was only 14.7 percent of Ford's British output in 1937 and 43.7 percent of its German production. Dollfus and the American Ford executives had trouble dealing with Emile Mathis and finally persuaded their headquarters in Dearborn to build a new factory west of Paris at Poissy to replace both Strasbourg and Asnières. This plant was under construction when the war broke out in 1939.[25]

TRUCKS AND BUSES

Trucks and buses competed with the railways more vigorously in France than in Britain or Germany. They forced many of the local rail lines and rural tramways to close down during the 1920s. Toward the end of that decade they began competing with the trunk rail lines for short hauls, under 50 miles. In the 1930s the introduction of diesel engines for trucks reduced their costs of operation, and by 1934 trucks carried about one-tenth as much freight as the railways.[26] The economy's failure to revive itself made the competition harder to accept, and the requirement that the government subsidize the railways' losses forced it to try to protect them from too much road competition. A decree-law of April 1934 stopped the creation of new bus lines or commercial truck services and encouraged the negotiation of local transport coordination agreements. These agreements provided that the railways would give up their short lines and investments in truck and bus firms and that the road haulers would renounce long-distance freight and passenger traffic. Progress came very slowly on these agreements, but after the government bought out the deficit-ridden railways and merged them into the new National Railway Company (SNCF) in 1937, most of the country was finally covered by passenger coordinating agreements. The 1939 solution for freight traffic was for the Transport Ministry to require that truck rates for freight could not be lower than rail rates.

Restrictions on truck freight applied only to common carriers, of course, and these firms owned less than 15 percent of French trucks. Although their growth was stopped, business firms and farmers could and did use their own trucks to move freight. The continuing economic stagnation probably had a greater effect on truck sales in France than did the anticompetitive policy. Truck sales failed to reach the level of the late 1920s before 1938.

French truck producers adopted diesel power quickly once the Germans demonstrated its feasibility. Peugeot made diesel engines on a license from the German Hugo Junkers and sold them for various purposes, including for trucks made by the smaller firms. Renault and Berliet made their own diesels and dominated the market for heavy machines. Both Peugeot and especially Citroën developed and sold a few small diesel-powered delivery trucks.

THE EXPLOSION OF LABOR

Most French autoworkers were paid by results – that is, according to various systems of piecework and bonuses – just like autoworkers in the rest of Europe. But it was France that saw the decade's most vigorous labor activity. Membership in labor unions or left-wing political parties was quite small among autoworkers, but an explosion came nevertheless. In the April-May 1936 elections the Popular Front left-wing political alliance won a comfortable majority in the Chamber of Deputies. Having learned from experience that leftist cabinets ultimately turned conservative, labor leaders hastened to confront management, hoping to bring the Popular Front government in on their side and together force concessions. Strikes began in aircraft plants in Le Havre (11 May) and Toulouse (13 May). In both cases, rather by chance, workers occupied the factories and won their quite modest demands. A similar short strike with occupation came at another aircraft firm in the Paris region on 14 May. Labor occupation of the factory put more pressure on management and prevented a lockout whereby management might not re-hire the workers' leaders. Thereafter came many more sit-in strikes in the metalworking industry, including at Citroën and then on 28 May at Renault. At the latter firm a small group of skilled workers who were Communists and/or members of the Metalworkers Union of the General Confederation of Labor (CGT) began and managed the action.[27] The strikes continued until mid-June, when Communist leader Maurice Thorez gave a back-to-work speech, and brought a great victory for labor. Collective agreements for all autoworkers and for workers in many other industries, ratified and extended by Popular Front legislation, guaranteed the right to organize and bargain collectively without reprisals, and for the election of shop stewards, a wage increase, a standard 40-hour week at the former pay for 48 hours, and two-week paid vacations. During and after the strikes workers flooded into the unions, especially the CGT, which, except for the 1940-44 Occupation, has been dominant in the French auto industry ever since.

For the next two years relations between auto labor and management were very tense, especially at Renault and Citroën, as labor tested how far it could go in controlling the shop floor and as management tried to reimpose the pre-1936 discipline. In 1938 the Popular Front alliance broke up, and a conservative-leaning government presided until the fall of France in June 1940. At the same time the need for rearmament exerted pressure for relaxation of the 40-hour week. A decree-law of November 1938 finally ended it. Striking against this, Renault work-ers again occupied the factories on 24 November, but the police forced them out, using tear gas and arresting nearly 300. The next day man-agement arranged a lockout and selectively rehired the workers it wanted. Among those not welcomed back were 843 union officials and militants.[28] The CGT called a general strike for 30 November against the attacks on labor's gains of 1936, but it failed. Thereafter manage-ment held the upper hand. All these events called forth almost no echo at the Ford operations in France. It paid higher wages than the French-owned firms and already operated on a 40-hour week in 1936. After a token walkout of seven hours, its workers returned to their tasks.[29]

ITALY AND ELSEWHERE ON THE CONTINENT

The Italian automobile industry suffered seriously in the early years of the depression. In the late 1920s about half its output had been ex-ported, but the higher tariffs, and small import quotas set up in much of Europe beginning in 1930 smothered most of this trade. Italian auto exports plunged from 28,000 in 1928 to 7,000 in 1933. Fiat, comprising about 85 percent of the industry at the end of the 1920s, had to react, for its production fell from 48,000 in 1929 to 19,000 in 1931. Giovanni Agnelli still headed the firm, assisted by Vittorio Valletta, an expert on factory management and finance who had taught at the University of Genoa and managed several small firms before joining Fiat in 1920. Their strategy was to introduce cheaper cars to expand the still very limited domestic market and move toward assembly and manufacture abroad to avoid the tariffs and quotas.

Fiat's first great success in the 1930s was the Balilla model of 1932, a four-seater with a 1-liter engine. Introduced in Italy at a price of 10,800 lire ($555), it was soon being assembled and then manufactured by NSU/Fiat in Germany and Simca in France, as well as in Czechoslo-vakia and Poland. Fiat made some 113,000 Balillas in Italy through 1937, its highest total for one model between the wars. The Model 1100 replaced it in 1937 and became a best-seller after the war.

After visiting the United States in 1933 and 1935, Agnelli decided to build a large new factory all on one level. He located in Mirafiori, in Turin's southern suburbs. Construction began in 1937, and the factory, with three times the floor space of the Lingotto works, opened in May

TABLE 7.2 INHABITANTS PER MOTOR VEHICLE

	1913	1930	1938
Britain	161-203*	30.2	19.7
France	318	28.5	18.5
Germany	950	95.5	39.6
Italy	1,889	166.9	116.0
Belgium/Luxembourg	–	49.8	35.6
Sweden	–	42.3	28.8
U.S.	77	4.6	4.4

* Because the number of registered motor vehicles cannot be determined, this ratio
must be a range.

1939. Moving away from Fordist principles to some degree, although inspired by the Ford River Rouge and Dagenham plants, the factory was organized for more flexible operation – that is, it could shift from one vehicle model to another without major disruption. Full-scale production at Mirafiori would come only after the Second World War.[30]

Meanwhile, Fiat presented its most innovative car of the 1930s, the 500 or "Topolino" (little mouse), unveiled in June 1936. Designed by Dante Giacosa and Antonio Fessia, this very small two-seater with a four-cylinder engine of 569 cc capacity (24 percent less than the Austin Seven) and a weight of only 1,050 pounds, caught the fancy of many Europeans. Its cheapest version cost 8,900 lire ($650).[31] Reliable and fuel-efficient, the Topolino was also considered "cute." As a stunt, two Frenchmen drove the Simca version 50,000 km in 50 days, all within the Paris city limits, changing gears 74,900 times and applying the brakes 82,400 times. In this urban marathon it traveled 47 miles/gallon. Commenting on a race for these "Mickey Mouse" cars in England, the British trade magazine *Autocar* remarked, "Pieces of cheese on a string had been prepared as bait, and there was talk of releasing a cat behind the runners at the start."[32] Fiat had made 83,266 of these cars by the time of Italy's entrance into the Second World War in June 1940.

The Balilla and Topolino cars revived Italian auto exports, which in 1937 rose close to late-1920s levels. The smaller car was especially popular in Sweden, Switzerland, and Britain, and several hundred even found their way to the United States. Italy's peak production year of 1937 easily surpassed its earlier record of 1926. Fiat models made in Germany by NSU/Fiat amounted to about 5,000 per year from 1937 to 1939, but in France Simca made at least 20,000 annually in these years.

In addition to several models of cars, Fiat in the 1930s also produced a variety of gasoline and diesel trucks, aircraft engines and aircraft, and, in conjuction with the Ansaldo company, small tanks. Its best years for trucks were 1936 and 1937, when it made a total of 17,599. Earlier, Fiat had taken control of Spa, Ceirano, and OM, small-scale truck makers, and it is not clear if their output is included in the Fiat totals.

Other Italian motor-vehicle firms operated on a small scale. Alfa Romeo made sports cars and engaged in victorious but costly racing. These expenses led to financial problems and government control from 1927. Thereafter both its labor force and management were colonized by Fascists. Its finances grew worse, and in 1933, on Mussolini's decision, the government brought it under the control of its Agency for Industrial Reconstruction (IRI), a public body that managed bankrupt enterprises. The IRI hired an executive from Fiat, Ugo Gobbato, to manage and modernize. Racing continued, but Alfa did more with trucks and buses. Both Lancia and Bianchi produced a few smaller cars in the 1930s and some trucks.

Like France, Italy had collective-bargaining agreements, written by the Fascist regime and fascist unions, covering labor-management relations for entire industries. To maintain some semblance of popular support for the regime, they incorporated worker improvements, including more holidays and welfare benefits. Piece rates and worker wage classifications were determined by joint committees of management and Fascist unionists. Under fascism, then, management did not extend its sway in the factories unhindered.[33]

Automobile manufacturing in the rest of Western and Central Europe amounted to little. In Czechoslovakia the Tatra firm and its designer Hans Ledwinka continued to innovate, introducing in 1934 a model with a rear-mounted, air-cooled V-8 engine. Skoda in the 1930s produced a new line of small cars, and the country as a whole made 14,000 motor vehicles in 1938.

In Sweden Volvo continued to make small numbers of passenger cars, but its trucks were more successful. Here it widened its range, moving into the heavyweights, where it competed with the Scania-Vabis company. Volvo lacked the funds to develop diesel engines but instead adopted the Hesselman-type engine. Here the fuel was injected directly but ignited by a spark plug. As the engine did not require high compression, ordinary gasoline engines with minor alterations could be used and low-grade fuels employed. Scania-Vabis also used Hesselman engines. In 1935 Volvo's parent, SKF, cut it loose, distributing the shares it held to SKF stockholders. The company found export markets for its trucks in the late 1930s – the Low Countries, the Mediterranean area, and South America. In 1939 it built 2,834 cars and 4,171 trucks.[34]

Switzerland's Saurer company was a successful example of an automobile firm operating in a small country. In the town of Arbon on Lake Constance it began making trucks and buses in 1903. With a fine reputation, it established branch factories in Austria (Vienna), France (Suresnes, near Paris), Germany (Lindau, just a few miles from Arbon), and the United States (Plainfield, New Jersey) to gain access to these markets. Between the wars Saurer's research and development and manufacturing were sited at Arbon and its production at Suresnes and Vienna. It also licensed production by OM in Italy. Saurer began producing diesel trucks as early as 1928. In Britain the Armstrong arms firm made Saurer diesels on license, 1931-37. Saurer's technical excellence and far-flung international ties enabled it to prevail despite a very small domestic market.

The Soviet Union, after trying and failing to develop an automobile industry by itself, relied on Western, especially American, guidance and technology in Stalin's first five-year industrialization plan (1928-32). In a decade it became a major European producer, but for domestic use only. The pre-revolutionary AMO factory in Moscow assembled a few 1912-model Fiat trucks in the 1920s and then was modernized by the Brandt company of Detroit, using American equipment (1929-31), and renamed the ZIS factory. Thereupon it made a copy of the American Autocar 2.5-ton truck (59,724 of them in 1938) and a much smaller number of larger trucks and large cars. Similarly, the Hercules engine company of Canton, Ohio, reequipped a truck factory in Yaroslavl, 160 miles northeast of Moscow, to make Fiat and its own trucks.

The Communist regime's major effort was with Ford. In the 1920s it imported some 1,400 Ford cars and trucks, usually assembled in Copenhagen. It also bought over 24,000 Fordson tractors and began making a copy of it in the Leningrad Putilov works. Although these rather light Fordsons were not especially suitable for Russian agriculture, the Ford mass-production mystique among Soviet leaders – and probably their hope to lure Ford into establishing a factory in their country – explain this policy. In May 1929 Ford and Soviet representatives did sign a major agreement, not for tractors but for cars and trucks. Ford agreed to license the Soviets to make model A cars and AA trucks. They would receive all the information they needed on equipment, tools, and manufacturing procedures. In addition, Ford would sell components to assemble 72,000 cars and trucks in the Soviet Union while the manufacturing facilities were under construction. Assembly of Ford vehicles from imported parts began in a former railway shop in Moscow and in a small plant in Nizhni-Novgorod (renamed Gorki in 1932) in 1930. The large manufacturing plant, also in Gorki (250 miles east of Moscow), was designed by the Albert Kahn company of Detroit and built by the Austin company of Cleveland, Ohio. Much of its equipment came from Ford's River Rouge Model A production lines, now obsolete as Ford moved to its V-8 models. As there were few actual or potential suppliers of automobile parts in the Soviet Union, a high proportion were made at the Gorki plant, much higher even than at Ford's River Rouge complex. In 1932 the Gorki factory (known by the abbreviation GAZ) slowly began producing light trucks. Their quality was low because of poor materials, but at least quantity expanded, and in 1938 about 35,000 GAZ workers produced 117,400 trucks, cars, and buses. The Soviets ended most of their purchases of Ford parts in 1933. They had obtained enough to assemble 28,351 vehicles, many fewer than originally anticipated. Ford received over $21 million for its goods and services on the 1929 contract.

Other Western concerns took part in the Soviet motorization effort. American, Swiss, and German companies designed and equipped separate factories for auto glass, lights, and electrical equipment. The Seiberling company of Akron, Ohio, helped establish a tire factory at Yaroslavl. At Stalingrad American firms built and equipped a large tractor factory to make International Harvester machines. A twin of this was erected at Kharkov and a factory for producing copies of Caterpillar tractors was built at Chelyabinsk, just east of the Ural mountains. In most of these cases Soviet engineers and technicians came to the United States to work and study in American factories in order to learn how to design and organize production.[35]

Although the quality of Soviet-made motor vehicles tended to be low in the eyes of Western observers, its engineering and military leaders kept abreast of innovations in the West. They began experiments with diesel engines in the early 1930s and soon decided to use only diesel engines in new Soviet tanks.

In 1938 motor-vehicle production in the Soviet Union reached 211,114, trucks accounting for 182,373 of these, according to official government figures, which tended to exaggerate reality. The country had become the fourth largest European producer, overtaking Italy. These vehicles went to the military, to industrial enterprises, and to government officials, and they were also used as taxicabs; they were not for private citizens, however.

Most of the workers in the new or modernized auto factories were unskilled, from a rural background. A few skilled workers leavened this mass, including some who had worked in West European or United States motor plants. Among the latter were the Americans Walter and Victor Reuther, who were employed at the Gorki factory in 1934-35. Upon their return to the United States, the Reuther brothers climbed to power in the United Auto Workers union and followed anticommunist policies. Wage differentials in Soviet industry, including the automobile industry, were quite wide. Despite Leninist rhetoric urging equalization of incomes, the differences were much greater than in Western Europe. One major reason was the shortage of skilled workers, who had to be paid well or would leave. Stalin insisted on such wide differentiation, asserting in 1931, "Equalitarianism has nothing in common with Marxist Socialism."[36] The ratio of wages for the least and most skilled metalworkers in 1927 was 1 to 2.8; in 1938 it was even wider, 1 to 3.6.

Lenin strongly admired Henry Ford, but like industrialists in Western Europe he favored Taylorism and especially piecework as a pay system that might better motivate workers. In the 1930s almost all Soviet autoworkers were on piece rates but without the guaranteed minimum that was standard practice in the West. Management also used a variety of bonus schemes to encourage quality and efficiency. From 1932 on the rates for piecework were determined exclusively by management, but the need to retain skilled workers tended to keep rates reasonable despite pressure from the government and the Communist party to cut them. To increase labor productivity, the government-sponsored Stakhanov movement from 1935 on encouraged and pressured selected workers to exceed work norms by large margins. This was the exact opposite of labor solidarity as practiced in the West.

A seven-hour day was standard in the 1930s, with premiums for overtime. Industrial firms operated on a six- rather than a seven-day week with five days of labor followed by one day of rest.

As unions had become cheerleaders for the regime and for management, strikes were forbidden, and absenteeism was punished by confiscation of food ration cards or eviction from company-supplied housing, the only option for dissatisfied workers was quitting. Many did, so turnover reached high levels. To combat this the regime used internal passports to control the spatial movement of workers. In 1938 it introduced Labor Books for each worker. Like a passport, a Labor Book identified the worker and included a record of jobs and performance. The worker had to present it before applying for a job.[37]

Within a few years the Soviet Union had an automobile industry. Moving with great haste and much waste, it imported the technology and applied untrained workers and managers to it. Among the industry's weaknesses at the end of the 1930s were a lack of service-after-the-sale facilities and a policy of almost fully integrated productive facilities that tended to slow down the diffusion of automobile technology.

Comte Albert de Dion and Georges Bouton in their two-cylinder cars at start of the Peking-Paris race, 1907.

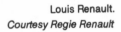

Louis Renault.
Courtesy Regie Renault

Steam tractor moving furniture, England, ca. 1913. *Courtesy R. A. Whitehead*

The Morris business in Oxford, ca. 1907. *Courtesy Basil Blackwell and Morris Motors*

A Ford Model T in St. Petersburg, ca. 1912. *Courtesy Henry Ford Museum and Greenfield Village*

Chassis assembly in the Renault factory near Paris, 1907. *Courtesy Regie Renault*

Citroën advertising on the Eiffel Tower. *Courtesy* Bulletin Citroën

Women winding magnetos, Marelli factory, Milan, 1930. *Courtesy National Archives*

Intersection in Milan, ca. 1930. *Courtesy National Archives*

Two novel forms of transportation, an ostrich and the Caterpillar, meet at Milan industrial fair, 1930. *Courtesy National Archives*

Citroën front-wheel drive model, 1934. *Courtesy S. A. Citroën*

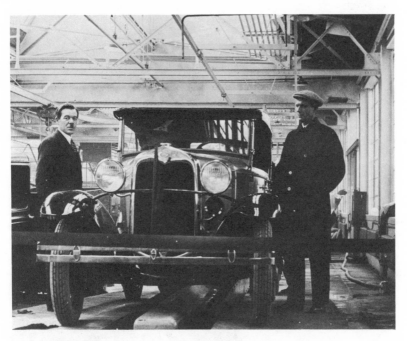

Ford Model A assembled in Moscow, 1930. *Courtesy Henry Ford Museum and Greenfield Village*

German Ford Eifel, 1937. *Courtesy Henry Ford Museum and Greenfield Village*

Ferdinand Porsche, 1930s.
Courtesy National Archives

Citroën 2CV in Tierra del Fuego, 1953. *Courtesy S. A. Citroën*

Heinz Nordhoff, architect of Volkswagen's success. *Courtesy Volkswagen AG*

Carl H. Hahn, Volkswagen chairman since 1982. *Courtesy Volkswagen of America*

Volkswagen plant in San Bernado, Brazil, 1986. *Courtesy Volkswagen AG*

Robot installing battery in Volkswagen car, 1983. *Courtesy Volkswagen AG*

William Morris in his first t 100 car. *Courtesy Basil Blackwell and Morris Motors*

8

MOTOR VEHICLES AND THE SECOND WORLD WAR

After the war one of the better British generals, Archibald Wavell, pointed out some of its lessons: "The more I see of war, the more I realize how it all depends on administration and transportation."[1] Wavell here expressed in a more elegant way the idea attributed to General Nathan Bedford Forrest of the American Civil War, "I git there the fustest with the mostest men."

The European automobile industry played a more important part in the Second World War than in the First. From the beginning armies were more motorized and mechanized. Air forces and navies required large numbers of gasoline and diesel engines. From the auto industries came trucks and other wheeled vehicles, tanks and other tracklaying machines, as well as aircraft and marine engines. Features that characterized the auto industries toward the end of the First World War were repeated with greater intensity–more government regulation of raw materials and factory location and more control of labor, including an increase in the use of women workers and, in some cases, the institution of forced labor.

GERMANY

The German regime did not use its motor industry to its full capacity although its military leaders well understood transportation's importance. Faulty planning by the political leadership explains most of Germany's difficulties. Hitler expected the war he began in September 1939 would be a series of limited and short conflicts that would not require the full mobilization of the German economy. So at first the motor-vehicle industry sharply cut output of passenger cars but did not fully engage in war production. Greater efforts did come in 1942, but even these did not require the full capacity of the industry. An underlying concern among the planners was the shortage of petroleum. Some of them wondered what good 100,000 more trucks would be if they had no fuel. (There was a good answer to this: they would replace vehicles that would be lost or damaged at a greater rate than expected.) There was no systematic plan to devote the industry to military ends, but a conversion by fits and starts. Sometimes this was due to unforeseen problems, such as the poor roads in the Soviet Union that required more half-track trucks and tractors than anticipated.

By spring 1940, just before the attack on the Low Countries and France, the German army comprised 165 divisions, of which 10 were armored but only four were motorized infantry, along with two motorized SS infantry.[2] At this point an armored division was supposed to have around 250 tanks, 561 passenger cars, 1,402 trucks, and 1,289 motorcycles. Assigned to a motorized infantry division were 989 cars, 1,687 trucks, and 1,323 motorcycles. These units used no horses, but the rest of the German army relied heavily on them. Each standard infantry division required over 5,000 horses, 600 to 1,000 trucks and cars, and 500 motorcycles. In these divisions the motor vehicles were used for officers, local supply, communications, engineers, and to pull antitank and field artillery. The enlisted men marched. Separate truck units provided long-distance supply from railheads to supply depots in the zone of operations. Altogether the German army mobilized 2.7 million horses during the Second World War, almost double the number in the First.

When the 1940 campaign began in the west the army had about 120,000 trucks, including at least 16,000 requisitioned from civilian use. Of course, Germany could in no way have motorized its entire army, but a shortage of motorized infantry to accompany its armored divisions in trucks or half-tracks did hamper its effectiveness. Early decisions that turned out to be crucial made the situation worse. The bulk of the army's standard trucks were 3-ton, two-wheel-drive gasoline machines made by Opel and German Ford. Heavier trucks with four-wheel drive and diesel engines did come from some of the other truck firms, but in much smaller numbers. If there had been a decision in the mid-1930s to standardize on diesel engines and four-wheel drive, it would have saved fuel and increased the efficiency of the trucks. More half-track trucks and fully tracked armored personnel carriers also would have strengthened the armored divisions, but this would have required unusual foresight by the military commanders, most of whom had doubts about the effectiveness of armored units. Almost all the tanks were powered by Maybach gasoline engines; diesel would have been better, for its fuel economy would have provided greater range and less chance of fire and explosion.

For the Russian campaign beginning in June 1941 Germany needed all the motor transport it could get. The army used French and British military vehicles captured in 1940; it seized more in the occupied countries and employed current French production in army units or to replace civilian German trucks called for military service. Three German armored divisions in the Soviet Union were equipped with French vehicles. But at the same time Hitler diverted two armored divisions and two understrength motorized infantry divisions, thousands of trucks, and much fuel to Rommel's North African campaign, which brought little benefit to Germany. In January 1943 the German army's stock of vehicles reached a reported peak of 715,000, 60 percent of which were trucks[3] and close to half probably French. That total very likely was inflated, however, for a month later it was reported as 587,000.

The Daimler-Benz group was the auto enterprise most important to the German war effort.[4] Before the war began Daimler-Benz produced many aircraft engines at Stuttgart-Untertürkheim and Genshagen. Almost all its car production stopped in order to increase the output of marine and aircraft engines, but Untertürkheim did produce some 10,000 1.5-ton trucks during the war. The Gaggenau factory concentrated on 4.5-ton trucks, 23,034 of them from 1940 to 1944 at a rate considerably below prewar. The Mannheim plant specialized in 3-ton trucks. The Mark III tank was designed at Daimler-Benz's truck plant in Berlin-Marienfelde, where production began in 1938. Late in 1941 the Nazi regime gave Daimler-Benz two additional factory complexes for more aircraft engine production. One was at Rzeszow in Polish Galicia, between Krakow and Lvov, and the other, Ostmark Aircraft Engines, had factories at Wiener Neustadt (near Vienna) and in Brno, Czechoslovakia. Ostmark's production record, however, was dismal.

An unusual controversy arose when Wilhelm Kissel, the Daimler-Benz chairman since the merger in 1926 and one of the most prominent businessmen in Nazi Germany, died in the summer of 1942. To replace him the firm's boards chose Wilhelm Haspel. This decision outraged officials of the Labor Front and the SS. No one challenged Haspel's loyalty to the regime or his competence. At issue was his wife's half-

Jewish ancestry. Heinrich Himmler, head of the SS, said he would lodge a complaint about this with Hitler and Göring. Nevertheless, the decision stood.[5]

As German men went off to war the automobile industry found new sources of labor: German women, foreign men and women who volunteered or more often were drafted to work in Germany, prisoners of war, and finally Jews and others from concentration camps forced to work in the factories. That this type of labor – most of it unskilled and much of it unwilling – could be used shows how far the German industry had gone in dividing jobs into simple tasks. Daimler-Benz engaged a maximum of 15,700 workers in Untertürkheim, and in 1944 over 5,300 of them were foreign, including 1,200 Soviet women. The number of German women employed in this establishment reached 2,130, although for ideological reasons the regime in public pronouncements discouraged German females from entering the labor market. The foreign workers were fed and housed in barracks and hostels. Some were paid, but most received little or nothing. The factory operated 11 hours on weekdays and eight on Saturdays, with very few people working at night.[6] The Genshagen and Rzeszow factories, farther east, had much higher proportions of foreign workers.

During the war both General Motors and Ford management in the United States lost contact with and all control over their German subsidiaries. German nationals managed these firms at the direction of government authorities. Throughout the war Opel's Brandenburg works made the standard two-wheel-drive, 3-ton-capacity truck using a six-cylinder gasoline engine. This plant assembled some 70,000 trucks from 1937 through 1945, from 1942 under the direction of Heinz Nordhoff, an employee of Opel since 1929. Nordhoff would become the most famous executive in the German auto industry after the war. At Rüsselsheim most of the Opel factory made parts for aircraft engines; the rest made cars and parts for the Brandenburg works. Its maximum wartime employment of 16,000 did not reach the peacetime high of 22,500. Ford had built a plant in Berlin in 1939 to assemble trucks that it was selling to the army at this time. It also put armored cars together there after the war began. At the larger Cologne operation it made 3-ton trucks and thousands of half-tracks. Ford-Cologne's total production, 1940-44, amounted to 79,619 vehicles.[7] Although Opel and Ford had excellent facilities and much experience at mass production, neither was converted to tank manufacture because of the regime's suspicions about their foreign connections.[8]

Of the two BMW facilities in Eisenach one produced cars, motorcycles, and aircraft-engine parts and the other made an American Pratt & Whitney aircraft engine, licensed before the war, and repaired BMW engines. At BMW's Munich operations it engaged in aircraft-engine development and production. BMW also labored to produce a jet-aircraft engine. By 1942 it had failed, and the Luftwaffe went ahead with one made by Junkers.

The Maybach firm in Friedrichshafen on Lake Constance gave up its small output of luxury cars and produced most of the gasoline-powered tank engines during the war. Because of the risk of depending on this single source, the authorities in 1943 contracted with the Wanderer plant of Auto Union in Chemnitz-Siegmar to begin making Maybach tank engines as a second source. In April 1944 the Maybach factory was bombed out of production. By the time Allied bombers crippled Siegmar in September, Friedrichshafen was back at work. Other Auto Union factories produced motorcycles, cars, half-tracks, and Junkers aircraft engines, but the regime did not use this firm to full capacity.

Truck makers engaged heavily in war production. Vomag, a truck firm of Plauen, Saxony, switched to tanks in 1941. Henschel, of Kassel, began making tanks in 1936. Thereafter it designed the "Tiger" tank, and production began in 1942. Henschel also operated another factory in Kassel, producing up to 600 Daimler-Benz aircraft engines monthly. Borgward and Büssing continued to make trucks, the latter specializing in 4.5-ton diesel models of which it produced 29,500 between 1939 and 1945. A Büssing factory also made Daimler-Benz aircraft engines, about 17,400 during the war, a quarter of all those produced. Krupp, a heavy-truck producer among other things, began making tanks at its Magdeburg works in 1934 and continued through the war. The MAN truck factory in Nuremberg also produced tanks from 1935 through 1945. It made some 2,000 of the 45-ton "Panther" models late in the war. In its Augsburg works MAN also resumed its manufacture of diesel engines for submarines–an area in which it had excelled in the First World War. The Volkswagen factory in 1940 began to produce the the Kübelwagen, a Jeep-like small scout car with two-wheel drive, along with an amphibious variant. A total of between 64,000 and 70,000 were made. VW also produced aircraft parts, V-1 flying bombs, mines, camp stoves, and other items, but it never operated at more than half capacity during the war. This failure to convert to full military production seemed to have come in part from a desire by the political leadership – Hitler himself? – to have the factory ready to make the VW car as soon as possible after the war.

The Czech vehicle firms had to join the German war effort. Skoda had made light tanks before German annexation and continued thereafter; ultimately, these evolved into self-propelled assault guns. Tatra developed a 12-cylinder, air-cooled diesel engine used in armored cars and trucks.

Labor shortages, spot scarcities of machine tools and parts, and air raids were the main problems facing the industry. And then its customers – the soldiers and airmen – had the problem of fuel that became desperate in June 1944. As mentioned in reference to Daimler-Benz, German women along with foreign and forced labor were the answer to the shortage of workers, although few of them were skilled. One estimate suggests that the proportion of skilled factory workers in the industry fell from 50 to 24 percent from 1940 to 1944, and that German women amounted to 18 percent and foreigners 48 percent of the motor-vehicle labor force in 1944.[9]

Parts shortages cannot be isolated from other factors slowing production, but this became a problem in 1943 and worsened in mid-1944 with heavier Allied bombing raids on railways, and factory dispersals brought about by attacks on aircraft-engine and tank-production facilities. From August 1944 on, most of the automobile plants in Germany sustained bomb damage. Usually a plant recovered to nearly normal output in two to 12 weeks after a major attack. Only persistent raids could keep it out of production. The Ford factory in Cologne was never hit, but its production collapsed in October 1944 owing to area raids that interrupted electric power supply and rail transportation. In the second quarter of 1944 German truck production was 26,214, the normal level for the undamaged industry; in the last quarter of the year it dropped to 12,189, reflecting the air attacks.[10] Reductions, but not as steep, also came in the production of tanks and aircraft engines, the industry's other major products in 1944.

GERMAN FUEL PROBLEMS

Germany began the war in 1939 with inadequate petroleum fuel supplies but managed to survive without a major motor-fuel crisis until

Lanfranco in the Fiat Mirafiore works took advantage of the prevailing defeatism to stage a strike in March 1943. Ostensibly concerned with matters of pay, this strike really was an end-the-war movement, and everyone understood this. It spread throughout Turin and to Milan. By April government wage concessions brought the workers back, but this affair marked the beginning of the end for Italian Fascism. Strategic bombing, therefore, did play a major role in ending Italy's participation in the war.[15] The coup of 25 July 1943 overthrew Mussolini, but German military forces immediately took control of northern and central Italy. Production by Fiat and other auto firms continued at a reduced level for the rest of the war.

FRANCE

The French motor-vehicle industry was largely out of the picture under German occupation from June 1940 on, but before France's defeat this industry generally met the military demands on it. Auto firms made a large share of its army's tanks. Renault had continued to produce tanks after 1919, in the 1930s making several hundred light reconnaissance models, about 260 of the rather mediocre 10-ton D type, over 1,500 of the 10-ton R35 of 1935 and over 300 of the excellent B tank of 32 tons. In 1936 the Popular Front government nationalized Renault's tank-design office, tank-assembly shop, and testing department, but Renault continued to supply most of the components for the R35 and B tanks as well as some 6,000 "chenillettes." Chenillettes were lightweight tracked vehicles used to bring supplies forward from depots, replacing the light railways of the First World War. Hotchkiss produced a light tank, and Somua, an affiliate of the important arms firm Schneider, made a fine 20-ton tank. Tables 8.1 and 8.2 show German (and Czech) and French tank production to the date of Germany's attack in the West. In addition, Panhard and Renault made several hundred armored cars while Renault, Citroën, Peugeot, Berliet, and other firms built trucks of various sizes. Engines for military aircraft came from Gnôme & Rhône and Hispano-Suiza. The latter company – like Rolls-Royce in Britain – also offered small numbers of luxury cars until 1938.

The French plan for military motor transport was, on mobilization, to augment the army's 60,000 vehicles with 240,000 requisitioned civilian cars and trucks and then gradually to retire the poorer civilian vehi-

TABLE 8.1   GERMAN (AND CZECH) TANK PRODUCTION TO 10 MAY 1940

Type	Manufacturer	Number
Pz I*	Krupp, Daimler-Benz, MAN, Henschel	1,605
Pz II	MAN	1,238
Pz III	Daimler-Benz, Henschel, Alkett	422
Pz IV	Krupp	348
Czech 35, 38	Skoda, CKD	447
	Total	4,060
	Tonnage	39,790

* light reconnaissance; equivalent to the French AMR and modernized Renault FT
Sources: R. H. Stolfi, "Reality and Myth: French and German Preparations for War,
1933-1940," Ph.D. diss., Stanford University, 1966; USSBS, *Tank Industry Report*, 3.

TABLE 8.2   FRENCH TANK PRODUCTION TO 10 MAY 1940[1]

Type	Manufacturer	Number
AMR[2]	Renault (largely)	400
Renault FT[3]	Renault	500
Renault 35	Renault	1,570
Hotchkiss 35, 39	Hotchkiss	1,055
FCM	FCM	100
D 1	Renault	160
D 2	Renault	100
Somua 35	Somua	416
B	Renault and others	337
	Total	4,638
	Tonnage	61,645

[1] French tanks had thicker armor and heavier guns than the German tanks.
[2] light reconnaissance; equivalent to Germany's Pz I
[3] modernized; equivalent to Germany's Pz I
Sources: R. H. Stolfi, "Reality and Myth: French and German Preparations for War,
1933-1940," Ph.D. diss., Stanford University, 1966.

cles in favor of new production. After the war began the army received about half of the maximum-capacity monthly production of 4,500 lightweight and 2,700 full-size trucks, supplemented by 7,000 trucks ordered from the United States – Studebaker, Dodge, and GMC. Of these, 5,000 were delivered by May 1940. Fiat also delivered some. Consequently, over 35,000 new vehicles joined the army from September to May 1940.[16] The French army, then, had more than double the number of wheeled motor vehicles than the German 120,000 in May 1940. The Germans moved faster nevertheless and prevailed in the May-June campaign over French forces fatally hampered by faulty planning and unaggressive leadership.

Once defeated, France had to give up some 700,000 existing cars and trucks to the Germans over the next few years, as well as most of its armored vehicles. Its auto industry worked primarily to fill German military orders. The Nazis wanted trucks and the repair of French tanks they had captured. The nationalized Hotchkiss firm agreed to repair its tanks. Louis Renault at first agreed to do the same to keep his workers and plant busy, but his associates, horrified at the implications, quickly won a reversal of this decision. The Germans insisted and François Lehideux finally arranged a compromise. The Germans requisitioned two Renault shops. There, under German command, workers of French and 16 other nationalities, previously unemployed, repaired about 100 R35 tanks and 150 B tanks, using parts drawn mostly from French arsenals. In this operation the Germans also refurbished a few Panhard armored cars and captured British tanks.[17]

Motor-vehicle production in occupied France was very small compared with prewar output, owing to shortages of materials, to the dispatch – forcible in most cases – of French workers to jobs in German factories, to bombing attacks by the Allies, and to resistance and sabotage by workers and managers. From June 1940 to mid-1944 French firms sold to the Germans 101,785 of a total of 121,493 trucks manufactured, and 15,595 of 16,773 cars. Some also supplied parts for German military equipment. Peugeot, for example, made a variety of parts for German military aircraft (Junkers and Focke-Wulf) and road vehicles, including tank treads. From February 1943 it was under the control of the Volkswagen management. That July there was an ineffective air raid on the Peugeot works at Sochaux. A British secret agent, Harry Rée, or Henri Raymond, alias César, who spoke French with a Manchester accent, had met Jean-Pierre Peugeot in May 1943 and received ƒ100,000 from him. British sources claim that sometime after the July raid Rée threatened to have the RAF attack Peugeot again unless he and his group were allowed to destroy certain key materials and machines that would stop production without loss of life and indiscriminate destruction of property. Whether J.-P. Peugeot agreed to this is not clear, but the plant was not bombed again, and a series of sabotages did begin with a fire in September 1943 that destroyed 5,000 rubber tires, followed by incidents that seriously damaged several key machines. Rée escaped to Switzerland in November 1943.[18] All the while, secret research and development work continued on new models for the postwar period.

Both owners and workers in the French auto factories faced a difficult, in some cases an agonizing, moral dilemma during the Occupation. Working to fill German orders meant helping France's conqueror, but keeping the factory busy and not quitting meant providing employment and an income to workers, as well as less chance of the machinery and men being shipped to Germany. At the liberation of France, some harsh judgments would be made.

The acute shortage of petroleum and German requisition of French motor vehicles led to the disappearance of most cars and trucks from the streets and highways. For most owners the only way to keep them operating was to install a gazogene. In France most of these burned charcoal, but Berliet had adopted the Imbert system, which used wood of any quality. From 1941 to 1946 this firm supplied 6,000 new gazogene trucks and 18,000 gazogenes to mount on trucks or buses in service.[19]

Life in Paris became onerous without many personal cars, taxis, or buses. Most former users of these vehicles dove into the already crowded Métro, but this subway system depended on the electricity supply, which became unreliable in 1944 and 1945. A few horse cabs reappeared along with bicycle taxis – a bicycle pulling a box on wheels in which the client rode, at a high price. For personal transportation most people used bicycles. A final alternative was to fill a large air-tight bag with stove or illuminating gas, set it on the roof of a car like a huge cake of soap and run the gas to the engine through a tube. The author's brother, serving in the U.S. army near Paris early in 1945, tells of "the arrival of a couple of friends at the Gare St. Lazare in a taxi so equipped, crawling up a slight grade, its rooftop bag flabby and almost empty and my friends leaning out the cab windows pressing and pummelling the bag for a last breath of gas to get them across the square and into the station."

With the largest output in Europe in the 1930s, the British motor-vehicle industry played a major role in military production, especially in aircraft-engine manufacture. As will be seen, the country's record in tanks was undistinguished, but aircraft rearmament began early, when in 1936 the Air Ministry determined that in a major war it would need many more engines and airframes than the industry could deliver with its current facilities. So it began a "shadow" factory program in that year, building and equipping a number of factories that could begin aircraft production quickly in case of emergency.[20] The ministry asked automobile firms to manage most of these plants because it assumed that they had more skilled managerial personnel available than the aircraft companies. Austin and Rootes would operate airframe factories; Daimler, Humber (Rootes), Standard, and Rover would manage shadow engine plants, making Bristol engines. All these were in production when the war began and others had been started. In 1938 Nuffield began building the largest of the new airframe factories to make Spitfire fighter planes in Castle Bromwich (on the eastern fringe of Birmingham). In this case construction progressed slowly, and when it was nearly finished, in May 1940, Vickers, the original producer of the Spitfire, took over the facility. In London, several auto-body firms joined forces to produce bombing planes. Ultimately, 12 shadow factories dotted the Coventry area, most involved in aircraft-engine production. The Standard company managed several of them, in the course of the war making 20,000 Bristol engines, 417,000 separate cylinders for engines, 1,066 Mosquito bombers, 12,800 armored vans and cars, and other military hardware.[21] Coventry's military importance was no secret to the Germans, who bombed it 40 times in 1940-41, but even these raids brought no lasting damage to the industrial plants.

Of the 100,000 Bristol engines made during the war, two-thirds came from plants operated by automobile companies. Rolls-Royce engines, especially the Merlin, were the other major type used in British military aircraft.[22] This firm's luxury-car operations were only moderately successful between the wars, and beginning in 1935 its sales revenue from aircraft engines exceeded that from cars. Under the leadership of Ernest Hives, general manager from 1933, Rolls-Royce began producing the Merlin in 1936. The original design had been faulty and required long development. In 1938 Rolls-Royce made 1,710 Merlins, primarily for fighter planes, but not until 1942 did this engine really run well. The company at first opposed shadow plants as a way to increase production, preferring to maintain closer control by expanding the use of subcontractors to make parts. But under government pressure it agreed to build a second factory that it would manage, at Crewe, between Birmingham and Manchester, with about two-thirds of the cost coming from the Air Ministry. The Crewe facility began making Merlins in 1939. A third factory near Glasgow produced its first Merlins at the end of 1940. Both the Crewe and Glasgow works used a much higher proportion of unskilled and semiskilled labor than the home plant at Derby, but the latter facility retained all development work on engines. This matched the arrangement that Daimler-Benz used in Germany—all development work at Untertürkheim, with Genshagen and other locations only doing production.

To meet an ever-increasing demand for Merlins, the English Ford company with government funds built and equipped a factory near Manchester to make them. Production began there late in 1941, using Ford methods of mass production. In 1943, 1944, and 1945 the Ford facility made more engines than any of the Rolls-Royce-operated establishments. Ford's Dagenham plant, east of London, was considered too vulnerable to German air raids to locate aircraft-engine manufacture there, but, cleverly camouflaged, it escaped serious bomb damage throughout the war. The British government also contracted with the Packard Motor Company in Detroit to make Merlin engines. It began production late in 1941 and altogether manufactured some 55,000 engines, 25,000 of them in 1944, almost as many as the four British factories combined in that year. About half of the Packard Merlins went into British and Commonwealth aircraft, the rest to American planes. The total number of Rolls-Royce aircraft engines made in Britain during 1939-45 reached 113,780 – 32,239 at Derby, 28,488 at Crewe, 23,808 at Glasgow, and 29,245 at Ford-Manchester.[23]

In 1939 Rolls-Royce had begun to look into the possibilities of gas-turbine aircraft engines. Its researchers made little progress, but RAF officer Frank Whittle did, and he demonstrated a prototype jet engine in that year. The Air Ministry asked the Rover company to cooperate with Whittle in developing and producing this engine for a fighter plane. Rover could not seem to manage this so Rolls-Royce took over and began producing Whittle's jet engines in 1943. The first Meteor jet fighters were delivered to RAF squadrons in July 1944. They proved to be inferior to the German jet fighters that appeared at the same time, but Rolls-Royce had gained a head start in the jet engine business. Ernest Hives's policy of hiring many talented engineers, unlike the other British auto firms, had paid off.

Although British military theorists between the world wars wrote a great deal about the use of tanks in warfare, the army had few of them by 1939. This was a consequence of a policy not to send a large army to the Continent (reversed only in 1939), of higher budgetary priorities for the navy and air force, and of disagreements over the type of tanks to make. The Vickers company was the sole tank supplier during most of the 1930s and continued as an important designer and producer during the war. The best of Vickers's wartime tanks probably was the Valentine, but the Harry Hopkins, a light tank, was an also-ran.

In 1936 the War Office asked the Nuffield organization to establish a tank-manufacturing operation. It created Nuffield Mechanizations in 1937 and delivered its first production model of a cruiser tank (A-13, or Mark III) the next year. This was the first entry by a motor firm into tank production, and Nuffield had many problems. By September 1939 it had built only 40 of these tanks. Eventually this model evolved into the Crusader tank, of which over 5,000 were made, but this tank was a disappointment in combat.

General Motors' Vauxhall concern in 1940 received the assignment to develop and produce a new heavy tank, the Churchill. Deliveries began in December 1941. Like Nuffield's cruiser tanks, the first ones had serious flaws, but by 1943 the Churchill was a satisfactory weapon. Vauxhall made 5,640 of them during the war, as the head of a group of firms supplying components. In the first part of the war British tanks lacked good engines. They even used many modified Liberty engines whose American design dated from 1917, but these proved unreliable. After much hesitation the army finally settled on the Meteor, a modified Rolls-Royce Merlin.[24] The British eventually used many U.S. Sherman tanks. In Normandy in 1944 two-thirds of the tanks in the British armored divisions were American.[25]

Before the war the British army also began to purchase many small, tracked, and lightly armored vehicles, like the French chenillettes, to move small amounts of supplies and troops in off-road situations. Often called Bren gun carriers, they were cheap and easy to make. The major producers included the carmakers Wolseley (22,000 of them) and Ford-Dagenham (14,000) and the truck makers Thorneycroft (8,230) and Dennis. Daimler, Humber, and AEC made armored cars, none of which was outstanding.

During the 1930s the British motorized their entire army, but since it was quite small this was not a major commitment at the time. When the war began, the War Office requisitioned many civilian trucks and vans. In addition, Canada supplied 386,000 motor vehicles to Britain from 1940 to 1944, and the United States supplied another 257,000. The British industry itself supplied somewhat under 90,000 trucks per year for military purposes, a total of 434,007 from 1940 through 1944, most of which were 1.5- and 3-ton vehicles. This output came without expanding production facilities but by reducing car output to low levels. Vauxhall-Bedford (almost 250,000), Ford, AEC, Thorneycroft, Leyland (also a major tank maker), Austin, and Nuffield were important truck producers. Total British output of 538,525 trucks and buses from 1940 to 1944, along with 138,969 passenger cars and vans, amounted to 677,494. Comparable German figures are 465,381 trucks and 184,515 cars for a total of 649,896.[26] The totals are surprisingly close to each other, and the British aid from North America was nearly balanced in numbers by the vehicles the Germans took from the occupied countries. With its much smaller army, the British forces were much more highly motorized than the Germans throughout the war.

Auto firms produced all sorts of other equipment, including mines, agricultural tractors (136,000 by Ford), aircraft-repair and small artillery by Nuffield, and 94,000 Ford V-8 engines for nonautomotive purposes.

The war production record of the British motor-vehicle industry was mixed. There were a few high-quality items such as the Rolls-Royce Merlin and Meteor engines, but British tanks, early tank engines, and trucks did not rise above the level of mediocrity often enough. Labor productivity usually fell behind that of Germany and North America. The basic reason for these difficulties was weak management, especially a serious lack of design engineers and a failure to achieve control over the production process.

One unusual aspect of the war was that different Ford and General Motors establishments produced equipment on both sides of the conflict. There were cases of German- and Italian-owned firms producing in Britain and the United States – Bosch, for example, and the Fiat assembly plant in England. With the proliferation of multinational enterprises in the twentieth century, such complexities were bound to occur.

Although independent labor unions did not exist in Germany or the Soviet Union during the war, they won considerable success in Britain. There, most employers lost control over wage rates to government officials and, under government pressure, frequently had to recognize unions as bargaining agents for their workers. In Italy and France unions and left-wing political parties rose from powerlessness in the early 1940s to a major influence in resistance movements and great power at the war's end.

THE SOVIET UNION

During the war the Soviet leadership placed a higher priority on tanks and aircraft than on trucks so the country produced relatively few wheeled vehicles. Choosing tanks over trucks was a major risk, but it worked out well because the Soviet tanks were first class and because the United States supplied the Red army with hundreds of thousands of trucks. From over 180,000 trucks per year from 1937 to 1939, Soviet truck output fell to 30,400 in 1942, 45,600 in 1943, and 52,600 in 1944, far below deliveries from the United States.[27] Most truck-making facilities were switched to making tanks, aircraft, or components for tanks and aircraft.

Assuming the official figures are correct, Soviet tank output was a startling achievement. From their beginning in the early 1930s, the three large tractor factories in Stalingrad, Kharkov, and Chelyabinsk also turned out armored cars or tanks. The Kirov (formerly Putilov) factory in Leningrad also made tanks. The Soviets built small and lightweight models at first, as in the rest of Europe; larger types with diesel engines came at the end of the 1930s. Officially the Red army had huge numbers of tanks, between 17,000 and 24,000, when Germany invaded in June 1941, but only about 6,500 actually could operate. Most of these in turn fell to the Germans in 1941, but new tanks of the T34 and KV models, using an excellent diesel engine and superior to the standard German III and IV types, appeared in growing numbers. Although the thousands of tanks the Soviets made in the 1930s turned out to have little direct military value, the soldiers had learned how to work with them, the factory managers had learned how to organize their facilities, and the suppliers had learned how to manufacture parts in large numbers, so that when new models became available, production was large almost from the beginning. In the first half of 1941, just before the German invasion, the Soviets manufactured 1,500 KV and T34 tanks; in the second half of the year, despite major disruptions brought by the German advances, they made 2,820.[28]

The tremendous German victories in the first weeks of the invasion triggered a general movement to evacuate Soviet industrial enterprises eastward toward the Ural Mountains or even beyond. The Kirov factory in Leningrad shipped its diesel-tank-engine machinery and workers to Chelyabinsk in August 1941; the rest of its tank equipment may not have escaped until months later, over the ice of Lake Ladoga. In October 1941 almost 12,000 of Kirov's tank workers and their families were flown out of Leningrad to the Soviet side of the battle lines; after considerable hardship they rejoined their machines in the Urals. Some went to Chelyabinsk, where the diesel-engine plant associated with the Kharkov tractor and tank factory also was shipped. This city became known as "Tankograd"; its factories produced an estimated 18,000 KV tanks and 48,000 tank engines during the war. The Kharkov tank-making machinery also went to the Urals, the last trains leaving just as the Germans poured in. Its tractor facilities ended up deep in Siberia at Rubtsovsk, some 275 miles south of Novosibirsk. The traditional industrial area in the Urals from Sverdlovsk north to Nizhni-Tagil became home to several plants making tanks and parts for them, especially the T34 model.

Equipment from the Stalin motor-vehicle factory in Moscow came to Miass, near Chelyabinsk, to establish a truck plant. Some departments of the Stalin works were relocated in Ulyanovsk on the middle Volga and in other eastern locations, although the Moscow plant continued to operate on a reduced scale. At Gorki motor-vehicle operations were converted quickly to tanks and tank engines in 1941. Two years later the Gorki complex sustained several German bombing attacks. The Stalingrad factory operated in the face of the German advance in 1942 until mid-September, in the last month repairing 200 tanks and 600 artillery tractors. In October the two armies fought each other around and even inside this factory for several days until the Germans finally took it. Some machinery from the Stalingrad tank fac-

TABLE 8.3 TRUCK AND TANK PRODUCTION IN THE SECOND WORLD WAR

	1939	1940	1941	1942	1943	1944[1]	1945
Trucks							
Britain	97,000[2]	112,531	124,738	137,339	127,713	113,251	102,623[3]
Germany	101,745	87,888	86,147	80,512	92,959	77,177	n.a.
U.S.S.R.	178,800	136,000	?	30,400	45,600	52,600	68,500[4]
Tanks							
Britain	969	1,399	4,841	8,611	7,476	3,604[5]	3,932[7]
Germany	247[6]	1,643	3,790	6,180	12,063	19,002	15,419
U.S.S.R	2,950	2,794	6,590	24,446	24,089	28,963	

[1] In 1944 the U.S. produced 595,330 army trucks.
[2] estimate
[3] 12 months
[4] 12 months
[5] 1944 and 1945
[6] last four months
[7] six months

Sources:
Great Britain, Central Statistical Office, *Statistical Digest of the War* (London: HMSO, 1951), 148, 159.
USSBS, *Effects of Strategic Bombing*, 278, 281.
Harrison, *Soviet Planning*, 118, 250, 253.
Zaleski, *Stalinist Planning for Economic Growth*, 604.

tory was probably shipped east during the summer of 1942. Soviet tank production continued to mount despite these serious problems, exceeding German and British output by wide margins (see Table 8.3).[29] Several thousand light tanks are included in the 1942 figure, but the 3,500 of this type made in 1943 were the last.

The Soviets made 106,000 airplanes during the war. Unlike the Western countries, the Soviet Union kept auto- and aircraft-engine development and manufacture separate in the 1930s, but during the war some auto-engine capacity was used to make aero-engine parts. Soviet designers took Western aircraft engines as their models, the Wright Cyclone from the United States and the Gnôme & Rhône and His-pano-Suiza from France. The output totaled between 175,000 and 185,000 engines during the war.[30]

To supplement the low level of Soviet truck production, the Western allies, especially the United States, furnished great numbers of them. A total of 466,968 vehicles reached the Soviet Union from the United States through the Lend-Lease program, including some 183,000 2.5-ton trucks, 149,000 1.5-ton trucks, 48,000 Jeeps, 629 tank transporters, and over 8,000 tanks and self-propelled guns.[31] Of these, 184,000 came through the Persian corridor, where General Motors erected two assembly plants in 1942 on Iranian territory at the head of the Gulf. Semi-knocked-down trucks from America were assembled there by Iranian employees and U.S. soldiers and were then driven, loaded with other supplies, by Soviet soldiers over roads improved by American and British efforts to the Transcaucasian region. When the flow of trucks and other supplies by this route ended in early 1945, the United States shipped both assembly plants to the Soviet Union.[32]

By the end of the Second World War the British, German, and Soviet motor-vehicle industries had expanded their manufacturing capacities. How the industry all over Europe would perform in the immediate postwar world would depend on raw-material availability and on political decisions about what would be produced and for whom.

9

RECOVERY

The automobile industries of the major European countries faced similar problems of reconstruction and reconversion at the end of the Second World War. In Germany and to a lesser degree in France and Italy, production facilities had been physically damaged, but in all countries greater problems arose from raw-material shortages and from the process of converting military factories back into car- and truck-making facilities.

The physical damage usually looked worse than it really was. Roofs and walls blown out by bomb blasts could be repaired cheaply. Complicated machine tools were the really expensive parts of an automobile factory, but it usually took a direct bomb hit on one to destroy it. Britain, Germany, Italy, and perhaps the Soviet Union had more machine tools at the end of the war than at the beginning. Britain and the Soviet Union made many tools and received large numbers of them from the United States. In Germany the stock of machine tools rose from 1.5 million to 2.3 million during the war, of which only some 2.5 percent or 58,000 may have been destroyed.[1] The Germans took as many as 80,000 machine tools from France and smaller amounts from other occupied countries, but after the war it lost many more than these as reparations, especially to the Soviet Union. The division of Germany complicates these assessments, but it is very probable that West Germany had more machine tools in 1946 than in 1939. France ended the war with fewer, and these were of a high average age. All European countries faced serious shortages of steel and other raw materials. Stocks of these materials had been depleted, demand for steel was immense, and these countries lacked the foreign exchange to import much steel or other materials.

Automakers had to work out a product policy. Should they emphasize trucks for the reconstruction effort or would surplus military vehicles ruin this market as they had in 1919-21? If they resumed

TABLE 9.1 Motor-Vehicle Production, 1945-1951*

	Britain			France			West Germany			Italy			Soviet Union		
	PC	CV	Total	PC	CV	Total	PC	CV	Total	PC	CV	Total	PC	CV	Total
1945	17	123	140	2	33	35				2	8	10	5	70	75
1946	219	146	365	30	65	95	10	13	23	11	18	29	6	96	102
1947	287	155	442	66	70	136	10	13	23	25	17	42	10	123	133
1948	335	173	508	100	98	198	30	27	57	44	15	59	20	177	197
1949	412	216	628	188	98	286	104	55	159	65	21	86	46	277	323
1950	523	261	784	257	100	357	219	82	301	100	29	129	65	294	359
1951	476	258	734	314	133	447	277	93	370	118	30	148	54	235	289

* in thousands

PC = private cars

CV = commercial vehicles

Source: B. R. Mitchell, *European Historical Statistics, 1750-1970* (New York: Columbia University Press, 1975), 467-69.

carmaking, should they go back to the prewar models or offer new ones, and should the cars be small and cheap for an impoverished clientele or medium-sized for the traditional middle-class market?

Many new people would meet these challenges. The pioneers of the industry were departing. Austin died in 1941, Perry of English Ford retired in 1948 and died in 1956, Nuffield retired in 1954 and died in 1963, Edouard Michelin died in 1940, Renault died in 1944, Robert Peugeot died in 1945, Marius Berliet died in 1949, Pierre Boulanger of Citroën died in 1950, Giovanni Agnelli died in 1945, Rasmussen of Auto Union returned to Denmark during the war and died in 1964, Kissel of Daimler-Benz died in 1942, and Ferdinand Porsche died in 1951. There were many changes in the Soviet industry because of military deaths and Stalin's continuing purges. In some cases the new people who took over showed greater ability than their predecessors.

RAPID REVIVAL IN BRITAIN

The Labour party won a clear majority in the first postwar election and maintained government controls over the auto companies. It required them to export a high proportion of their output in order to earn scarce foreign exchange. It enforced this policy by government allocation of steel. Those companies that failed to export adequately would receive less steel. World markets welcomed this British effort to export motor vehicles: in most of the world new cars had not been available since 1940. The United States did not supply much of this postwar craving for cars because American producers concentrated on filling the home demand until 1950, and American cars were too expensive and burned too much fuel for most of the world anyway. Into this fortunate situation drove the British carmakers, at first resuming production of prewar models as the fastest way to satisfy customers who desperately wanted cars. The British Big Six continued to dominate the business. Whatever bomb damage they had suffered early in the war was more than offset by the shadow factories that became available at the war's end. Already in 1947 Britain turned out as many vehicles as in 1938 and rapid expansion continued until 1951.

There was a drawback to this initial success, however. The only cars the British firms had available for export were those designed in the 1930s for domestic service – that is, for slow speeds on good roads.

They found buyers nevertheless, and exports reached a high of 66 percent of production in 1950, but the hard usage these cars experienced
overseas and the inadequate service facilities brought them a poor reputation. This situation made them vulnerable to competition, especially
from German manufacturers, in the 1950s.[2] The success of the Land-
Rover and some British sports cars that were designed for the use to
which they were put in export markets shows that with time and planning the British automakers could do it right.

DIFFICULTIES IN FRANCE

Among the few benefits of the war for France were the 50,000 military
vehicles the Americans left behind in 1945 that were sold by auto manufacturers and dealers. The French automobile industry had to overcome some damage problems and resolve some ownership issues. The
Peugeot works had been bombed and sustained some sabotage, and
then, in the fall of 1944, it lay in the midst of several weeks of fighting in
the Montbéliard-Sochaux area. These events destroyed 101 machine
tools, but in 1944 the Germans carried off 1,545 more machine tools
(about one-third of the total), 2,155 electric motors, and a variety of
other equipment. When the war ended Peugeot engineers went looking
for their machines, finding some in Alsace, Germany, and even
Czechoslovakia. They also brought back some 700 German machines
and bought at bargain prices several dozen used American machines.
By 1946 Peugeot had the machinery to resume the prewar level of output but could not because of labor and raw-material shortages.[3] The
first vehicles – lightweight trucks and vans – came in September 1945. In
1946 output rose to 14,000, mostly commercial vehicles, but gradually a
larger number of a prewar-model passenger car.

During the Vichy regime and after the war, government economic
planning was in high favor as a way to allocate scarce resources and
improve efficiency. Drafted by the Ministry of Industrial Production,
the Pons Plan of February 1945 for the postwar automobile industry
aimed to concentrate production among fewer firms and have them
specialize in certain segments of the market (see Table 9.2). Peugeot
was supposed to take over Hotchkiss and two small truck firms, but this
scheme never worked out. For passenger cars the plan assigned a

TABLE 9.2   THE PONS PLAN FOR POSTWAR FRANCE, FEBRUARY 1945*

	Fiscal HP (CV)				
	Under 6 CV (very small)	6/8 CV (medium small)	10/12 CV (medium)	Over 12 CV (large)	Light utility
Renault	X	X			X
Citroën			X	X	
Peugeot		X			X
Simca/					
Panhard	X				X
Ford				X	

* passenger cars
Source: J.-L. Loubet-Loche, "Les Automobiles Peugeot," Ph.D. thesis (Lille: ANRT, 1988), 48.

medium-small car to Peugeot, along with light utility vehicles. This suited the company's desires, for it believed it could do well against the prewar Renault car in this class but preferred not to compete against a projected small car (the 4 CV) proposed by the nationalized Renault company or against the midsize Citroën front-wheel-drive car that retained great popularity.[4] Production of Peugeot's new 203 model began in 1948 as truck output ended. In 1950 the company surpassed its prewar record output with over 62,000 cars, almost all of one model, for in the seller's market a company needed to offer only one type. Recovery was achieved; henceforth it would be growth.

While Peugeot's tasks were to rebuild its physical plant and then find steel, Renault went through a complete change of ownership and attitude. Louis Renault expected to take full command of his firm upon the liberation of Paris in August 1944, but a large fraction of the public thought otherwise. He was arrested in September on a charge of dealing with the enemy during the war, but his real fault was to incur the wrath of the political Left, riding very high in France at this point. To the Left and probably to a majority of the public, Louis Renault had become a hated symbol of French capitalism. Unwisely, during the war he had made no gesture of friendship to labor, to the Left, or to the Resistance. In the political situation of 1944 he was alone; there was no constituency to defend him. Immediately after Louis Renault's arrest, before he had been tried or convicted of anything, the government of President Charles de Gaulle requisitioned the Renault factories and appointed a provisional administrator. After several weeks of poor treatment in prison, Louis Renault died in a hospital in October 1944. The legal case against him thereupon died with him and logically his enterprise should have gone to his heirs, but the government kept it and issued a nationalization ordinance in January 1945, with little compensation ultimately going to the Renault family. The government had no realistic alternative to these extralegal procedures. Labor generally demanded nationalization, the Socialists and Communists insisted on it, and de Gaulle's primary aim was to maintain unity. Louis Renault and his property rights were sacrificed to reasons of state.[5]

French Socialists had a long tradition of pushing nationalization of major sectors of the economy, arguing that public ownership would bring better and more progressive management. French Communists had come late to the policy of nationalization – in 1938 – and usually urged it as a negative sanction, to punish capitalists and weaken capitalism. If Louis Renault had lived, his lawyers probably would have been able to defeat the charges against him and win restitution of his enterprise (an investigating judge examined the case against Renault and his chief administrator until 1949 and then dropped it for lack of evidence). Even so, Renault's health was such that the firm would have gone into other hands soon.

The Renault nationalization ordinance created the Régie national des usines Renault, a *régie* being a government-owned enterprise. In this case its management was independent of direct state control and its employees were not considered civil servants. To fill the crucial position of president of the Régie Renault, the de Gaulle government chose Pierre Lefaucheux, a successful engineer and enthusiastic manager who had played a major part in the Resistance but was not closely identified with any political faction. Lefaucheux insisted that the nationalization ordinance grant almost complete autonomy to the Régie Renault, as he feared that normal government control would entangle it in bureaucratic molasses and make it subject to the pet experiments of government officials and politicians. He succeeded, but he had his own agenda; he wanted to make Renault a showplace of industrial modernization and social progress. He also hoped to justify public ownership of the firm by making a new "people's car" as soon as possible, despite the view of some government planners that the economy really needed trucks at this juncture. Lefaucheux also pressed for exports to earn the foreign exchange France needed.[6]

A small car was available. Renault executives had decided early in the Occupation to prepare a small, 4-fiscal-hp (4 CV) car for the post-war market. They had to proceed secretly, and Louis Renault had shown no sympathy for the project. They followed the Volkswagen lay-out with the engine in the rear but made the car smaller and lighter. Gradually prototypes were built, tested, and improved. In November 1945 Lefaucheux finally decided to go ahead with the 4 CV, but then the minister of industrial production insisted that Ferdinand Porsche, a French prisoner at this point, be brought in to advise the Renault peo-ple on designing and manufacturing a small rear-engined car. Under-standably, the French engineers at Renault reacted coldly to Porsche's presence for several months, and apparently he had no influence on them.[7] Renault introduced the 4 CV at the 1946 auto show, and deliv-eries began late in 1947. The car was a big winner for the Régie, which made over a million of them by 1961.

The Berliet case in Lyon began like that of Renault, but it followed a different and a fascinating evolution.[8] In September 1944 the Resis-tance leader Yves Farge, a left-wing journalist appointed by the de Gaulle government as commissioner of the republic for Lyon, ordered the arrest of Marius Berliet for collaborating with the enemy. On the same day Farge called in Paul Berliet, Marius's son and second in command, and without telling him of his father's arrest requested more of the company's trucks to help bring food into the city. Paul Berliet agreed, but a few days later he and his three brothers also found them-selves in prison. Marius Berliet had paid even less attention to changing political circumstances during the war than Louis Renault had, making no effort to contact those who might take power when Germany and the Vichy regime collapsed. In May 1944 he even welcomed Marshal Pétain, the Vichy head of state, to tour his recently bombed factory.

Yves Farge wanted to push the Berliet family out of the way so he could install in their factories a new kind of humanitarian industrial enterprise under workers' control. He requisitioned the firm on the ba-sis of a 1938 law on mobilization in time of war and appointed a new administrator on the basis of a Vichy ordinance that allowed the gov-ernment to so act when the management of a firm was not available. Farge chose one of his Resistance associates, the Communist Marcel

Mosnier, to run the operation. Mosnier had been sales manager of an electrical appliance company. He consulted daily with a council of management that included his technical director Alfred Bardin and representatives of shop-floor workers. Each building had a workers' committee that sent delegates to an enterprise works committee. The CGT union controlled these committees, which had important advisory functions. Socialists dominated the CGT at Berliet until March 1946, when Communists took it over.

From the Liberation until May 1947, the Communist party held certain portfolios in the French government, and its watchword to the workers was "produce." The CGT followed this line, and few strikes or other disputes arose in these years. At Berliet production did recover, held back only by a lack of raw materials and equipment, not labor reluctance. The new administrator encouraged widespread factory welfare services along with vigorous social and sports activities. Piecework wages continued, supplemented by an annual bonus based on a complex formula aimed at rewarding the assiduous. The CGT propagandized vigorously in the factories, promoting Communist political views as well as production speedups.

The principle of worker-management of the firm – "the Berliet experiment" – achieved only a partial success. Intellectuals found the idea charming, but a close investigation by a fervent supporter of the principle concludes that only a small minority of the workers showed enthusiasm for it.[9] These supporters included some in middle management who believed their ability to contribute to the firm had not been recognized by the old bosses, some of the workers from prewar days who retained a strong negative attitude toward the Berliet family, and some new workers who came to the firm after 1944 with hopes of a social revolution. In time the strongest supporters of worker-management were found among the Communists, who constituted as much as 10 percent of the employees.[10] In the company house organ and in CGT publications, workers were confronted with sermons and moralizing: "Those workers who restrict their output are playing the game of the trusts and the reactionaries. Workers, do not tolerate the bellyaching of these bad comrades, real parasites, agents of the 5th column." A group of metalworkers from the Soviet Union was brought to Lyon to show the French how to do their jobs. Some toolmakers who asked for more pay were called "agents of reaction in the service of the Berliet family."[11] Mosnier had appointed a militant young Communist as head of plant security. Marching about in breeches and boots, he gave the impression that the party really controlled the enterprise.

In 1946 Marius Berliet and his sons Paul and Jean came to trial, charged with producing for the Germans, sending workers to obligatory service in German factories, and denouncing members of the Resistance to the police. The Berliet works had sold 2,389 vehicles to Germany (in some cases on direct orders from the Vichy government), of a total production of nearly 9,000. These deliveries were only a tiny proportion of the 101,875 trucks sold by all French auto firms to Germany during the Occupation and were dwarfed by those of Renault, Citroën, Peugeot, and French Ford. One might compare the Berliet deliveries over four years to the 5,800 that the company supplied the French army over just nine months, from September 1939 to June 1940. The Germans had drafted workers from all large metalworking establishments, and the prosecution had difficulty finding workers who were denounced by the accused for Resistance activity, although the head of plant security during the Occupation was found guilty of this sort of thing as well as of membership in the anti-Resistance Militia and was shot in 1946. In any event, Marius was convicted and sentenced to two years in prison and loss of all his property. Paul and Jean Berliet received five-year sentences. Because of his age Marius was allowed to live under house arrest in Cannes where he fought back, writing hundreds of letters and sending angry pamphlets to persons who might help him reverse the court decisions.

After the Berliet convictions the government failed to propose a law nationalizing the Berliet works. The Communist minister of industry, Marcel Paul, later explained that he had higher priorities and that there was opposition to the step in the cabinet and by pressure groups.[12] He did, however, reappoint Mosnier as provisional administrator. By 1946 the strong Resistance and public antagonism to capitalism had cooled from the winter of 1944-45, and the inconsistency of nationalizing Berliet but not hundreds of other industrial establishments was obvious. Then came the major shift of national politics in May 1947 when the Communist ministers left the government to go into opposition. This move ratified changes in public opinion and the development of the cold war.

At Berliet the Communists now began to act in a more sectarian way and in October attacked in their works newspaper several members of the management council as enemies of the working class,

Pétainists, agents of Berliet, and even fascists. Mosnier, who sometimes had been embarrassed by the presumption of his Communist comrades, refused to discipline them in this case, so the split between the non-Communists and Communists in the firm, which had already begun to open, cracked much wider. Technical director Alfred Bardin, a Socialist who had ardently favored worker management, was one of those attacked by the Communists. He and others organized an opposition to the current management, finding most of their support in middle management, technicians, and white-collar workers. When Mosnier then discharged Bardin the latter's supporters went on strike, 5 November 1947. Most of the shop workers remained on the job, but then they too walked out on 25 November, joining the great national strike led by the Communists for economic improvement and against the Marshall Plan and American economic aid.

This general strike ended in early December, and on 10 December the middle management strikers won their point. The Socialist minister of industrial production, Robert Lacoste, replaced Mosnier with Henry Ansay, a bureaucrat from his ministry who had worked with Lefaucheux at Renault in 1945-46. The firm remained in a provisional legal status until July 1949, when the Council of State, the highest court with jurisdiction over government actions, declared that the 1946 appointment of Mosnier was illegal because the owners of the firm were then ready to take control of it. This opened the way for the Berliet family to regain its property. Marius Berliet died in May 1949, but he had anticipated this outcome. It came gradually as there was an effort to avoid antagonizing the labor force. Paul Berliet, pardoned in 1948, returned to head the Berliet enterprise in 1952.

Under different circumstances the Berliet worker-management experiment might have continued. As it was, internal contradictions fatally weakened the effort. Many workers believed that the CGT union, committed to supporting top management, paid little attention to their grievances. The administrator Mosnier had both professional and party loyalties, and when the chips were down he went with his party. Middle management came to feel threatened by the parallel hierarchy of the Communist party in the works.

The Michelin, Citroën, and Peugeot firms also sold products to Germany during the war, but there was no serious effort to punish their owners. The Michelin family had some Jewish ancestry. Some members engaged in the Resistance, and four were deported to Germany where one died. Two others made their way to England and joined the RAF, and one died fighting for the Free French in Corsica. The Peugeot family helped local Resistance groups and sent information to England, and one of Robert Peugeot's sons served with the Free French and U.S. armies. The other two sons escaped to Switzerland during the 1944 fighting. So it was more difficult to pin the collaborationist label on these families and their companies.

After the war Citroën resumed making its front-wheel-drive cars along with trucks that it had produced during the Occupation. Its introduction of the very small 2 CV vehicle (once scheduled for 1939) was delayed until 1948 by the Pons Plan to let Renault and Simca concentrate on small cars. The 2 CV became a unique character in European automobile history. Looking somewhat like a bug-eyed camel, it was a low-powered, humpbacked economy car. Made to be a dependable means of transport for farmers and other country folk, its legendary reliability–like the Ford Model T and the VW Beetle–won for it a place of esteem in the popular culture of motorcars. The 2 CV had a canvas top that rolled up like the lid of a sardine can, its windows did not roll down but flipped up, the shift lever emerged from the dashboard, and the air-cooled, two-cylinder engine drove the front wheels, but not very fast. While the minister of industry publicly grumbled how it was a shame that a company like Citroën could produce such an ugly car, and a British journalist concluded that "it takes genius to achieve such ugliness," the people began to buy it by the thousands in Europe, Africa, and South America. Only a few were sold in North America.[13] By the time production in France stopped in 1988 after 40 years, some 7 million 2 CV cars and variants had been made. Assembly continued in Portugal until 1990. Expressways and rising incomes finally ended the career of the 2 CV; it was too slow for life in the fast lane.

Like the other French companies, Simca began by turning out its prewar models. It had been equipped with new machine tools in the late 1930s, and it received Marshall Plan aid for more new equipment as it expanded its facilities considerably. French Ford in Poissy under Maurice Dollfus's leadership repaired its serious bomb damage and began making V-8 cars and trucks in 1945. In January 1946 its output was third in France after Citroën and Renault. But it failed to build on this strong start. Its cars were too expensive for the French market. Dollfus retired in 1948 and was succeeded by François Lehideux, who in 1940 had broken with his uncle Louis Renault and during the Occupation had managed the Vichy-sponsored committee to coordinate the automobile industry. His thorough experience did not help, and French Ford declined.

By 1949 French motor-vehicle output had made its recovery, and, as in Britain, the structure of the industry had little changed. At Renault, however, there was more vigor, a narrowing of the focus to concentrate more on motor vehicles, and a greater taste for risk.

GERMANY

Motor-vehicle production in Germany recovered quite slowly after the defeat. In the Soviet-occupied zone the best machinery from the auto plants went to the Soviet Union as reparations, and the local regime was in no hurry to repair and reequip the factories. The West German industry also revived slowly, for a number of reasons. The occupying powers at first discouraged a rebirth of German industrialism; there was a severe shortage of steel, whose output the occupiers restricted, and new networks of component suppliers had to be developed. The market was small, as many people had suffered severe financial reversals during the war and especially immediately thereafter. Many had lost their homes to aerial bombing or as refugees from the East needed housing. Securing a home came before a private automobile. In this situation none of the major German manufacturers was ready to offer large numbers of a small and inexpensive car.

In 1948 the West German economy began to revive rapidly when most price and production restrictions were ended and there was a major currency reform. By 1951 the automobile industry regained its prewar level of output, two or three years after the other major continental producers.

Opel lost its truck factory in Brandenburg – the surviving machinery was shipped to the Soviet Union, and the plant was taken over by the East German regime. The company could not resume production of its small Kadett model in Rüsselsheim, for the Soviets took as reparations all the tooling and drawings for this car, which soon appeared in Moscow as the Moskvich. (In the 1950s the Soviets sold Moskvich cars in Western Europe. Customers were advised that for spare parts they could apply to their local Opel dealer.) Opel's first postwar vehicle was a 1.5-ton truck in July 1946, joined in December 1947 by the prewar

Olympia car. Some in General Motors management wanted to abandon Opel, discouraged by Germany's weak economic situation and finding a connection to the Nazi regime distasteful, but company chairman Alfred Sloan persuaded his colleagues to hang on until 1950 to see what might happen. An economic boom began, of course, and in 1950 Opel made some 73,000 vehicles. This was over five times the 1948 level and second to Volkswagen, but still only about half the prewar record.

Ford lost its facilities in Berlin as the war ended. At Cologne it first made several thousand trucks. Passenger-car production began in 1948, and production of the prewar Taunus model reached 11,000 in 1949. Ford could have expanded its facilities and output much faster, but a lack of interest and assistance from its American parent held it back. Only in 1951 did it begin to approach its prewar level of production.

The Auto Union combine's plants all fell within the newly designated East Germany and were taken over by the new regime. Most of its managers turned up in the West and arranged to recommence manufacturing in Düsseldorf in 1950, making DKW cars with a small, two-cylinder engine.

Aerial bombing had damaged all of Daimler-Benz's plants. At first it repaired cars and then slowly resumed production of its prewar Model 170, making 214 in 1946 and 831 in 1947. Thereafter growth accelerated. It concentrated truck and bus production at Mannheim until the Marienfelde plant in West Berlin could be rebuilt in 1950. In that year the firm produced 33,900 cars and 8,500 trucks.

Adler of Frankfurt am Main revived its typewriter and motorcycle production but had to relinquish its efforts with cars. Karl Borgward, however, did succeed in producing trucks and small but expensive Hansa cars in the late 1940s.

A new player emerged in the German car business after the war – Volkswagen. The autoworks' owner, the Nazi Labor Front, had vanished, and at first no one knew what to do with the huge factory. Because it and the new town for its workers, soon to be called Wolfsburg, lay in the British zone of occupation, British army officers took control of it, made essential repairs, and began building small numbers of the original VW cars. Through 1947 the plant supplied a total of 20,000 cars to the British occupation forces; to the French, U.S., and Soviet armies; and to local German officials. At first Volkswagen had to barter cars for steel, parts, and supplies, but with an occupying power's authority behind it, the firm probably found steel more easily than the did. Another reason for keeping the plant operating was for the many refugees in the area.

h officers in charge of the firm came to admire the VW Bee.. identify with their job, and they worked diligently to keep the company in business. When asked, neither British nor American auto firms showed any interest in buying the plant or its machinery, although some Soviet officials did suggest that the border dividing East and West Germany be moved just five miles to include the Wolfsburg plant in their zone. Colonel Charles Radclyffe, the officer in charge, instead found Heinz Nordhoff, the former Opel executive, and made him director of the factory at the beginning of 1948. Knowledgeable, ambitious, and autocratic, Nordhoff expanded production and now sold Beetles to Germans as the low-price leader. As the only cheap car widely available, the VW sold easily, and production rose to 90,588 in 1950, continuing to lead the German industry in output as it had since 1945. Nordhoff did not have to pay interest or dividends on the huge original investment, so he could reinvest profits in equipment repair and renewal. This was the only way to finance investment, as banks hesitated to lend to this legally uncertain enterprise. When a new West German government appeared, the British turned the VW operation over to it in September 1949. That government would now have to determine the ownership issue through legal processes.

The West German motorcar industry reached the prewar rate of German output in 1951 thanks to Volkswagen, about which Nordhoff once remarked, "By one of those ironic jokes history is sometimes tempted to produce, it was the Occupation Powers who, after unconditional surrender, brought Hitler's dream into reality."[14]

ITALY

Motor-vehicle production in Italy resumed quite slowly after the war ended. When the Germans withdrew from Turin at the end of April 1945, the local liberation committee accused Fiat leaders Giovanni Agnelli and Vittorio Valletta of collaboration with the Nazis. It removed them from the firm in favor of a committee of four, including two of the firm's leading engineers, a sales executive and a Communist labor representative.[15] Later, in August, the American military authorities appointed a local physics professor to chair this management committee. In this period an aggressive Communist and Socialist effort to carry out a de facto nationalization of Fiat and some other major industrial firms might have been attempted, parallel to the Renault and Berliet cases in France late in 1944. It did not occur for several reasons. The Italian Communist leader Palmiro Togliatti had come from Moscow with Stalin's orders to cooperate with non-Communist groups, even with King Victor Emmanuel. Allied forces and the American money and food they represented had more political influence in Italy than in France in 1945. Finally, perhaps because Italians had already experienced some nationalizations of economic enterprises by Mussolini and had observed that this policy did not deliver the utopia it promised, they did not press it.

The new management committee at Fiat had trouble finding the materials to expand production but had to maintain the high wartime level of employment. The Communist labor leaders in the Fiat factories urged the workers, a large majority of whom voted Communist in plant elections, to roll up their sleeves and work to save Fiat and the Italian economy. They preached a mixture of Taylorism and Stakhanovism, pointing out Lenin's admiration of Taylorism, but they had slight success. The Communist member of the management committee in December 1945 exhorted his militants to work harder, declaring that the company had a 40 percent surplus of workers and that many should be fired. "Too many people are doing nothing. This must stop."[16] But many workers opposed the reimposition of discipline and responsibility. Some were reported as sleeping all afternoon and responding to challenges by their Communist leaders to work harder by calling them Fascists. As one labor leader lamented, the men "interpreted liberty as doing nothing."[17]

As for Agnelli and Valletta, they showed in their defense against charges of collaboration that between the overthrow of Mussolini in July 1943 and the liberation of Turin in April 1945 they had secretly financed partisan (resistance) organizations, contacted Allied agents, and tried to protect Italian workers and equipment from deportation to Germany. The court was leaning toward exonerating Agnelli when he died at age 79 on 16 December 1945.

Giovanni Agnelli compares well with Henry Ford, Herbert Austin, and Louis Renault as a long-term captain of the automobile industry. Less stubborn and jealous of his own authority than Ford, less a mechanic and more a businessman of the world than Austin, bolder and

e political sense than Renault, he had led his firm for
ry. Through major economic and astonishing political
ept Fiat at the forefront of industrial development in
opting some of the policies of those three men.

against Valletta were dropped, and he returned to Fiat
in 1946 after an arrangement early in that year where he accepted that
an administrative council representing workers and middle management would consult with him on policy matters. There was concern that
without Valletta and a more traditional management structure Fiat
might not recover and would be bought by foreign capitalist interests,
perhaps by General Motors.

A year later Prime Minister de Gasperi excluded the Communists
and Socialists from his cabinet and began receiving special financial aid
from the United States. The Left, trying to get back in power and fearful of the American economic aid and influence, began a series of
strikes. But these obviously political actions irritated many workers and
split the labor movement into several factions, weakening it on the local
and national levels. At Fiat the Communists politicized – and thereby
weakened – the administrative council, which disappeared in 1949. A
last spasm of postwar labor militancy occurred in July 1948 following an
attempted assassination of Togliatti, the Communist leader. To protest
this act, workers occupied Fiat and many other Italian factories, but in a
few days this burst of anger faded, and management resumed control.

As in France, shortages of coal and steel held back autombile production in Italy. By 1948 conditions improved considerably with Marshall Plan aid, and in 1949 Italian output regained the prewar level. Fiat
dominated the industry even more than before the war and offered
three prewar models. The lack of variety gave an opening to specialized
body firms such as Pininfarina, Bertone, Ghia, and others to offer dis-
tinctiveness to these cars, for a price. The flair for body design that
these companies demonstrated soon won contracts for them from other
European and American producers.

THE SOVIET UNION

Recovery of the motor-vehicle industry in the Soviet Union proceeded
at about the same pace as in Western Europe, and faster than West
Germany. None of the prewar centers of the industry – Gorki, Moscow,

Yaroslavl – had been overrun by the invaders, although considerable equipment had been evacuated eastward from the Moscow Stalin truck factory. Plants in these centers resumed production of prewar trucks along with newer models resembling the U.S. army trucks received during the war. Some new cars appeared: from Gorki came the Pobeda (Victory) car, and from the Moscow small-car factory originally established by Ford to assemble the Model A came the Moskvich (Opel Kadett). Plants created during the war with equipment shipped out from Moscow continued to make trucks at Miass and Ulyanovsk. The latter factory put together a Jeep-like vehicle with parts supplied by Gorki. Four new truck-assembly plants began production at Minsk, Odessa, Mytishchi (a Moscow suburb), and Kutaisi (in Georgia). The Odessa plant was probably a combination of the two U.S. plants that operated in Iran during the war.[18]

Of the equipment from Germany, it is not known by Western observers where the Opel-Brandenburg truck plant finally was moved, nor the equipment from the six Auto Union factories in Saxony, three BMW plants, a KHD diesel-engine factory from Oberursel, Austrian auto factories from Graz and Steyr, and equipment from many others. Generally, the Soviets chose as reparations the most modern equipment, such as the Brandenburg truck and Opel Kadett machinery. With their experience gained in evacuating machinery before the advancing Germans in 1941-42, the Soviets probably handled this operation with few mistakes and little damage.[19] It is likely that all this automotive machinery taken as reparations equipped the new Soviet truck plants as well as modernizing the prewar factories. It explains how the country was able to regain quickly the prewar level of output.

The motor-vehicle industry's diffusion from its original center in the Gorki-Moscow-Yaroslavl triangle, at first forced by the evacuation from Moscow in 1941, continued. It appears that little of the evacuated machinery came back to the original factories. These were reequipped with the large wartime deliveries of American machine tools as well as the massive amount of German reparations machinery.

In 1949 output of Soviet trucks and passenger cars surpassed the prewar level, with trucks far in the lead – 230,000 of them to 46,000 cars. This traditional Soviet bias for capital goods over consumer goods would continue until Stalin's death in 1953 and be followed by a slow growth in the proportion of passenger cars produced. The trucks engaged primarily in short-haul and construction operations. The poor condition of highways and bridges precluded much long-haul activity, a situation confirmed by the fact that intercity bus manufacturing began only in the mid-1950s.

By about 1950 the European automobile industry had recovered. In the West most of its leaders had decided to go ahead for mass motorization with small and very small cars, using American manufacturing technology to do it.

10

THE GREAT BOOM: BRITAIN
AND GERMANY

From the achievement of recovery by 1950 until the first oil-price shock in 1973, the European automobile industry celebrated its bonanza years. Growth was astonishing by earlier standards. Considering only the four major western producers – Great Britain, France, Germany, and Italy – motor-vehicle output rose from 1.57 million to 11.67 million, or a 7.4-fold increase. In 1970 these four countries outproduced the United States for the first time.

This increase traced the path of Western Europe's postwar economic expansion. The growth of auto production at first came primarily in small or very small cars – VW Beetle, Fiat 600 and 500, Renault 4 CV and Citroën 2 CV, Morris (later British Motor) Minor and Mini. The engines of these machines ranged in size from the 2 CV's 375 cc to the Beetle's 1131 cc. Europe was adapting to its own soil Henry Ford's dream of a car for everyone. In time, as European personal incomes continued to rise the "people's cars" grew larger and more powerful, just as in the United States the Ford Model T had given way to the Model A and the V-8, the Chevrolet, and the Plymouth.

Europe's carmakers also rediscovered exports. The continental producers followed Britain into North and South America, to Asia and Africa, to the smaller countries of Europe, and finally to each other when the customs barriers began to shrink in the 1960s. The European Economic Community (or Common Market) began to function in 1958. Until this point the tariffs levied on imported cars by the six countries in the Common Market ranged from 17 percent for West Germany to 45 percent for Italy. Gradually these tariffs and other restrictions began to fall, customs duties reaching zero in 1968, with a common external tariff of 17.6 percent. This policy provided European auto firms opportunities for more trade within Europe but at the cost of losing some of their home markets to imports. Consumers benefited from the com-

TABLE 10.1 EXPRESSWAYS IN SERVICE, 1974*

West Germany	3,260	Belgium	626
Italy	3,210	Switzerland	567
France	2,046	Sweden	376
Britain	1,060	Spain	317
Netherlands	776	U.S.	31,310

* in miles

petition in price, advanced technology, and reliability. Manufacturers benefited by the opportunity to sell the same model over a broader market and thereby take advantage of economies of scale. West Germany in 1956 and then France in 1966 surpassed Britain as an exporter. After 1970, when Germany's great export success, the VW Beetle, began to grow obsolete and its sales faded, the French caught up and in 1974 became Europe's leading exporter of passenger cars.

The European penetration of the U.S. market was probably the least predictable aspect of this export boom. The American producers' abandonment of the small, economical car, based on the assumption that used cars would satisfy the less-well-off consumer, left an opening for the European firm that could provide cheap and *reliable* new cars. Volkswagen could, and Beetles began to arrive in large numbers in 1956, but the Japanese followed a decade later.

As European producers expanded to satisfy the strong domestic and export demand, they eschewed the policy of constructing larger and larger factories. Except for the Soviet Union, they followed the U.S. pattern and decentralized to several assembly plants supplied by a number of specialized parts and subassembly factories. Further, they did more subcontracting for parts, as this was cheaper than investing in a new factory of their own, depending on close inspection to ensure reliable quality. Some of the major carmakers – British Motor, Renault, and Fiat – did not watch these incoming parts as rigorously as they should have, and quality difficulties began to surface. A general problem toward the end of the boom years was labor unrest, and auto managements ventured several tactics to regain the loyalty of their workers.

The growing congestion on highways brought by the passenger-car boom led to demands for expressways all over Western Europe. Left-wing politicians had preferred to invest public funds in government-owned railways, but when more and more of their constituents became motorized they acquiesced. West Germany recommenced building autobahns in 1957, Britain opened its first motorway segment in 1958, and France built some short routes around major cities in the 1950s. To build and operate long intercity *autoroutes* the French established mixed government-private companies, financed in part by public funds but primarily by loans to be serviced by tolls. Italy built its *autostrada del sole* from Milan to Naples, finished in 1964. The smaller West European countries also constructed expressway networks. All of the postwar expressways had dual roadways. As in North America, the trucking industry took advantage of these highways to expand its long-distance business.

BRITAIN LAGS

In the 1950s Great Britain lost the motor-vehicle industry lead it had achieved in the immediate postwar years, and its growth began to lag behind Europe's other major producing countries (see Table 10.2). This development generated much concern in that country, and it appears that industry observers have spent more time trying to explain Britain's decline than focusing on the successful growth in the other European countries.

One reason for this decline has already been suggested: the relatively low reliability of British cars when subjected to hard usage. This hurt export sales generally, and especially in North America, where a boomlet in British sports cars in the 1950s and 1960s faded away because of frequent repair problems and weak service arrangements. The large Australian market for British cars began to weaken between the wars as GM and Ford set up facilities to make local bodies for imported chassis. After 1945 GM and later Ford and Chrysler began manufacturing chassis and engines there to escape protective tariffs, but British firms hesitated until 1954 to take this step.

At home, the two largest British firms, Nuffield and Austin, merged in 1952, as Lord Nuffield and Leonard Lord, his former subordinate and now head of Austin, negotiated intermittently for several years before reaching an agreement. Their creation of the British Motor Corporation (BMC) was supposed to bring efficiencies of scale and

TABLE 10.2 WEST EUROPEAN MOTOR-VEHICLE PRODUCTION, 1950-1973*

	1950	1954	1958	1962	1966	1970	1973
Britain	784	1,038	1,369	1,689	2,053	2,098	2,164
France	357	600	1,128	1,537	2,024	2,750	3,596
West Germany	301	674	1,488	2,343	3,035	3,842	3,949
Italy	129	217	403	947	1,366	1,854	1,958

* in thousands

defend against the growing might of English Ford (officially styled Ford Ltd. since 1928) and GM's Vauxhall. It did not work out that way. Nuffield retired at the end of 1952, and Lord, the actual leader, reduced the number of engines and bodies, hiring Pininfarina to design some of the latter, but none of the BMC factories was closed. They were reorganized to produce more cars with, in most cases, traditional machinery. Labor productivity did not increase significantly.[1] The failure to invest heavily in new types of machinery continued a policy of most British-owned auto firms since the 1930s and is a key to the later difficulties at BMC. Lord did not try very hard to get the managerial and engineering staffs of the two partners to work together and lost some of the best of them by his abrupt decisions based on hunches and whims. There was little product planning and market analysis, and no effort to hire clever young people from the universities to strengthen these areas.

The brightest spot in the BMC picture was Alec Issigonis, born in Smyrna, Turkey, to a naturalized British father of Greek descent and a mother who was the daughter of a Bavarian brewer. Issigonis arrived in England in 1922 at age 16 and became an automobile design engineer, joining the Nuffield organization in the late 1930s. During the war Issigonis designed the Morris Minor car, which was introduced in 1948, despite Lord Nuffield's intense dislike of its appearance. The Minor went on to become the first British car to reach 1 million sales, although it was not vigorously promoted overseas. Of greater consequence, Issigonis designed the Morris Mini, which appeared in 1959, the British champion in the very small car sweepstakes. Again, the Mini had great appeal at home, where the people have a continuing love for very small cars, but also on export markets, which took a majority of those manufactured. The most interesting aspect of the Mini was Issigonis's placement of the engine in front in a transverse position to drive the front wheels – not the first time this had been done but the first time such a car became a major factor on the market. By the late 1980s over 5 million Minis and derivatives had been sold, and its principle adopted by many of the world's carmakers. A major error that Lord and BMC made with this car was to set its price too low; hence it did not generate the profits it should have. This in turn was due to poor cost accounting and a lack of market research.[2] An arrogant man, Issigonis disdained those aspects of cars that might attract consumers who were not engineers: comfortable seats, heater, radio. So sales might have been even larger. The Mini's 10-inch wheels, stubby appearance, and high-quality performance eventually made it a cult car, rather like the VW Beetle and the Citroën 2 CV.

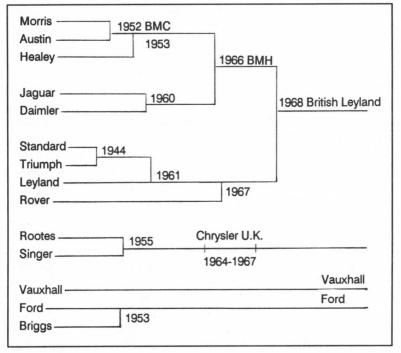

FIGURE 10.1 RESTRUCTURING THE BRITISH AUTO INDUSTRY, 1944-1968

The 1960s saw a series of mergers among the British-owned automobile and truck makers, a shakeout that had largely occurred on the Continent from 1930 to 1945. In Britain it came in this decade when competition grew keener and the smaller firms realized they did not have the engineering staff or production facilities to offer new models at competitive prices. Jaguar had found a profitable niche with its sports cars and expanded by buying English Daimler from its parent BSA in 1960, along with some component makers. In 1966 Sir William Lyons, owner of Jaguer, merged his company into the BMC, which changed its name to British Motor Holdings for a brief period. Lyons retained control of the Jaguar operation until his retirement in 1972, but quality problems had begun to infect the cars. The Standard company under Sir John Black had done very well during the war and bought the failing Triumph motorcycle firm toward the end of the war. The company benefited from the seller's market to dispose of undistinguished vehicles and manufactured Ferguson tractors profitably until 1959. Black became quite erratic, and finally his board of directors dismissed him in 1954. Without the earnings from the tractor contract after 1959, Standard-Triumph could not seem to make much money, so it sold out to the very successful truck maker Leyland in 1961.

The Wilks brothers had revived the Rover company during the late 1930s and the Second World War. In 1945 it moved from Coventry to the shadow factory it had operated in Solihull, near Birmingham. Its wisest decision was to develop a rugged Jeep-like four-wheel-drive machine introduced in 1948 as the Land-Rover, a go-anywhere work vehicle. To the firm's surprise and delight a large export and home demand appeared for Land-Rovers, and from the outset Rover made more of them than cars. Over a half-million were produced by 1966, most for export and many assembled in small overseas plants. Rover could have sold many more of them.

Leyland, seeking to expand its car business, bought out Rover in 1966 and just the next year, with government encouragement, merged with the unprofitable British Motor Holdings to form British Leyland Motor Corporation. The new company at this point ranked as the fifth largest auto firm in the world after the U.S. Big Three and Volkswagen. Sir Donald Stokes of Leyland took command of British Leyland, but the firm continued its short-sighted policies. Stokes was unwilling to take the unpopular step of closing the least efficient factories. The company's new models targeted the middle range where Ford already was very strong and did not sell well on the Continent because the firm had not established extensive dealer networks in France and Germany in anticipation of low Common Market tariffs.[3]

The remaining British-owned group, Rootes, made a few middle-price-range models but in 1960 began construction of a new factory in Linwood, near Glasgow. The government had refused permission to expand except in high unemployment areas. At Linwood, Rootes built an entirely new small car, the Hillman Imp, to compete with the BMC Mini. The Imp proved to lack reliability, sold poorly, and the American Chrysler company began to move in. Chrysler under Lynn Townsend wanted to enter the rapidly expanding European market, where Ford and General Motors already had firm bases. It had obtained a majority holding in the French firm Simca in 1963 and in 1964-65 purchased a substantial interest in Rootes at the time of Lord Rootes' death. Chrysler soon bought a controlling interest in Rootes and changed the name to Chrysler (UK), but it was not sure what to do with this operation. One major asset the firm held was a contract to assemble Hillman Hunter cars in Tehran under the local name Peykan (Arrow). Production of Peykans began in 1967 and continued for over 20 years, amounting to several hundred thousand vehicles. Despite this, the British operation cost Chrysler much money and its new management in Detroit from 1975 began wondering how to get rid of it.

Ford Ltd. proved to be the most successful large auto firm in Britain from the 1950s to the 1970s. Dagenham exported vigorously after the war: 79 percent of its cars went overseas in 1950. The firm even exported to the United States and gained more autonomy from its masters in Dearborn. The Americans allowed it to develop its own engineering staff and encouraged it to hire academically trained staff, unlike at BMC. In 1948 Sir Patrick Hennessey (he was knighted 1945) took over leadership of English Ford from Percival Perry. Hennessey had begun his Ford career in 1919 as a laborer in the Cork factory and rose through merit to the top. Ford began to introduce new models by 1950 along with a stripped-down prewar Anglia now called the Popular. The latter was offered at the lowest price on the British market and sold well. Hennessey bought his body supplier, Briggs, in 1953, but needed more space for expansion as Dagenham went far beyond its original capacity of 200,000 annually. A new assembly plant had to be built near Liverpool at Halewood, an area of heavy unemployment, in 1959-62. Dagenham in 1960 turned out 575,417 vehicles. In 1962 Ford offered its extremely successful Cortina model, a midrange car completely designed in England. It became the company's largest seller through 1987, with 4.3 million, second to the BMC Mini's 5.1 million.

Upon the direction of Henry Ford II, the firm in 1967 reorganized its European operations into one company, Ford of Europe. Essentially, this merged the British and German firms to gain economies of scale in engineering and manufacturing, now that trade barriers in Western Europe were shrinking. Ford of Europe would have one line of vehicles for the entire continent, with the design and manufacturing carried on in those places where it could be done most efficiently. Sir Patrick Hennessey strongly opposed the idea but he was overborne and then retired in 1968, the most significant leader of the British motor industry in the postwar years. At first two British-designed models were also adopted in Germany, the Escort (1968-80) and Capri (1969-87).

The GM entry in Britain, Vauxhall, made few waves with its passenger cars until it introduced its small car, the Viva, in 1963. It assembled this best-seller in a new factory in Ellesmere Port, near Liverpool. Opel and Vauxhall had engineered the car jointly, a straw in a later strong wind of Britain importing automobile engineering from elsewhere. It appears that GM had less interest in Vauxhall cars than in Bedford trucks. These remained the leaders in the small and medium ranges. Bedford adopted diesel engines in the late 1950s, mounting its own or employing those from Perkins or the Detroit Diesel division of GM.

Rolls-Royce emerged from the war a leading manufacturer of jet engines. It had no German competition, little from France for several years, and with government encouragement took over its British competitors. And yet its triumphs with jet engines ultimately turned to ashes. After several years of public subsidies required by some financial and engineering miscalculations, it went bankrupt in February 1971, and the government had to nationalize it. Meanwhile, Rolls-Royce continued with a small output of cars, about 2,000 annually, making them in the factory at Crewe and using more and more components from suppliers, including bodies, electrical equipment, and even transmissions from General Motors or Chrysler. Its new Silver Shadow model of 1965 showed that the firm had not lost its flair for elegance. After two years of government ownership the car division, Rolls-Royce Motor Holdings, was sold back to private investors in 1973. Additional facilities expanded output to some 3,500, but it found financial independence difficult. In 1980 Rolls-Royce became a division of Vickers, the armament firm.

LABOR DIFFICULTIES

The British auto industry from the late 1950s on was unique in its high incidence of labor disputes. Major factors in this were unwise government policies, weak and ineffective management, and weak labor unions. The government tried to manage consumer spending on the national level by often changing the rules on hire-purchase (installment sales) and the purchase tax (a special sales tax on consumer goods). The many changes in these regulations did affect car sales sharply, but they also made it very difficult for the carmakers to schedule production. Scheduling problems brought, in turn, unpredictable employment for the workers, with sudden shifts from overtime to short-time or layoffs. This boom-and-bust cycle of employment along with relatively high wages seems to have encouraged workers to get higher pay during the boom periods through strikes, "get it while you can," with little consideration for the long term or loyalty to the firm. The workers were countered by supervisors who held that all claims or demands must be opposed or discipline would be lost.[4]

Except at Ford, management had little presence on the shop floor. In most auto firms, shop stewards played a major role in managing production and tended to work for the interests of those who elected them, a single shop or department, not the factory as a whole. Management tended to be weak in organizing production, in arranging it to reduce the sudden stop-and-go policy that so antagonized workers.

Contrary to the general opinion, the industry was not highly unionized at the end of the war in 1945,[5] but the unions did enroll more members from 1956 on, when layoffs became more frequent and workers wanted support. Three national unions competed for members among the semiskilled operatives, along with several others enrolling skilled workers. Their rivalries reflected weakness and led to more demands for better wages and conditions. Most workers, however, found the national unions unhelpful in local disputes and followed the lead of their shop stewards. In quarrels over perceived inequities over pay, earnings fluctuations, work procedures, and personality clashes, workers in one shop frequently downed their tools and walked out.

A strong union would have taken the dispute immediately to management and insisted on a decision without a work stoppage. Generally, a strong union would have been able to achieve significant gains without frequent strikes. A union leader described the system: "The negotiating procedure as it then was almost invited direct action because of the long time it took to exhaust the procedure, at the end of which there was inevitably a failure to agree. Workers quickly found they got a solution quicker by direct action than by negotiation."[6] The direct action would be an unconstitutional (wildcat) strike in one department that might shut down production of an entire factory in short order. The unions could not discipline the shop stewards, and it became more and more difficult for management to dismiss them without provoking a larger strike. In the late 1960s more and more of the shop stewards became political radicals, sometimes Communists, Trotskyites, or Maoists, and were accused of promoting strikes to bring down the capitalist system in Britain. Some certainly aimed at this, but in most cases the rank-and-file workers did not strike for political ends but for what they perceived as real work-related grievances. In the late 1960s the strikes grew more frequent and brought significant cuts in production. They may have had some effect also on investment decisions and exports, but poor management decisions in export marketing probably outweighed them in weakening the industry.

By 1971 British Leyland was the only auto firm left that used piecework pay arrangements. This system caused great difficulties in modifying production methods because rates had to be changed with new procedures or new machinery and such a change might bring a wildcat strike. The company began shifting to day rates, but this in turn generated more disputes, which reached a high point in the early 1970s.

By the early 1970s the British auto industry was no larger than it had been a decade earlier, and its output was headed into a decline. Home demand for passenger cars continued to rise gradually, but it was met by imports, which climbed to 31 percent of the market in 1973.

WEST GERMANY

While the British were snatching decline from the jaws of victory, the West German auto industry rose from apparent disaster to brilliant success. Output contined to climb at a rapid pace after 1951, when it exceeded the prewar production record for all of Germany. About half of this expanded production usually went to exports, where the VW

Beetle led the way. In 1971, 58 percent of the country's motor-vehicle output went abroad, with the United States taking 38 percent of these German exports, or 872,000 vehicles.

Volkswagen remained the largest German auto firm. With large production facilities and a reliable, cheap car, which was gradually improved with larger engines, better brakes, and more sophisticated transmissions, it continued to dominate the low end of the price range despite challenges from Opel, DKW, and Fiat's German subsidiary. To accommodate a powerful demand from domestic and foreign markets, Director Heinz Nordhoff established new factories, in Hannover in 1956, followed the next year by a reconditioned aircraft-engine plant in Kassel he bought from Henschel, and in 1964 a large new factory in the port city of Emden on the North Sea to supply the export market. In December 1961 VW produced its 5 millionth car, and its 10th millionth came as soon as September 1965.

Many of these sold abroad. Export sales had begun on a very small scale, to the Netherlands, in 1947. Nordhoff expanded them to get foreign exchange to buy new machinery not available in West Germany. Exports rose from about one-third of output in 1950-51 to over half in 1955. These cars went at first to Germany's small neighboring countries and then to Canada (1952), Australia (1953), and many other countries. Assembly of knocked-down VWs began in South Africa in 1950, in Brazil in 1953, in Australia in 1954, and in Mexico in 1964.

At first American companies importing European cars disdained the peculiar-looking Beetles, but in 1953 VW decided to make a determined effort to penetrate the United States. It dispatched talented representatives who established VW's own distribution network. Emphasized from the very beginning was an effective service and parts system that VW had worked out in Germany and in earlier export ventures. In 1958 VW sold 100,000 cars in the United States, and in the following year all imported cars took one-tenth of the U.S. market. VW constituted about one-fourth of the 614,000 imports. Detroit struck back in 1960 with its first generation of compact cars in order to regain the small-car segment of the U.S. market. They succeeded in winning back those who had been seduced by most of the small European imports except VW, which hung on and ultimately increased its U.S. sales to reach a record 582,573 in 1970. In its best years it unloaded a freighter full of them almost every day of the year. VW won success in the difficult American market for a number of reasons: the car was reliable, having been thoroughly tested before the war and improved in the early 1950s from experience; the service was unusually good; in both reliability and service it outdid British, French, and Italian imports; and at a low price, it filled a niche that for a time the American manufacturers ignored, and it established itself before they reacted. VW's unusually clever advertising, claiming that this was an honest car, never pretending to be something else, was done with wit and understatement, reassuring VW owners and attracting new buyers. The Beetle's odd appearance and low price soon brought a rash of VW jokes, a reprise of the humor of an earlier generation about another odd-looking cheap car, the Ford Model T.

Slowly and painfully the legal status of Volkswagen was determined. In 1960 the West German parliament made it a public corporation, with the West German government and the state of Lower Saxony each holding 20 percent of the shares and the rest sold to the public in small lots. The income from this sale went not to VW but to the Volkswagen Foundation, chartered as a philanthropy to promote science and technology. After 13 years of legal battles, those who had bought VW savings stamps achieved a settlement in 1961, giving them some credit toward a car or cash.

In the 1960s Heinz Nordhoff began considering a successor to the basic Beetle. The 1930s technology it represented had to give way to a new generation, but, untypically, he could not make up his mind, and upon his death in 1968 the problem remained. The company developed several contenders and finally in 1974 introduced the Golf (Rabbit in the United States) with a transverse water-cooled engine driving the front wheels – the Issigonis layout. The last Beetle emerged from Wolfsburg in July 1974. At this point 12 million had been built, but production continued elsewhere in Germany and overseas.

General Motors invested large sums in Opel in the 1950s, finishing reconstruction of the old works and building new ones. Production expanded rapidly from 1953. Opel chose to exploit the middle-price range between VW and Mercedes-Benz, with the Rekord of 1953 outselling Ford in this market segment. Then the new Opel Kadett of 1962, made in a production complex newly built in Bochum in the Ruhr area, challenged VW with considerable success. Opel even tried to compete with Mercedes-Benz in the high-price range. GM exerted greater control over the company than before the war, sending American engineers and managers to do stints in Rüsselsheim. New factories came on-line in Strasbourg, France (1968), in Kaiserslauten (1969), and in Antwerp, Belgium (1969). Just in time for the first oil shock, Opel introduced a diesel-engined Rekord in 1972, to compete with Peugeot and Mercedes oil-burners.

Ford expanded more slowly in Germany than had Opel, and it did so without a general European strategy, for Ford companies in Britain, Germany, and France all had their own noninterchangeable designs. Finally, in 1954 Henry Ford II began a large expansion program in Cologne and in 1964 opened a new assembly plant for the Ford-Werke in Genk, Belgium. This plant began production just two years after Ford's new English assembly factory in Halewood. The establishment of Ford of Europe in 1967, encompassing the German, British, and other operations, would lead to more integration of the different establishments.

Daimler-Benz enjoyed the best years of its life during the great boom. It began offering new models in 1950. In that year a diesel passenger car reappeared, soon followed by redesigned standard models. These dominated the upper range of the market in Germany until the 1970s. At first these models had no competition at home, but Daimler-Benz wisely maintained strong engineering to develop and solidify its image of quality. The major owners of the company were the Deutsche Bank (25 to 28 percent) and Friedrich Flick (39 percent). Flick was an industrialist who lent vigorous support to the Nazi movement in the 1930s. He emerged from prison in 1951 to rebuild his industrial empire. Both the bank and Flick took the long view, accepting low dividends in return for better quality and a growing market share. Exports became an important part of the firm's business; trucks and buses were sold everywhere and cars in the United States especially. In the mid-1950s Daimler-Benz had Studebaker distribute Mercedes-Benz cars in the United States, hoping this would be cheaper and simpler than building their own sales network, but this did not work out well. When Studebaker went out of business the German firm established its own distribution system in the mid-1960s. By 1969 Mercedes-Benz passenger-car sales in the United States reached 29,191. Some were diesels, and the firm's experience with them would be a great advantage during the 1970s.

Most of the smaller German firms disappeared during these years of expansion. DKW cars with two-stroke engines made by the new Auto Union company during the 1950s competed with VW and Opel in the lower price ranges. Friedrich Flick acquired an important owner-ship interest in Auto Union, and in 1958 Daimler-Benz bought it. Then in 1964 Daimler-Benz arranged to split Auto Union with VW, with D-B retaining the Düsseldorf factory, where it would make trucks, and VW gaining the name Auto Union and a new facility in Ingolstadt, north of Munich. At the latter factory VW assembled Beetles and soon brought back the Audi name for some mid- and upper-range cars. The DKW badge disappeared. The Auto Union company brought to VW water-cooled engines with front-wheel-drive technology. VW soon would use these in its models of the 1970s.

The NSU firm resumed motorcycle manufacture after the war, but when it met tough competition from Japan it moved up to cars in 1957 and offered very small models attacking VW from below. It began using Wankel rotary-piston engines in 1962. Developing an old idea, Dr. Felix Wankel made this engine practical, or so it appeared. In addition to NSU, several other auto firms tried the Wankel, including Citroën, GM, Ford, and the Japanese Toyo Kogyo. Because of engineering problems, all ultimately abandoned it save for some of the last firm's Mazda models. NSU continued to expand in the 1960s, gradually mak-ing larger machines, including about 40,000 rotary-engined cars before giving up on them. In 1969 VW-controlled Auto Union bought NSU, and the name soon disappeared. Borgward also left the picture, closing its doors in 1961.

The BMW firm returned to automobiles in Munich in 1955, build-ing three-wheel Isetta bubble cars powered by a motorcycle engine. It made 160,000 in a few years but gradually moved upmarket with more conventional cars using larger engines. In 1966 BMW bought the Hans Glas company, which also had been producing very small cheap cars, some of which went by the name Goggomobile. BMW had tried some expensive prestige cars in the 1950s that failed to win favor, but it launched another attack on this niche of the market in 1968.

The Porsche organization moved to Gmund in Austria late in the war. It began making a few cars there in 1948 based on the VW chassis and soon moved back to Stuttgart, where Ferdinand Porsche passed his company on to his son Ferry before he died in 1951. The Porsche firm specialized in racing and sports cars with sales climbing to 4,264 in 1956. It continued this risky policy and succeeded with it thereafter.

By the 1970s Germany had three volume carmakers – VW, Opel, and Ford – with two of them entering cars in the upper rank – VW's

Audi and Opel's Senator – along with Mercedes-Benz and BMW in the high-price category and Porsche for wealthy sportsmen. But difficulties began to creep in as the 1960s drew to a close. The economy's growth began to slow down from the earlier rate, imports began to appear on the home market, and costs rose. A law of 1969 made it extremely hard to dismiss workers at a time when demands for higher wages and benefits were being granted. A powerful blow to exports came when the exchange rate of the deutsche mark to the U.S. dollar rose 40 percent from 1969 to 1973. This required much higher prices for German cars in the United States, hitting the Beetle especially hard, for it lost its competitive edge on price.

Labor relations in the German auto industry went more smoothly than in Britain, Italy, or France. One union – Industrie Gewerkschaft Metall – represented the workers and it bargained on a national level with the employers association. Wildcat strikes were illegal, and unions were fined for encouraging them. Every company had a works council elected by the employees, legally separate from the union. These councils did not become politicized and served as valuable means of communication and as resolvers of grievances. By law, representatives of the workers also sat on the supervisory boards of the companies, where they had a voice in their firms' grand strategies. Paid at low rates just after the war, by the 1970s German autoworkers received relatively high pay and extensive fringe benefits.

The large, strong union and the worker participation in company decisions probably account for the absence of severe friction in the German motor firms, even in the wake of the technological changes that kicked off so many difficulties in Britain.

11

THE GREAT BOOM: FRANCE, ITALY, AND ELSEWHERE

FRANCE

RENAULT

Into the 1970s the four major firms in France made more and more cars, but two of them, Simca and Citroën, ran into difficulties. The Régie Renault continued to lead in output, as its managers felt obliged to run the firm as France's champion in world competition. The company's management did not fear technical innovation and economic risks as some might expect of a nationalized enterprise, and as Louis Renault had between the wars. Nationalization had eliminated private stockholders who might have encouraged management to concern itself more with short-term profits than long-term strategy. The concern's only stockholder was the state, and it did not need the state's prior approval of decisions. Nationalization also brought engineers into greater influence in the firm, and they were encouraged to show their prowess. Renault introduced automatic transfer machines to its engine-block line in 1947, the first in Europe. The work of Pierre Bézier, these moved the blocks automatically along a series of machines that performed various cutting operations on them. When everything on the line worked the way it should, it required only one or two workers to load and unload the blocks.

From the beginning, Pierre Lefaucheux wanted to decentralize Renault's operations from Billancourt. Between the wars the firm had established a plant 115 miles west of Paris in Le Mans for tractor manufacture, and other operations had been transferred there as well. In 1946 it obtained land at Flins, down the Seine 27 miles from Paris. A factory opened there in 1952, doing body stamping and final assembly. By the 1970s it had expanded several times to employ 20,000, many housed in Renault-built apartments.[1] In later years the Régie added

191

TABLE 11.1 IMPORTS AND EXPORTS OF PASSENGER CARS*

	France		West Germany		Italy		Britain	
	Exports	Imports	Exports	Imports	Exports	Imports	Exports	Imports
1955	140	10	320	17	69	3	391	18
1960	509	26	781	89	198	18	570	58
1965	529	147	1,259	274	308	103	628	56
1970	1,394	299	1,706	660	632	460	690	158
1973	1,782	463	1,996	768	656	418	599	505

* in thousands

several more factories along the lower Seine and in Brittany. The work force at the mother plant in Billancourt would never increase above the 35,000 that it had reached in the late 1930s. By the 1970s those at Billancourt would be only about one-third of the Renault employees engaged in car production.

After the Communists left the coalition government in France in spring 1947, the CGT union at Renault dropped its cooperative attitude toward management and became demanding and obstructionist. So the Renault experiment with a new kind of arrangement between labor and management gave way to the more traditional adversarial relationship. Both Lefaucheux and the workers had dreamed of something different, and both were disillusioned.[2]

Lefaucheux died in an automobile accident in 1955. His aggressive leadership had brought success to the Régie Renault, rather as Heinz Nordhoff had done at VW. Both had taken command of a partially damaged auto producer, more or less government owned, depending on their own earnings to pay for expansion and staking everything on "people's cars." Nordhoff ultimately did better – he had a better car, was not challenged by labor leaders with political priorities, and showed greater skill in foreign marketing than Lefaucheux and his successor.

Pierre Dreyfus replaced Lefaucheux. A Socialist and longtime Ministry of Industry official, he had presided over the board of the nationalized Lorraine coal mines and had served on the board of the Régie Renault. Dreyfus was not as forceful as his predecessor and preferred diplomacy to confrontation. He did not let government officials tell him what to do but kept them sympathetic by advising them of important developments ahead of time. Consequently, his relations with the bureaucrats were much smoother than those of Lefaucheux. Dreyfus's two basic goals for Renault were to introduce careful long-term planning and other aspects of modern management, and to expand exports sharply.[3]

In his first move he tried to stabilize labor relations with a contract that granted the workers significant advantages: three weeks (rather than two) of paid vacation, pay for legal holidays, a new retirement plan, and a procedure to try to avoid recourse to strikes and lockouts. Annual labor turnover did drop to very low numbers, and in the mid-1950s Renault's own wage workers began to buy cars in significant numbers. In 1956 the Régie introduced its very popular Dauphine model, an expanded 4 CV with an 845-cc engine, and in 1959 adopted front-wheel drive in a van.

Early in 1957 the French government, concerned about a deteriorating balance of payments, asked the auto industry to expand exports sharply. To add force to this request, it threatened to increase taxes on cars and gasoline if auto exports did not rise. Dreyfus agreed with this policy, and Renault shipped its cars out vigorously, especially to the United States, where the VW Beetle had found a market. But Renault's experience there echoed the earlier British example. Cars designed for Europe did not withstand rough American usage, and Renault did not take the time to develop a solid network of service-oriented dealers. Its large American sales of 1959 – 118,000 – gave way to huge stocks of unsold machines rusting away on East Coast docks. Dreyfus the export-oriented planner had plunged into the U.S. market with little investigation and planning. The consequence was to brand French cars with the reputation of mediocrity in American eyes. Exports elsewhere expanded nevertheless, and Dreyfus achieved his goal of exporting half of Renault's output from 1959 on. In 1962 West Germany became the largest importer of Renault vehicles in the Common Market, but Spain was Renault's largest European market outside France. Assembly began there in 1953 in Valladolid, and Renault achieved full manufacture in 1965. Renault owned just under half of its Spanish affiliate, Fasa, which made 182,000 vehicles in 1973, the second largest output in the country.

Dreyfus expanded Renault's line of models, gradually covering the low- and middle-price ranges with several types and later the upper reaches as well. He aimed to have models ready for changes in the market, and this policy proved its value in the 1970s when VW stumbled and the oil shock shifted demand to small cars. He received help with the expenses generated by this policy and by the new factories when the French government accepted the argument that as the sole shareholder in the company it should invest some money in it, in lieu of a public issue of shares, and receive an appropriate return in lieu of dividends. Critics of the firm angrily denounced this as an unfair subsidy.

Renault also diversified, although it did not go as far as Fiat in this direction. The Renault truck line had been merged in 1955 with some smaller French producers in the Saviem affiliate. The Régie owned the major French producer of ball bearings. It expanded its manufacture and sale of machine tools – a move that eventually led to designing and equipping automobile factories abroad, especially in the Soviet Union. It also continued to build agricultural tractors and established a car rental company.

PEUGEOT

In the seller's market of the 1950s Peugeot stayed with one model in the middle of the range and tried to build a reputation for reliability. Top management determined that it could sell its cars at a somewhat higher price than the competition as customers learned that they would make more on the resale. The company began introducing a new model every five years from 1955 on, keeping each one in production for about 10 years. It focused all of them in the 6- to 9-fiscal-hp niche and expanded output annually. Labor shortages in its Montbéliard region led to more and more operations elsewhere in France and, in 1962, in a large new manufacturing complex in nearby Mulhouse.

Maurice Jordan, the operating head of Peugeot until 1965 and very conservative about investment and expansion, found exports unprofitable for the firm. As he viewed the matter, their value was primarily to keep the home factories busy and bring greater economies of scale.[4] To spread the risk of fluctuations in foreign markets, Peugeot shipped cars in small numbers to about 100 countries in the 1950s rather than concentrating on a few where it might build solid sales and service systems, as VW did in Brazil and the United States. Jordan wanted to spend as little as possible on exports, exclaiming as late as 1957, "We shall never invest a franc in a foreign plant."[5] The early Peugeot foreign assembly factories in Australia, South Africa, and Belgium were financed by local interests, but gradually the firm did put funds into small assembly operations in Ireland and several Latin American countries. Peugeot also bowed to government pressure and expanded exports in the late 1950s, selling in the United States through Renault dealers, with about the same result as its partner.

In the mid-1960s Peugeot decided to move to a multimodel policy and a more rapid expansion. This strategy shift coincided with the death of Jean-Pierre Peugeot in 1966, Maurice Jordan's move up to replace him as chairman of the board, and younger executives taking control of operations. There was concern over the serious competition threatened by Ford and General Motors in Europe as well as that by VW, Fiat, and Renault. Peugeot's leaders concluded that it must expand or die.

By 1972 the firm had a range of five models extending from the small to medium-large and in the next year was the sixth largest producer in Western Europe. The company had become one of the volume producers rather than remaining a French Mercedes-Benz or Volvo.

In its expansion Peugeot began to cooperate with other French firms. From 1963 to 1965 it worked with Citroën on joint purchasing and planned to jointly produce certain parts. This arrangement broke up when Peugeot suspected Citroën of trying to take it over. Then Peugeot and Renault in 1966 began the same kind of cooperation and took it further, establishing a jointly owned transmission factory in northern France near the Belgiam frontier, along with a nearby three-way-owned engine factory with Volvo. Peugeot continued as the most profitable of the major French firms, so it could take advantage of unexpected opportunities in the 1970s.

CITROEN

Citroën continued after the war to make its 1934 *traction avant* model, producing a total of 759,000 by the end of its run in 1957, along with the odd-looking 2 CV introduced in 1948 and its derivatives with more conventional body styles. After Pierre Boulanger died in 1950, Pierre Bercot took over at Citroën. He gained the full confidence of François Michelin, who gradually assumed command of Michelin, Citroën's parent company, in the 1950s. Bercot was very sure of himself but rather doubtful about most everyone else. He wanted Citroën to make cars that he knew people needed, not what they thought they wanted. He had little interest in selling or servicing cars but was fascinated by technical innovation.[6] Bercot's attitudes paralleled those of his predecessor, Boulanger, and the Citroën company in the 1960s reflected them – technology first, marketing last. In 1955 the Citroën engineers produced another sensation, the DS model in the medium-high price range with a 2-liter engine. This had hydropneumatic suspension; disc brakes; power-assisted steering, brakes, and transmission; and an unusual streamlined shape. The experts were enchanted by this innovative model, and it sold well, but some customers were put off by its complexity.

Meanwhile, Citroën expanded, by taking over Panhard & Levassor in stages in 1955 and 1965 and then, at a stiff price, the sports and racing car firm Maserati of Modena, Italy, in 1968. It also opened factories in the provinces – a manufacturing and assembly plant at Rennes in

Brittany in 1960 and several other parts-making plants. In 1967 Citroën bought control of the Lyon-based Berliet firm, the largest heavy-truck producer in France. Paul Berliet remained in command while Citroën added new capital and new factories to the Berliet operations. Citroën also invested heavily in facilities to produce the Wankel engine.

In 1968 François Michelin committed Citroën to a major change. The company's sales and earnings had slipped because of vigorous competition from Renault, and it looked for a savior. François Michelin and Gianni Agnelli of Fiat agreed to have Citroën and Fiat coordinate their activities to better compete on the European market against the aggressive General Motors and Ford. The companies would work together in planning, investment, research, purchasing, and sales. Fiat would invest funds in the Citroën operations, and it was generally assumed that the move would soon lead to a takeover by Fiat. President Charles de Gaulle refused to permit such a final step, but the companies did work together uneasily for a few years. Citroën continued to lose money, and Bercot retired in 1970. Fiat did not find the Citroën people cooperative enough and finally decided to end the marriage in 1973, selling Fiat's share in Citroën back to the Michelin family. But Citroën still needed a financial protector. The Wankel adventure had failed, it was building a large new factory northeast of Paris at Aulnay-sous-Bois to replace the obsolete works on the Quai Javel (since 1958 renamed Quai André Citroën) in Paris, and the first oil shock reduced demand for cars. A deal was struck in 1974. Peugeot agreed to take over Citroën, while Renault took Berliet and merged it into its Saviem truck affiliate under the name Renault Vehicules Industriels. Large loans from the French government lubricated these transfers.

SIMCA

Like the other French volume carmakers, Simca expanded rapidly from 1950. Its impresario, Henri Pigozzi, bought the Unic truck firm from the Rothschild interests in 1952 and then in 1954 took over the French Ford operations. Ford management in Dearborn had decided to sell out in France (just before the beginning of a major economic boom in that country). It sent a capable manager to make some cosmetic improvements to Ford's factory in Poissy and then sell it. Simca, cramped for space in Nanterre and eager to expand quickly, bought it and moved all its assembly facilities to the Poissy site. Simca took advantage of all this new production capacity and became the second largest car producer in France until 1960. In that year Pigozzi split his firm, with the truck and other noncar facilities becoming the separate Simca Industries. Chrysler acquired a minority interest in Simca Automobiles in 1958 and then bought out Fiat's share in 1963 to obtain a controlling interest, while Fiat took a majority holding in Simca Industries that soon took the name Fiat-France.

ITALY

After 1950 Fiat began to introduce models of postwar design. Its 1100 model of 1953 scored a major success, for, including its variants, it sold over 2 million by 1970. The new 600 model of 1955 was Fiat's first car with the rear engine arrangement. This best-seller was followed by the even smaller 500 model, a two-cylinder car of 1960. These three models – small, utilitarian types – were aimed primarily at first-time car buyers in the protected Italian market and in Spain and Latin America. These simple and cheap cars motorized Italy, and by the early 1970s the country had about as many autos per thousand people as the other major Western countries. Fiat built larger models also, to defend against imports. Vittorio Valletta (*Il professore*) expanded operations in Turin, which absorbed most of Fiat's employment of 158,000 in 1968 in Italy. Some 60,000 worked at the Mirafiore plant alone. Most of the many new workers migrated to Turin from southern Italy and brought major strains to the housing, transport, and other facilities of the city. Fiat indirectly employed thousands more, for it subcontracted for many of its parts with hundreds of small shops in the area. Often former Fiat workers owned and operated these concerns, frequently using second-hand machinery and hiring unskilled labor at very low wages.

Fiat continued its prewar efforts to sell elsewhere in Europe. It revived its operations in Germany (NSU/Fiat); in France with Simca, which since 1951 had sold a French-designed and manufactured Aronde model; in Spain with a new company in Barcelona, Seat, 51 percent owned by Fiat; in Austria; and in various Latin American countries. Fiat also expanded its production of trucks, aircraft, and ships. In 1965 it produced over 1 million vehicles for the first time.

As Vittorio Valletta approached his eighties, Giovanni (Gianni) Agnelli – familiarly called *l'avvocato* because of his law degree – the playboy grandson of the builder of the firm, Giovanni Agnelli, began to move into command of Fiat.[7] In 1963 Gianni became managing director, and when Valletta finally retired in 1966 Gianni took his place as chairman. Valletta died the following year at age 83. Using the principles of administrative and geographic centralization, he had vigorously and autocratically brought Fiat back from the depths of 1943-45 to resume its position among the handful of major European automakers.

Just at the time of this transition at the top, Fiat signed an agreement with authorities in the Soviet Union to build and equip a very large automobile plant at Tolyattigrad. Fiat officials certainly had experience with a huge, centralized concern of this kind. The Soviet complex would make a sturdier version of the Fiat 124 model, a front-engine 1,200-cc car introduced in 1966. Most of the plant's tooling was imported from Western Europe and America, and a large share of it was financed by an Italian government lending agency. The Tolyatti deal was followed by others in which Fiat equipped smaller factories in Eastern Europe to make versions of Fiat cars – in Poland, Yugoslavia, Bulgaria, and Romania.

Gianni Agnelli in 1967 approved construction of still another large Turin auto plant, Rivalta, in the southwestern suburbs. He led Fiat into the "trial marriage" with Citroën in 1968 and in the following year took over the debt-ridden Lancia company, but a time of troubles soon arrived. In a "Rampant May" and a "Hot Autumn" of 1969 came a series of strikes and other labor disturbances, including sabotage. Within a few years Fiat faced a multiyear siege by radicals and terrorists claiming to represent the labor force. Valletta's policies had weakened the unions at Fiat, especially the Communist CGIL, and they had slight influence on the workers. Largely single young men under age 25, unused to disciplined factory work, they had little commitment to their jobs or to the firm's long-term health. Their lives off the job in overcrowded Turin gave them little stability. Many short strikes and considerable violence marked labor relations, but in terms of days lost, absenteeism was a much more serious problem for Fiat than strikes. In the early 1970s it was usually over 12 percent and sometimes climbed to 20 or 25 percent.

Fiat had little difficulty with domestic competition. Alfa Romeo made about 65,000 cars per year in the mid-1960s and Lancia about 30,000 before climbing into the Fiat fold. Imports became a concern late in the decade, however, as they rose from 11 percent of sales in 1966 to 21 percent in 1969 and 33.7 percent in 1970. Although the ᴜROPEAN MOTOR-VEHICLE PRODUCTION, 1973*

	Cars	Total vehicles
Fiat	1,504,147	1,635,537
Volkswagen	1,364,154	1,463,489
Renault	1,290,000	1,414,563
British Leyland	875,888	1,012,492
Opel	839,542	845,303
Peugeot	684,538	765,978
Citroën	658,829	751,457
Ford (Germany)	679,324	728,514
Ford (Britain)	453,440	590,668
Chrysler (France)	519,822	546,779
Daimler-Benz	339,040	503,895
Audi-NSU	409,793	409,793
Seat	361,100	363,900
Chrysler (Britain)	307,549	336,505
Volvo	242,036	272,632
Vauxhall	151,955	258,721

* For comparison, in 1973 the largest U.S. producer, General Motors, built 6,514,419
vehicles, and Toyota, the largest Japanese producer, made 2,308,096.
Source: Ward's Automotive Yearbook, 1974, 91.

imports cut Fiat's share of its home market, for which it had always sought protection, Fiat remained a powerhouse in the European auto industry by leading Europe in output in 1972 and 1973.

The labor upheavals of 1969-70 catalyzed some major changes in Fiat's strategy.[8] Gianni Agnelli quickly reversed the firm's 70-year policy of centralization and announced plans to build nine small- and medium-size factories in southern Italy. The company also began to make more parts and assemble more cars abroad – in Poland, Spain, and Latin America. Fiat decided to reduce the amount of semiskilled labor in its factories by introducing more automation and robots. In the midst of these major shifts came the oil shock of 1973-74.

The Alfa Romeo firm, owned by the government through its IRI holding company, revived after the war. At first it produced commercial vehicles but returned to cars in the 1950s, offering relatively expensive sports and prestige machines that provided upwardly mobile Italians an alternative to Fiat. During the 1960s it gradually shifted its operations to a new plant in Arese, eight miles northwest of Milan. In 1968 it produced 97,000. Then the government poured more funds into Alfa, financing a second and larger plant near Naples where it would make a new, less expensive family car, the Alfa Sud. This establishment, planned for a capacity of 380,000, began production in 1972 and soon ran into troubles, which are treated in the next chapter.

NEW MANUFACTURING COUNTRIES

Alongside the four major auto-producing countries just discussed, three other West European countries developed important auto industries after the Second World War – Sweden, Belgium, and Spain.

SWEDEN

In Sweden the Volvo company entered the postwar period as a small producer of cars and trucks (905 cars and 5,150 trucks built in 1946) without very good prospects for either, considering the long-run trend toward concentration of the business. Its first postwar-model car began to sell briskly in 1947 when imported components and sheet steel from the United States became available. Volvo's 1949 car output of 5,362 exceeded its truck production and continued to rise. In the years of scarcity after the war Volvo had no trouble selling all the cars it could make, and their reliability won the company a strong reputation. Volvo knew it could not depend on the Swedish market alone and worked to expand exports in the 1950s. Its cars developed a following in the United States, where some 10,000 Volvos were delivered in 1957, almost one-quarter of the total output of 42,192. Volvo continued to expand, gaining control over some component manufacturers in Sweden, and in the 1960s began assembly at Halifax, Canada; Ghent, Belgium (to get into the Common Market); and 11 other locations by 1973. In 1960 the firm sold 65 percent of its 80,100 cars in Scandinavia and 20 percent in North America. By 1970 the Scandinavian share had dropped to 37 percent and the North American climbed to 24 percent, but the rest of Europe had risen to 30 percent of the 210,000 total. Volvo's policy of high-quality mid-priced cars filled a niche that grew larger as European incomes rose. Its truck sales expanded more slowly than cars and remained more concentrated in Scandinavia and Europe.

The second Swedish carmaker, Saab, appeared on the market in 1949.[9] This firm, Svenska Aeroplan Aktie Bolaget, dated from 1937 when it was established with private capital but on government initiative to build military aircraft. In 1944 Saab decided to diversify into automobiles. It planned to make a small sports model that would not compete directly with Volvo and would receive some protection from foreign cars by the Swedish tariff of 15-20 percent. Inspired by the prewar German DKW, Saab in 1949 offered a front-wheel-drive car. It had a two-cylinder, two-stroke engine mounted transversely in front. Saab made only a few thousand cars a year at first and began to export to the United States in 1956. After Saab reached a peak of sales at 29,000 in 1964, customers began to turn away from the two-cycle engine. Consequently, the firm in 1966 introduced a four-stroke type designed and built by German Ford. In 1969 sales recovered to 30,000, and Saab presented a new model that revealed a shift in product policy away from small and inexpensive sports cars toward mid-range family or executive cars. This one had an engine designed by the Ricardo consulting organization in England and manufactured there by Triumph (British Leyland). Also in 1969 Saab merged with the Swedish truck maker Scania-Vabis to form Saab-Scania. The Wallenberg family financial empire controlled Scania-Vabis and henceforth dominated Saab-Scania. The Scania division delivered about 10,000 trucks a year during the late sixties and early seventies.

Saab kept its cars in the public eye by racing but also placed more than the usual emphasis on safety. In 1971 it introduced headlight washers and wipers, an improvement taken so seriously in Sweden that before long all new cars sold in the country had to have them. Its most spectacular safety stunt came in February 1962 when the firm got someone to drive a Saab off a Norwegian ski jump before television cameras. After falling with a serious bump and rolling over several times, the car settled on its wheels – its body only lightly damaged – and was driven away.

Sweden in this period presents a rare case of auto manufacturing developing in a small country under local control. Its success did not depend on a very high protective tariff but can be attributed instead to first-class engineering skill, a local network of component firms, and capable marketing.

BELGIUM

Belgium traditionally welcomed assembly plants of the major European and American producers. Until the Common Market began to cut tariff barriers among the major continental countries, most of the cars assembled went to the Belgian market itself or to the other small, low-tariff states such as the Netherlands, Switzerland, and Scandinavia, or overseas. In 1958 car and truck assemblies in Belgium amounted to 140,000. Thereafter Common Market tariffs fell, and the Belgian government lured auto firms with convenient port facilities, low labor costs, and other incentives as the government tried to encourage alternative industries to declining coal mining and heavy metallurgy. Ford opened its plant at Genk near the German frontier in 1964 as a satellite of its Cologne works. Ford built nearly 300,000 cars there in 1973 and gradually integrated the plant's operations with other Ford facilities in Western Europe. General Motors concentrated its efforts in Antwerp and assembled more than 300,000 vehicles there in 1973. VW, British Leyland, Volvo, and the major French firms also assembled vehicles in Belgium, in numbers ranging from 25,000 to 114,000 in 1973, with the total just over 1 million.

SPAIN

The motor industry in Spain, as in Belgium, eventually came under the control of large foreign firms, but the Franco government and its successors tried harder to develop an independent domestic industry with loans to local operators and protective tariffs. The National Industrial Institute, a government agency, in the late 1940s promoted the Seat company to make passenger cars and encouraged other Spanish companies to assemble foreign components. But a lack of engineering skill and capital eventually brought foreign firms into Spain to take control, if not majority ownership, of these concerns—Seat by Fiat, Fasa by Renault, Barreiros by Chrysler, and others. Output rose from 49,000 in 1958 to 235,000 in 1965 and 822,000 in 1973. This was far from maturity, however, for Ford was beginning to build a large plant near Valencia, and General Motors would soon follow as Spain became a larger carmaker than Great Britain.

By the early 1970s in Western Europe the manufacturing operations of the automobile industry were spreading out geographically, but managerial and financial control were becoming more concentrated.[10]

12

COMMUNIST CARS

THE AUTOMOBILE INDUSTRY IN THE SOVIET UNION

Soviet car production expanded slowly until the late 1960s, making the Moskvich in Moscow and the Volga, which replaced the Pobeda, in Gorki. The Soviets also took a leaf from Western Europe and in 1962 began to make a very small car, modeled after a German NSU, in the Ukrainian city of Zaporozh'e, but these machines never gained a good reputation. Both Stalin and Khrushchev opposed the spread of passenger-car ownership to ordinary citizens. Khrushchev tried to compromise somewhat by setting up a rental-car system, but crippled it with restrictions: only certain people received authorization to rent cars, reservations could be made only one hour in advance, and one had to pay cash in advance. The system failed.

For ordinary citizens cars were expensive. A typical engineer, with an income well above the average worker, would have to pay the equivalent of 23 months' salary, in cash, for a Moskvich in 1966. The regime sold the same car abroad for about half the domestic price. However, in the Soviet Union the selling price of a new car had less importance than in the West. To obtain a car, most persons had to sign up on a waiting list at the place of employment and wait several years for delivery, at which time they paid cash. This arrangement gave considerable power to the employer who might manipulate the list or insist on a bribe. The scarcity of new cars led to high prices for used ones, well above the official rate.

Meanwhile, truck output grew as the truck assembly plants that had opened after the war expanded their output, began making more of their own components, and were joined by new factories. The Yaroslavl factory lost its truck manufacture to Minsk and to a new (1958) plant in the Ukrainian city of Kremenchug and devoted itself exclusively to diesel engines. The Odessa truck assembly works shifted to making

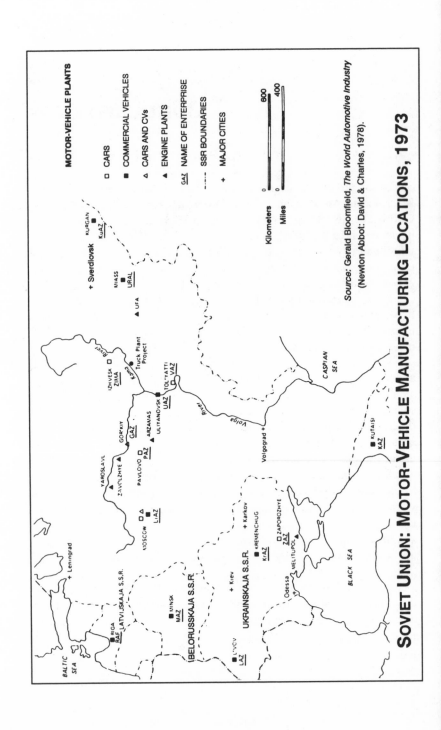

SOVIET UNION: MOTOR-VEHICLE MANUFACTURING LOCATIONS, 1973

MOTOR-VEHICLE PLANTS

☐ CARS

■ COMMERCIAL VEHICLES

△ CARS AND CVs

▲ ENGINE PLANTS

<u>GAZ</u> NAME OF ENTERPRISE

---- SSR BOUNDARIES

+ MAJOR CITIES

Kilometers
0   400   800

Miles
0   400

Source: Gerald Bloomfield, *The World Automotive Industry*
(Newton Abbot: David & Charles, 1978).

trailers. At Zhodino east of Minsk a factory built very heavy trucks from 1959. Both trucks and cars remained quite old-fashioned in their technology as compared with West European models. In 1965 the industry produced 201,000 cars and 415,000 trucks and buses. The car output was slightly more than that of Sweden in this year, but in Europe only Britain produced more commercial vehicles.

In the mid-1960s the new leadership of Kosygin and Brezhnev placed a much higher priority on the automotive industry than earlier. They decided that Communist party members, government officials, and ordinary citizens needed more material incentives such as automobiles to reward their efforts. So they devoted the largest single investment of their economic plan for 1966-70 to a major new car factory on the middle Volga River near Kuibyshev. The political leaders thought so little of their own automobile industry after 35 years of operations that they contracted with Fiat to design and equip the complex, named VAZ for Volga Automobile Works.[1] The new town that housed it and the workers was called Tolyatti, after the Italian Communist leader, no friend of Fiat's management. Within a few years this town numbered 500,000 people. The plant made a sturdier version of the Fiat 124 model, called the Zhiguli in the Soviet Union and Lada on export markets. Soviet engineers designated which parts of the car had to be modified, and Fiat enginers in Turin developed the new parts. Lower-quality Soviet steel, for example, required larger cross sections, and the scarcity of gasoline stations led to enlarged fuel tanks.

The VAZ complex at Tolyatti was another example of Soviet gigantism, huge industrial establishments like Ford's River Rouge or Dagenham or Berliet's Vénissieux works. At a time when Americans and West Europeans were beginning to realize that such large establishments were almost impossible to manage efficiently, especially the labor force, the Soviets continued to build them. The Tolyatti works included foundry, forge, stamping, engine-making, and assembly. The assembly hall for the Zhiguli car was 1.25 miles long, and a trolleybus coursed along its length to bring workers to their stations. Fiat worked more closely with the Soviets than Ford had at the Gorki works in the early 1930s. Some 1,500 Fiat specialists and 1,000 from other Western firms worked in Tolyatti as consultants, and 2,500 Soviet technicians went to Italy for training. Fiat was not only general consultant for the entire project but supplied designs for each aspect of the production process. It provided much of the machinery itself and obtained equipment from other Western firms for the Volga works. It supervised installation of this machinery and brought Soviet materials to Turin for testing.

Although the VAZ had a high level of vertical integration at Tolyatti, the planners wanted more than the usual supply of parts to come from vendor factories. This strategy, normal in the West and Japan, was intended to diffuse technology more widely and bring more efficiency, perhaps even competition, in the long run. With the help of Western and Japanese firms, the regime modernized or built many new factories to supply Tolyatti. Suppliers in Poland, Hungary, and Bulgaria also furnished parts, which they bartered for finished cars. The Soviets had difficulties operating this subcontracting system in order to obtain satisfactory quantities and qualities at the right time, however. What sort of discipline could the VAZ exert on a supplier who fell short, a supplier that the planners had designated as the only source? In 1974 the head of the Gorki car and truck works revealed some of the difficulties a Soviet factory manager confronted. He confessed to all sorts of problems – waste of materials, slow workers, delays in introducing new methods – but he laid most of the blame on the lethargy of the three government ministries he had to deal with: those for the motor vehicle industry, construction, and installation and specialized construction.[2] In the late 1970s an industrial reform placed each of the major vehicle-building enterprises at the head of a production group of supplier firms and sometimes a branch assembly plant. This reform aimed to reduce the role of the engineering section of the Communist party's Central Committee and the State Ministry of the Motor Industry in day-to-day operations and to grant more autonomy to the actual productive establishments. The risk of this restructuring was that the automotive production groups would become autarkic entities, heedless of the needs of the industry as a whole.[3]

Originally designed for an output of 600,000 units a year, with 85,000 workers on two shifts, production at the Volga works reached 650,000 in 1974 and 830,000 in 1979. It also made a considerable effort to develop after-the-sale service, adopting the Western practice of owner's manuals and a one-year warranty. It slowly opened a network of service centers supplied with Western equipment. It appears that the delivery of repair service fell far behind the standards of the West, however. In 1988 a Moscow newspaper reported a story from the far-northern city of Archangel. There, one Aksenov brought his Zhiguli to the repair station for some bodywork on 9 June. It appeared that other work also was needed on the mechanical system of the car. The standard time to complete these repairs was 45 days. After this period Aksenov went for his car and found that nothing had been done, and that his battery had disappeared. Friends suggested that he should have "greased the skids," but he waited for several more weeks. Late in August, with the driving season coming to a close, Aksenov had had enough. After warning the head of the repair station and local government officials, he began a hunger strike outside the repair station. This brought the media and the director of the Provincial Auto Repair Service running.

Promises were made; a new battery was ordered. Then, on 9 September, three months after Aksenov had brought his car in, it was ready. Made cautious by his ordeal, he asked if the mechanical repairs had also been finished. No, he was told, that must be done on a new repair order. "Couldn't it all have been done at once, to avoid taking the engine out again?" No, he was told, that's not the way things are done.[4] Around major Soviet cities informal and illegal auto-parts flea markets appeared as private dealers and their customers met at night to strike bargains they thought were better than at the official repair stations. A large fraction of private Soviet autos operated on stolen government fuel because service stations were few and inconveniently located. For many years Soviet car owners kept their windshield-wiper blades inside their cars. When rain began they would stop, get out, and attach the blades. It is not clear whether this custom began because of a shortage of blades and was spread by movies showing the practice, or whether it began as a comic episode in a film and thereafter was widely adopted as a defense against possible theft.

The VAZ also took part in Soviet efforts to raise labor productivity and reduce traditional overstaffing. Norms of output were raised, something that in the West is called a speedup, but more novel in the Soviet context was the brigade organization of labor. Individual piecework and time rates of pay were abandoned. Instead, all VAZ workers were assigned to brigades of from 35 to 300 persons; no one was attached to a permanent job or machine but shifted about according to the brigade's needs. Jobs were enlarged and combined. Workers received 60 per cent of their pay according to their individual qualifications and 40 per cent on the collective result of the brigade's efforts.[5] Presumably social pressure within the brigade would encourage greater individual effort, but it might also work in the other direction. Other auto firms also tried to raise labor productivity by careful time-and-motion study. Specialists at the Miass truck factory filmed processes for a full day to analyze them better, then raised output norms by over one-third and required workers to meet them.[6]

One aim of the Volga works was to earn foreign exchange by exports, which led to a strong emphasis on quality. Sold abroad as the Lada model at very low prices, these Soviet Fiats did not in fact find many buyers except in the East European countries where government agencies bartered auto parts and other goods for them. The same car, known as the Zhiguli, at home cost a sum equal to 3.5 years of the average worker's wage in the 1970s.

In the economic plan of 1966-70 the Soviet authorities hired Renault to modernize and expand its Moskvich factory in Moscow. Renault also designed and equipped a new 220,000-capacity car factory in Izhevsk, about 170 miles northeast of Kazan, to make variants of the Moskvich models, and it opened in 1971. Much of the equipment for these two plants also came from Western suppliers.

In 1972 the number of passenger cars produced in the Soviet Union for the first time exceeded that of trucks, and in 1975 the auto industry made 1.2 million cars, six times the 1965 level, or about the same as Britain, Italy, or Canada in that year.

With the 1971-75 plan came the turn of truck manufacturing for modernization and expansion. The large majority of Soviet trucks still were standard models of 2.5 to 5 tons capacity made in Gorki and Moscow. To end the shortage of heavy trucks the regime proposed a huge manufacturing complex requiring an even larger investment than the VAZ. They located it on the Kama River, about 150 miles above its confluence with the Volga near the town of Naberezhnye Chelny. The town's name eventually was changed to Brezhnev. About three-fourths of all the machinery, equipment, and technology for the Kama Automobile Works (KamAZ) came from Western and Japanese suppliers. The foundry was designed and equipped by an American firm and the transmission shop by a German firm; Italy provided the conveyor systems and Japan the presses. Originally, Soviet specialists from the diesel-engine plant in Yaroslavl designed the new diesel that would power KamAZ trucks, but difficulties ensued and a call went out to Renault to improve the engine and manage the equipment of the engine factory. The KamAZ was to have a capacity of 150,000 heavy trucks and 250,000 diesel engines, the largest such production complex in the world by far. New housing for some 300,000 people also had to be constructed.

The three new establishments in the Volga-Kama river area – at Tolyatti, Izhevsk, and Brezhnev – show that the regime expected to use river transport during the open season to ease the strain on the overburdened railways. Hydroelectric facilities on the rivers also supplied power to the plants.

By the mid-1980s Soviet passenger-car output of 1.5 million per year and truck production of 800,000 made the industry the third largest in Europe and the fifth largest in the world. Demand for passenger cars in the Soviet Union remained strong, but waiting periods had shortened and credit terms even became available on an old Moskvich model. With assistance from Porsche, the Volga plant introduced a new front-wheel-drive model in 1987, the Samara, the first of this type in the Soviet Union.

There were some 13 million private cars in use by 1987. A research institute calculated that in 1985 there were 45 cars per 1,000 inhabitants, about half the 93 per 1,000 that the State Planning Committee decreed was the norm of rational consumption. However, in the three Baltic republics the average was higher than the Union average, ranging from 81 to 96 per 1,000, and in some republics it was lower – Azerbaijan (30), Moldavia (33), Kirghiz (34), and Tadzhik (35).[7]

In addition to the obstacles Soviet citizens encountered in obtaining a car, driving it outside major cities raised difficulties because of the poor roads. Only some 135,000 miles of the country's 850,000 miles of roads were paved in the mid-1970s, although the first limited-access highway, a beltway around Moscow, opened in 1962. The low load limits on roads and bridges continued to restrict long-distance trucking.

In the age of *glasnost* there was plenty of self-criticism of the Soviet automobile industry. In a discussion in the Supreme Soviet in 1987 on the nation's automotive industry, the head of the ministry admitted that its labor productivity was about one-fourth that of leading firms in the capitalist countries and that its trucks lagged behind foreign models in service life and reliability. Some knowledgeable deputies uttered harsher criticisms, asserting that only 20 per cent of the country's vehicles measured up to world standards, that KamAZ truck engines wore out too rapidly, that the Coal Ministry preferred to use Japanese over Belorussian trucks, and that Soviet vehicles could be sold abroad only when priced 30 to 50 percent below similar models. Speakers complained that it took 10 to 15 years to develop a new model, that investment in the industry was too low, that such funds were inefficiently allocated, and that new equipment was installed too slowly. They claimed that the return on research and development spending was low or even negative and criticized the motor-industry ministry for spending too much money importing foreign manufacturing equipment, especially from capitalist countries.[8]

THE AUTOMOBILE INDUSTRY IN EASTERN EUROPE

In the countries of Eastern Europe dominated by Communist parties, East Germany and Czechoslovakia were the only ones with significant prewar auto manufacturing. Poland and Hungary had some industrial base from which to develop this industry, but Yugoslavia, Romania, and Bulgaria, with little metal manufacturing and few engineers, had to start almost from scratch and depended largely on foreign technology. The East European countries at first devoted more resources to trucks and buses than to passenger cars.[9] In 1949 the Council for Mutual Economic Assistance – CMEA (often called Comecon) – was established to encourage some integration of the economies of these countries, including the Soviet Union. For two decades Comecon accomplished very little in this line, however. Each of the communist countries followed the Soviet system of allocating resources and establishing production schedules by centralized planning, not by the market, and each country had its own national plan into which it was awkward to fit foreign trade. It proved difficult to mesh these national plans very thoroughly.

The motor-vehicle industry seemed appropriate for Comecon integration because of the important economies of scale gained by producing large numbers of the same-model car, at least up to 200,000 annually, and the possibilities of having each of the several countries specialize in a few types of motor vehicles, or components, and then distribute them to each other. Reality was more difficult. Each of the countries wanted its own cars for reasons of nationalist prestige and wanted its own auto industry in order to expand manufacturing employment and spread modern technology. The currencies of the various countries were not convertible, so multilateral trade was very complicated. For a car firm in one country to import from a producer in another required agreement between the planning bureaucracies in each country as well as between the enterprises themselves. Complex negotiations about quality, delivery dates, and the type of goods to be used for payment were necessary.

Generally, it seemed simpler although more expensive to establish small-scale suppliers in one's own country, or to buy some parts from vendors in Western countries. Despite these roadblocks, in the 1960s and especially the 1970s integration of the East European auto industries did make progress.[10] A turning point came when the leadership of the Soviet Union legitimized private motoring and hired Fiat and Renault to expand and modernize its car production. These decisions gave a green light to those who favored expansion and integration in the East European auto industries, but much more specialization and integration came with commercial vehicles than passenger cars.

Quality and productivity remained quite low in these countries' auto industries. The planners usually gave a monopoly to the factory making a certain type of vehicle, for competition was considered wasteful. But without competition there was no spur to raise quality and no need for investment to make new models. Overstaffing was rampant, for it was a way to achieve the system's promise of full employment, and there was little incentive to reduce costs.

The East German auto industry had to overcome its losses of machinery to the Soviet Union at the end of the war and the flight westward of managers and engineers. In 1949 auto making recommenced. At Eisenach small numbers of prewar BMW and then Audi models were built until 1955. They were joined by a small prewar DKW with a three-cylinder, two-stroke engine, called the Wartburg. At Zwickau even smaller DKW types were produced, under the name Trabant. In 1973 the East Germans built some 147,000 cars and about 32,000 trucks. For at least a decade the East Germans and the Czechs negotiated on the joint production of a passenger car, but it never appeared.

The major East German truck maker, in Ludwigsfelde, near Potsdam, was at the center of a network of suppliers of engines, bodies, and other components. A heavy-machine builder in Erfurt began to supply its presses and other machinery to car and truck factories all over Comecon in the 1970s.

In Czechoslovakia the Skoda factory in Mlada Boleslav (halfway between Prague and the Polish frontier) was the largest in the East European countries. Modernized with machinery from Western countries in the 1960s, this plant turned out some 150,000 cars annually in the mid-1970s. In that decade it was joined by a new Skoda car plant in Slovakia near Bratislava, which had a capacity of 100,000 vehicles. Czech output rose little, however, amounting to only about 170,000 annually in the late 1980s. An unusual postrevolutionary event slowed production at Skoda early in 1990. The new president, Vaclav Havel, declared an amnesty, and some 1,500 convicts who worked under guard on the paint line received their freedom. Unable to find anyone else to do the painting, management got the army to order its recruits into the factory. Skoda's large truck-making activities, Liaz, were located in Jablonec near the Polish border. The Avia firm in Prague and the old Tatra firm in Koprivnice made trucks, some on license from Renault. The 12- and 14-ton Tatra trucks were exported widely in Comecon, especially to the Soviet Union, and subassemblies for Liaz trucks went to Bulgaria for assembly there.

Hungary's vehicle industry became the most integrated with the other Comecon countries. Its leaders decided that, with a population of just 9.3 million in 1950, a national car-production program would be too expensive a luxury,[11] and they chose instead to concentrate on trucks and especially buses. Considering the anti-individualist bias of the Communist regimes, it appeared that buses would find a strong market. But the country had to cooperate with the other Comecon countries to find markets for its buses and to obtain the cars its people wanted. Three major companies dominated the Hungarian vehicle industry, all with roots extending back several decades. Raba in Gyor made diesel engines and rear axles for trucks on license from the West German firm MAN and assembled small numbers of trucks; Csepel of Budapest made truck and bus chassis on license from the Austrian firm Steyr; and Ikarus of Budapest assembled and put bodies on these components for its line of buses. Ikarus also imported some chassis and engines from such Western firms as Volvo, Scania, Leyland, and Perkins. Knowing that it had to export most of its output, Ikarus emphasized quality but may also have received government export subsidies. It became one of the major bus builders in all of Europe, in the same quantity category as Daimler-Benz and Bedford. Exporting some 85 percent of its buses, Ikarus found its best markets in the Soviet

Union and East Germany, with about 1,000 a year going to capitalist countries.[12] For its exports of buses and auto parts to other members of Comecon, Hungary received cars and trucks. All did not go well under the political and economic reform of the late 1980s, however, for in early 1990 Ikarus declared bankruptcy. On the other hand, the Japanese firm Suzuki was preparing to assemble cars in Hungary in 1992.

Poland in the 1970s imported large amounts of Western technology and expanded its automotive industry manifold. Its passenger-car production rose from 27,000 in 1967 to 326,000 in 1978. Most of these were Fiat types, made near Warsaw and in two new factories in Silesia. There was some specialization of manufacture of Fiat parts among Poland, the Soviet Union, and Yugoslavia, which all made Fiat-designed vehicles. The Poles also wanted to make a nearly full line of trucks and buses, using Western components and manufacturing licenses. Poland led the East European countries in commercial-vehicle production in the 1980s.

Romania under Ceausescu showed the least interest in cooperation within Comecon. In 1966 it arranged a license with Renault to build the Dacia passenger car, eventually making over 80 percent of its parts domestically. A similar arrangement with Citroën led to production in 1979. Romania's truck production began with derivatives from Soviet models, but in the 1970s it began working with such Western firms as Renault and MAN, although it did employ some Hungarian parts.

Bulgaria, even less populated than Hungary, chose to specialize. It did assemble small numbers of Soviet trucks and cars, as well as Fiat and Renault cars. It also assembled Skoda trucks and buses with parts shipped from Czechoslovakia, paying for them with its own rear-axle assemblies. But Bulgaria's primary activity in the automobile industry was to specialize in electrical equipment, especially industrial forklift trucks and other types of materials-handling equipment. It dominated the Comecon market for these vehicles and tried to sell them in the West through Daimler-Benz. In the 1980s Bulgaria was Europe's largest producer of factory trucks and the second largest maker of electric hoists.

Yugoslavia was an associate member of the Comecon, but most of its foreign economic ties have been with the West. In 1954 it arranged to make Fiat models on license in Kragujevac, a Serbian town south of Belgrade, under the name Zastava. By 1976 Fiat had invested several million dollars in this facility and imported large amounts of its parts for Fiat's operations in Italy. In the 1980s Zastava exported a Fiat-derived model called the Yugo to the United States. Yugoslavia also began assembling vehicles from other Western companies – Citroën, British Leyland, Renault, and VW. From 46,000 cars produced in 1967, Yugoslavia increased to 180,000 in 1975 and 228,000 in 1985. For its commercial vehicles it depended largely on licensed manufacture from Western firms.

By the late 1980s East European countries other than the Soviet Union were making about 1 million cars and 225,000 commercial vehicles a year – numbers of moderate significance for Europe and the world. These vehicles served the local area and the Soviet Union primarily, for their quality, with few exceptions, remained below that of producers in Western Europe, America, and Japan. The gradual development of international specialization among these countries demonstrated the growth of economic logic over political dogma, but the revolutions of 1989 brought sharp challenges and changes.

13

CRISES AND COMPETITION

The oil shock of 1973-74 ended the great boom of the European automobile industry. Petroleum prices, forced upward by the OPEC cartel, in January 1974 reached $11.65 per barrel in the Persian Gulf, up from $2.59 a year earlier. Early in 1974 gasoline grew scarce in Western Europe and the United States; governments tried to reduce consumption with various kinds of rationing schemes. West Germany even put a speed limit (100 km/hour) on the autobahns, but only for a few months. Although the shortages eased by midyear, oil prices stayed high (see Table 13.1).

This first oil shock brought two major effects. First, it suddenly amputated demand for cars all over the world, especially the larger, less fuel-efficient models. A corollary to this was relatively firm demand for small, economical cars and for those with diesel engines – a demand that began to increase in mid-1974. Total car sales in Western Europe regained normal levels in the late 1970s. Second, it brought a restructuring of the car market in the United States as auto producers there speeded production of small cars and under federal government pressure gradually reduced the size, weight, and fuel consumption of their entire fleets. Many American car models by the late 1970s came to resemble typical European and Japanese cars. This led to efforts by General Motors and Ford to design mass-market cars that with little alteration would suit both the European and American markets. The "world car" became an objective, with components mass produced by specialized factories in several countries brought together for assembly in one or more plants, and then the cars sold all over the world. It was Henry Ford's Model T déjà vu. The shift in American demand to cars of the same size and power as were common in Europe provided a great opportunity for the major European producers, but in fact the Japanese took much more advantage of it. In the United States Japanese cars had earned a higher reputation for reliability than the

217

TABLE 13.1   GASOLINE RETAIL PRICES, 1973-1988*

	1973	1975	1980	1985	1986	1988
France	1.06	1.56	2.97	2.37	2.58	3.60
Italy	0.99	1.66	3.08	2.62	3.25	3.96
Britain	0.78	1.27	2.60	2.09	2.07	2.52
West Germany	1.18	1.25	2.46	1.85	1.88	2.06
U.S.	0.40	0.57	1.19	1.02	0.93	0.95

* including taxes; in U.S. dollars per U.S. gallon of regular leaded gasoline, except
  regular unleaded gasoline for the U.S., 1985-88
Sources:
1973-80: U.S. *Statistical Abstract*, 1988, 583.
1985-88: *1989 Energy Statistics Sourcebook* (Tulsa, Okla.: Pennwell, 1989), 320.

European volume-produced models, and several of the Japanese firms had developed effective dealer networks, originally based on low-priced cars. Of the European-owned firms, only VW was capable of challenging the Japanese on the U.S. market, but it was in the midst of dropping the Beetle for entirely new models. In the event, the Japanese kept their dominance over the import trade to the United States.

In 1979 came the second oil shock as the OPEC countries raised prices sharply again following the Iranian revolution that replaced the shah by Khomeini. This cut demand for autos once again, and the producers continued their efforts to reduce fuel consumption. Interest continued in diesel-engined cars, where the Europeans were ahead of American and Japanese technology. Many firms looked about for alternative products to make as it appeared that the car market would not continue to expand. They also stepped up their investigations of alternative sources of power: petroleum produced from coal or organic matter and especially electric batteries. The OPEC cartel's high prices, sometimes over $30 a barrel, slowed the growth of demand for gasoline and fuel oil, encouraged some of its members to sell more than their quotas, and brought more sources of petroleum onto the market from the North Sea, Alaska, Southeast Asia, and elsewhere, so by the mid-1980s there was talk of an oil glut, and prices fell back to $20 a barrel and even as low as $10 on brief occasions. By this time car owners had digested the higher gasoline prices, which in markets such as the

United States were back to the early 1970s levels in constant dollar terms.

European automakers also confronted major changes in labor and manufacturing methods. Although autoworkers in Europe received relatively high pay, the jobs were not eagerly sought after, as evidenced by high absenteeism and turnover rates. As a result, the auto companies began hiring immigrants desperate for work: Yugoslavs and Turks in Germany, North Africans in France, Southern Italians in Italy, and Caribbean blacks in Britain. In 1990 Soviet authorities hired over 1,500 contract workers from the People's Republic of China to do the toughest jobs in the Gorki and other automotive plants. Quite another policy was to attack a reputed cause of labor alienation in the auto factories – the jobs on the assembly lines or elsewhere that involved ceaseless repetition for an entire shift. Antidotes included the rotation of workers among different jobs, incorporating more content and responsibility in a job, and reorganization that required a team to perform a large task so as to promote camaraderie. Two schools of thought emerged on these matters. One argued that workers wanted more content in the jobs to remain interested in them; the other alleged that increasing the intellectual content of a job, raising the number of decisions to make, was more tiring. The probable answer was that workers were different – some preferred repetition so they could think of other things, others wanted to become more involved in their tasks.

Another approach to the labor problem involved a major manufacturing development that appeared in the 1970s: electronics. The introduction of electronics, where the Japanese often were the leaders, involved computer-aided design of cars, which accelerated this process. Electronics technology helped management schedule deliveries and processes, and it changed production itself, for computer-controlled machines – robots – could do certain awkward or unhealthy jobs such as body welding or painting as well as complex installation of parts during assembly. The computer-controlled machines not only relieved semiskilled workers of unpleasant tasks but provided greater flexibility in production – a machine could be programmed to perform differently on consecutive parts or in assembly. This provided for mass production of nonstandardized items.[1] There was a negative side: the occasional (or frequent) malfunction of these machines and the complaints from labor leaders about the loss of jobs for humans.

An innovation in materials – ceramics – was on the horizon in the early 1990s. Such materials can withstand very high temperatures and were being developed for use in parts of engines, in particular in diesels. The Japanese again appeared to be leading in the arduous development of ceramics for automobiles.

THE VOLUME PRODUCERS

By the early 1970s seven major firms dominated the European mass-market for cars: VW, Fiat, Renault, Peugeot-Citroën, and British Leyland, along with the U.S. multinationals GM and Ford. They had to share a market that was not growing as fast as in the 1960s. What some firms gained in sales tended to be at the expense of others. Through the 1970s and 1980s the American multinationals and a new player in Europe, Japanese imports, would gain market share. The big loser was British Leyland. Key elements of success would be frequent introduction of new models and a reputation for reliability, both of which stemmed from the greater experience of car owners. No longer would a potential customer be attracted to the idea of just owning a car, but rather to owning a particular car that had attractive features and would not require frequent repairs. British Leyland, Renault, and Fiat were slower than the others to appreciate the market shift toward quality.

THE AMERICAN MULTINATIONALS

General Motors and Ford were the most international of the major producers in Europe, with important production facilities in Germany and Britain. Chrysler tried to follow its American rivals into Europe in the 1960s when the market there was growing much faster than it was in North America. But Chrysler's Simca and Rootes operations did not grow into major competitors in Europe. Its only chance with them was to integrate manufacturing and marketing, as Ford was doing in Germany and Britain. This did not happen, partly because the home company in Detroit, a victim of mismanagement, did not have the money to invest in such projects. In fact, the Chrysler British operation became such a drag on the stumbling Chrysler Corporation that it decided on a major change. Just six months after the British government had bailed out British Leyland and nationalized it, Chairman John Riccardo of the Chrysler Corporation came to London in November 1975 with an ultimatum: either the British government had to take over Chrysler (UK) or it would be closed. Fearful of the social and especially the political impact of losing up to 25,000 jobs, the Labour government scurried about for a softer solution. The upshot was a scheme for substantial government subsidies and loans – $300 million – and a Chrysler promise to continue manufacturing in Britain, in part by assembling components shipped from its French subsidiary, Simca, to make a new model. Chrysler (UK) sales continued to fall nevertheless, and in 1977 it won only 6.2 percent of the British market.

In Detroit, Chrysler continued to search desperately for cash, and Riccardo finally sold its entire European holdings to Peugeot in 1978. Peugeot primarily was interested in the Simca operation in France, partly to keep another foreign firm out of the country, but it had to accept the British and Spanish companies as part of a package deal. Peugeot paid Chrysler $230 million in cash, assumed $400 million in debts, and gave Chrysler 15 percent of its capital stock, worth about $200 million. So ended Chrysler's European efforts, at least for a decade. It had lost money on this adventure, and selling out did not bring in enough to save the jobs of the Riccardo group, which gave way in 1979 to Lee Iacocca and his team.

Ford expanded in Europe in the 1970s. Spain was a target, one of the most rapidly expanding markets. The Franco regime there wanted a larger automobile industry but sought to maintain domestic control over it. No foreign firm could own over half of a Spanish concern, local content had to amount to 95 percent of a car's value, and there was a 30 percent tariff on imported parts. Ford negotiated for several years to turn aside these regulations and establish a base in Spain before this country joined the Common Market. The Spanish government and Ford finally struck a compromise. Ford would maintain 100 percent ownership of its Spanish subsidiary, its cars there would have 66 percent domestic content, and the tariff on imported parts would fall to 5 percent. Ford agreed to export at least two-thirds of its output and to protect the auto producers already in Spain by limiting sales on the local market. Spain was pleased to get the industrial jobs, to find a client for many small firms that made or would make auto parts, to obtain the foreign exchange from exports, and to receive the technology transfer.[2]

Construction of the new factory began near Valencia in January 1974, and the first car, a new model called Fiesta, rolled out in October 1975. This plant made the engines, with the transmissions coming from

a new factory in Bordeaux, France. Another new Ford factory, in Saarlouis, Saarland, Germany, also made Fiestas, and the demand expanded
so swiftly that some were assembled in Dagenham as well. Later Ford
models such as the Escort and Sierra also were made and sold interna-
tionally. In 1990 Ford of Europe proposed to expand its operations in
Spain again, this time to make a sport-utility vehicle in conjuction with
Nissan. At the same time, Ford and VW planned to establish an assembly plant in Portugal to produce small vans.

In the 1970s the bulk of Ford's European design and development
of cars shifted to Germany, where it had more well-trained engineers.
At the same time productivity in Ford's English factories declined,
while in Germany it rose.[3] The many labor disputes in the English
plants bore some responsibility for this, but they in turn sprang from
poor shop-floor management. This situation led the Ford company to
reduce the British content in its cars offered on that market, selling
more that were imported fully built from the Continent or were assembled from imported parts. Nevertheless, Henry Ford II did not give up
on manufacturing in Britain and with a substantial government subsidy
began building a new engine plant in South Wales at Bridgend in 1978.
In the 1980s productivity began to rise in Ford's British factories as
workers and management finally absorbed the probability that some of
the plants would close if operations did not improve. From Halewood,
Ford flew some 2,000 employees to Saarlouis to observe how Germans
did similar tasks. Workers and managers put aside their mutual distrust
and set up joint committees to solve problems rather than fight over
them. The consequences were startling. From 1980 to 1988 the annual
output per employee rose from 15 to 31 cars; nevertheless, at Saarlouis
the figures showed an increase from 31 to 42 per year.[4] The rising efficiency in England led the firm to increase the proportion of manufacturing done there.

With tariffs and other restrictions eliminated or minimized among
the West European states by the 1970s, a multinational could move
some aspects of auto manufacturing among its plants in several countries to take advantage of currency exchange rates, labor costs, and
productivity, but its options were limited by the heavy expenses and loss
of goodwill from laying off workers and professional staff, and by the
need to keep costly machinery operating.

General Motors revised its European strategy in 1979. It established a European headquarters in Zurich and began to integrate fur-

ther the design and manufacture of vehicles among its national affili-
ates. It built an engine factory at Aspern, near Vienna, which opened in
1982, and ended most engine production in England. In Spain it followed the path Ford had broken to build a car-making factory near the
northern city of Zaragoza and three smaller parts-making plants to
produce small cars for the southern European market. GM reduced its
Vauxhall operations largely to assembly and sales. It concentrated its
car designing at the Opel facilities where German and American engineers worked on European and world cars. An Opel Kadett model of
1975 became the Chevette, made in Germany, Britain, Australia, Japan,
and the United States. Starting in 1979 all Vauxhall cars in Britain were
Opels, with the Vauxhall badge on them, either imported fully built up
from Germany, Belgium, or Spain, or assembled at Luton or Ellesmere
Port. GM also expanded its marketing effort in France and Spain. The
model GM designed in the United States as the J-car was modified with
a better engine for Europe and introduced there in 1981 as the Opel
Ascona/Vauxhall Cavalier. This car surprised everyone by its sales success. Its engines came from Australia, transmissions from Japan and
the United States, stampings from Germany, and carburetors from
France. On occasion it did pay GM to expand assembly in Britain, as in
1987 when exchange rates shifted and Vauxhall exported cars with the
Opel badge on them.[5]

Looking for engineering help and some prestige names for its cars,
GM-Europe under the leadership of Robert Eaton bought the British
Lotus sports-car firm in 1986 and a half interest in the Swedish Saab in
1990. When Eastern Europe opened to Western firms, General Motors
moved aggressively while Ford held back. GM's sales were climbing,
especially in Germany, where Opel was challenging VW for leadership.
GM needed more manufacturing capacity and decided to find it in
Eastern Europe, where it might lead to increased sales. It arranged to
make engines and assemble a few thousand cars in Hungary. In
Eisenach, East Germany, it agreed to build a new assembly plant and
decided to build a new transmission plant at Aspern, Austria, near its
engine plant there. GM also hoped to assemble cars in Poland. In the
meantime several GM assembly plants in Western Europe began
operating three shifts a day to meet the demand for cars.

THE DECLINE OF BRITISH LEYLAND

Although each of the major European-owned volume car producers went through a time of troubles in the late 1970s or the 1980s, all emerged to post larger profits by the late 1980s except British Leyland. When the British car industry began losing its tariff protection its clientele began buying foreign cars. In 1973 the country entered the European Economic Community (or Common Market). By 1975 cars entering from the Continent paid just 4.4 percent tariff that would soon drop to zero, and cars from elsewhere, primarily Japan, paid 10 percent. British Leyland's management under Donald Stokes realized that some of its 48 plants should be closed and some 30,000 personnel laid off, but fearful of the reaction from labor and the government, it kept postponing the strong medicine. If it had produced some popular models in addition to the Mini, increased sales might have absorbed the surplus workers, but these did not appear. Rover, the best managed division in British Leyland, in 1971 launched the Range Rover, a four-wheel-drive station wagon and the only real design success of the 1970s. But the company could not organize itself to meet the strong demand for this model. Table 13.2 shows the low level of investment and suggests the overstaffing in British auto firms generally, and especially in British Leyland.

The flood of imports, from 8.3 percent of the British market in 1968 to 33.2 percent in 1975, and the oil shock cost British Leyland sales and quickly brought a financial crisis. By November 1974 the firm's banks had become reluctant to extend their loans, and it asked the new Labour government for help. This was just what many Labourites wanted, especially the leftist secretary of state for industry, Tony Benn. For years they had prescribed nationalization as an antidote to industry's troubles, and now they had an opening. The government guaranteed British Leyland's loans and appointed a committee to investigate. Headed by Sir Don Ryder, from the paper industry, the committee reported in March and April 1975, blaming the company's problems "on poor management (Stokes would have to go), grotty [shabby] machinery and bad industrial relations." It proposed that the government pour very large sums into British Leyland to modernize, rationalize, and expand it. "The alternative was to accept the unemployment of nearly one million people and the abandonment of a comprehensive motor industry."[6] The government accepted this argument,

TABLE 13.2 INVESTMENT IN AUTOMOBILE COMPANIES, 1972

	Fixed assets per employee (£s)
Volvo	4,662
Volkswagen	3,632
Opel	3,612
Ford (West Germany)	3,608
Fiat	3,160
Daimler-Benz	2,694
Ford (Britain)	2,657
Renault	2,396
Chrysler (Britain)	1,456
Vauxhall	1,356
British Leyland	920

Source: Karel Williams et al., *The Breakdown of Austin Rover* (Leamington Spa: Berg, 1987), 35.

and in return for huge subsidies the company was effectively national-ized in June 1975, with the new name BL.

Its situation did not improve, however. The Ryder plan depended on expanding sales to avoid laying off workers, but the company did not have attractive new models ready. Labor was brought into the decision-making process, but strikes continued. Government officials, especially Ryder, interfered with investment decisions and labor relations. Finally, the Labour government asked an aggressive businessman from the chemical industry, Michael Edwardes, to take over. He insisted on a free hand and received it, in October 1977.[7]

Edwardes turned out to have a different vision from what the unions and left Labourites had had in 1975. He did what tough execu-tives would do later at the other major European auto firms (Romiti at Fiat, Calvet at Peugeot, Besse and Lévy at Renault) – establish realistic goals, close plants, lay off personnel. He also replaced or moved around many executives, sometimes hiring new people from English Ford where they had learned modern management. Edwardes refused to back down in the face of threats from labor; he turned the tables and threatened to close down the firm or parts of it if labor did not accept layoffs, changes in work rules, and only modest pay increases. After he had closed several factories labor took him seriously. When in November 1979 he fired the Communist chief shop steward at Austin-Long-bridge, "Red Robbo" Robinson, for obstructionism, he convinced the workers to stay on the job. Although Edwardes dismayed sentimental-ists by ending production of MG and Triumph sports cars – both big money losers – his policies convinced Margaret Thatcher to keep him in the top job when her Conservative government came to power in May 1979.

Edwardes kept going back to the government for more money be-cause it was costly to close factories, give severance pay, and develop new models. The second oil shock of 1979 and the rising value of the pound sterling in that year, making British exports more expensive, brought very serious sales declines. In 1980 both export and domestic sales of BL cars were about half the 1973 figures. Under Edwardes, British Leyland had great success with one new car, the Metro (1980), and arranged to assemble and sell a Honda Civic model under the name Acclaim (1981). Later, its Rover 800 of 1986 was a variant of the Honda (Acura) Legend and appeared in America as the Sterling.

When Edwardes left BL in September 1982, its employment in Britain had dropped to 83,000 from 130,000 in 1977. Car production had fallen from 650,000 to 405,000. Edwardes had turned BL into a small-scale producer of cars for the mass market, along with some spe-cialized vehicles. Manufacturing processes had been updated and work practices reformed. A major failure was a loss of export markets, espe-cially in Europe.

One of the Thatcher government policies was to sell public eco-nomic enterprises to the private sector, where they believed they would be more efficiently operated, a point of view that would be reflected on the Continent as well in the 1980s. The Jaguar privatization exemplified this policy. Jaguar found itself in deep trouble in the late 1970s. Its sales had dropped sharply as quality problems irritated customers. Edwardes persuaded a young engineer, John Egan, to take it on. Egan soon found that 60 percent of the faults in the cars came from poor-quality parts bought from subcontractors. Egan read the riot act to his vendors and made them liable for full warranty costs following failure of their com-ponents.[8] Vigorous efforts to improve in-house quality and to raise productivity by laying off surplus workers brought the company back to profitability by 1982. Jaguar had almost lost its U.S. market, selling only

2,951 vehicles there in 1980, but this revived to 20,528 of total production of 38,378 in 1985.

Jaguar's success led to its flotation as a private enterprise in 1984 with some shares given free to the workers. It continued to prosper, and Egan plowed much of the profit back into investment, an unusual practice in the British car industry. Egan's revival of Jaguar so impressed the automobile world that Ford bought it in 1989 for the very high price of $2.56 billion. Ford expected to invest large sums in Jaguar and eventually raise its output from 50,000 to 200,000. After some hesitation Egan decided not to work for Ford and left the company.

The rest of BL did not recover as well as Jaguar. Its Honda-derived models had a mixed record. The Sterling was supposed to compete in the U.S. luxury-car market but ran head-on into the new Japanese models and had to be withdrawn in 1991. The once successful and proud Leyland truck division was set up in a joint venture with the Dutch truck maker DAF in 1987 after the British government cancelled its debts. BL adopted a new name, Rover Group, in 1986, and the Thatcher government finally sold it to British Aerospace in 1989 for $280 million after paying another $1.5 billion in Rover's debts. During its 14 years of ownership the British government had paid a total of $5.4 billion in subsidies. The European Economic Commission challenged the transaction with British Aerospace as involving unfair subsidies, so the government had to reduce them by several hundred million dollars. British Aerospace had been another nationalized concern, but after privatization in 1981 it had prospered.

In 1990 Honda and Rover knit closer ties, with the Japanese firm becoming 20 percent owner of Rover and 20 percent of Honda Limited (its British operations) going to Rover. Great Britain in the early 1990s was the major portal through which the Japanese carmakers entered Europe and the European Community. They found this country, desperate for more manufacturing employment, willing to accept them. In 1986 Nissan opened an assembly plant in the northeast, near Sunderland, and soon claimed its cars had 80 percent local content. The British Nissans proved to be high-quality vehicles, made with rather conventional machinery but with innovative labor policies. Workers were treated with respect although closely supervised. Most of the executives were British, often recruited from Ford. Meanwhile, Honda built an engine factory near Swindon, and Toyota began construction of engine and assembly plants, as well as a design center in Belgium. By the mid-1990s the three Japanese car builders will have the capacity to make a half-million cars a year in Britain, many for export to the Continent.

The British car industry by the 1990s had become largely foreign owned and controlled. Weak management from the 1930s on explains this. Its failures were many: poor recruitment and training of engineers and other management personnel, a very low level of investment, amateurish foreign marketing, and an inability to manage on the shop floor. It is interesting to note that to run BL-Rover the government twice went to persons who had come from abroad – Michael Edwardes from South Africa and then Graham Day from Canada.

FIAT IN TRANSITION

Problems abounded for Fiat in the 1970s.[9] Sales fell as fuel prices rose, efforts at even more diversification did not appear to be successful, foreign investment had not paid off, and labor problems did not improve despite large concessions on pay. In 1976 Gianni Agnelli and his brother Umberto brought in Carlo De Benedetti, a very successful young Turinese businessman, to help them run the enterprise, an admission that they found it too much for themselves. De Benedetti prepared to take strong measures – sharp cuts in the factory labor force and in white-collar employees, tight controls over spending, and heavy investment in new models. All this change all at once was too much for the Agnellis, unused to decisive management, so De Benedetti left Fiat after 100 days and soon gained fame by turning around the Olivetti company. A few months later, in December 1976, Gianni Agnelli announced a deal with Libyan strongman Muammar Qaddafi to sell him 15 percent of Fiat's equity for $415 million, much above the market price for these shares. Qaddafi also received representation on Fiat's board of directors. This tie with a reputed supporter of terrorism aroused considerable comment at a time when terrorism was beginning to threaten Fiat itself. Agnelli later regretted, and subsequently reversed, this step.

In 1975 Fiat reorganized its truck operations into a new company called Iveco (Industrial Vehicle Company) that included its various activities in Italy, Unic in France, and Magirus in West Germany. It became the second largest truck firm in Europe behind Daimler-Benz and sold a few thousand midweight trucks on the U.S. market yearly. A decade later, in 1986, Ford of Europe transferred its heavy-truck divi-

sion to a joint venture with Iveco, in which the latter
trol. Ford heavy trucks had a sizable market only in E

The Agnelli brothers did find two able executive:
manage the Fiat empire. As the head of car operations they chose Vittorio Ghidella, who would preside over the revival of Fiat autos in the
1980s. Cesare Romiti, a very tough executive from the finance side and
a complete opposite to Gianni Agnelli's smoothness and charm, became managing director. These men stiffened the resolve of the Agnellis to fight back against terrorism.

This plague had revived in Italy in 1969, fostered by disaffected intellectuals and journalists, and lasted until the early 1980s. Terrorists
targeted Fiat in the mid-1970s, murdering four of its executives, including the director of automobile planning, and wounding 27 others;
they also engaged in sabotage at the firm. In October 1979 the company
fired 61 suspected terrorists and saboteurs, and when a wave of wildcat
strikes, demonstrations, and terrorism recommenced in September
1980, Cesare Romiti announced the dismissal of 13,000 workers, a huge
and unprecedented number for Italy. When politicians protested, the
company agreed to lay off 24,000 for three months instead, an arrangement where these workers would receive 90 percent of their
wages from a government unemployment fund. The unions struck anyway, but this made them look unreasonable and bent on destroying the
company, so public opinion shifted to favor management. After five
weeks of the strike a midlevel executive took the initiative and organized a march in Turin against the strike. To everyone's surprise this
affair attracted some 40,000 people – white- and blue-collar Fiat
employees along with people from other local firms. The unions quickly
backed down and signed an agreement that resulted in 23,000 layoffs
for up to 34 months and labor's approval of a permanent reduction in
the work force through early retirements and no new hires. The "march
of the 40,000" gave Fiat management more confidence in itself and
encouraged other firms to move against overstaffing and against
allegedly overpowerful labor organizations.

Fiat rebounded in the 1980s. New models appeared; productivity
and quality improved, making it harder for wags to translate Fiat as
"Fix it again, Tony"; and the company made healthy profits. Its new
factories in the south expanded, and it was able to reduce the labor
force at Mirafiore. Fiat withdrew from the U.S. car market and finally
gave up its investment in the Spanish company Seat in 1980. At that

point Fiat owned 41 percent of Seat, but after Seat suffered a string of losses owing to an excess labor force, Fiat pulled out and sold its share back to the government holding company INI. Several years later, and after more heavy losses, the Spanish finally worked out a deal with Volkswagen.

For a time Fiat considered the idea of merging with the Ford operations in Europe, but the scheme collapsed when it became clear that both sides wanted control. Then, when the Italian government tried to sell Alfa Romeo to Ford, Fiat – hitherto not interested in this firm – reacted strongly. After Ford submitted its bid in 1986 Fiat made a counter offer, wrapped in the Italian flag. Although Fiat's bid was less than Ford's, especially considering that it provided for Fiat to begin payment only in 1993, the government had no real option. Italian consumers probably would have benefited from a strong domestic competitor to Fiat, but in the Common Market Fiat already faced vigorous competition in Italy. Fiat took over Alfa in 1986, but there was a sting in the tail. The European Economic Commission ruled that a large subsidy the Italian government paid to Alfa before the takeover violated fair competition in the Common Market and that Fiat would have to pay it back. This government subsidy problem bacame an issue again with the Rover Group in Britain in 1989 and with Renault in France. Fiat kept its good reputation in the Soviet Union and in 1989 contracted to establish another large new car factory at Elabuga, near the KamAZ truck complex. In 1991 this major project was shelved, and Fiat agreed to take a 30 percent share of the VAZ (Tolyatti) auto works that was being privatized. In Poland Fiat equipped a new assembly plant in the South in the early 1990s and arranged to buy a controlling interest in it.

To deal with the labor problem on a long-term basis, Fiat at Mirafiore and in its newer factories in southern Italy experimented with heavy doses of automation. Its engine plant at Termoli was highly robotized so that both machining and assembly time were well under half those at Mirafiore. This success encouraged the company to install even more automatic machinery in a reorganized assembly plant in Cassino. In the early 1980s this factory built 1,000 cars a day with 10,000 workers. After reorganization it employed 7,000 to make 1,200 cars daily in 1989 – in the same range as the Ford plants in Halewood and Saarlouis – but the Cassino rate was scheduled to climb to 1,800 a year later. A journalist described some aspects of the Cassino factory:

Fiat has sought to minimize use of traditional assembly lines at Cassino, relying instead on 14 highly automated sub-unit assembly islands. Pre-assembled modules move via robot-trailers and automatic guided vehicles to stations for mating with car bodies.

For example, dashboard cables, instruments, electronic parts and trimming are automatically assembled and later joined to heating, ventilation and air-conditioning units, steering columns, pedals, and the brake system.

A robot tests all functions of the dash, which is then automatically mounted as a unit onto the body.

Another key operation is automatic off-line assembly of the front sub-unit, which consists of powertrain, crossbeam with suspension arms and spring/damper/hub carrier. Robots add the radiator, rear suspension and central section.

Next, mechanical underbody components are automatically bolted to the bodyshell after having been positioned on pallets, computer-matched with each shell.

Robots then install the wheels – using optical detectors to find the holes for the bolts – and add the bumpers. Seats are mounted automatically and fixed into place, and assembly is completed with the fitting of pre-assembled doors.

Final adjustments and checks are handled automatically. A simulator replicates rough-surface driving and then automatically adjusts the suspension.

Fluids are added automatically, including gasoline. A robot pushes up the flap and reads engine specifications to determine what type of fuel is needed.[10]

This plant in 1989 had 439 robots, 481 automatic guided vehicles, and a large variety of other high-technology features.

From the late 1970s to the late 1980s Fiat's overall labor productivity in cars approximately doubled. It managed to become both a volume and a specialist carmaker, with the Alfa badge for sporty cars and Lancia for luxury, like VW with its Audi marque, and Peugeot with some Citroën models. British Leyland failed to succeed with this strategy.

VOLKSWAGEN

Volkswagen gradually phased out its Beetle model in the 1970s. In Germany the last one was made at the Emden plant in January 1978 for a total of 19.3 million, of which some 5 million found buyers in the United States. Production of this car continued on a small scale in Brazil, Mexico, and Nigeria so that over 20 million had been built by 1990. In a difficult transition VW began selling new models, such as the Golf starting in 1974, with water-cooled engines in front. Its competitive situation in the United States crumbled, by 1976 selling just 203,000 (along with 46,000 Audi models), compared to 583,000 in 1970, and its dealers there were defecting to Japanese makes. From 1970 to 1976 Toyota and Nissan alone increased their U.S. sales by almost exactly the number that VW lost. VW's management decided the only way to protect its franchise in the United States from further erosion was to manufacture there, to offset high German labor costs and the high rate of the deutsche mark against the dollar. In 1976 VW bought a vacant factory in Westmoreland, Pennsylvania, from Chrysler, and, with generous subsidies from Pennsylvania, it equipped and opened an assembly plant in 1978. It was a disappointment. Only once (in 1980) did this branch turn out over 200,000 cars, and from 1983 it usually made less than 100,000, so VW finally closed it in 1988 and returned to direct shipments of its cars from Germany or from its plants in Mexico or Brazil. The Japanese had overwhelmed VW in the U.S. market. In 1990 the Sony company moved into the Westmoreland factory to make television tubes.

VW's operations in Brazil were troubled by that government's financial mismanagement, and in 1986 VW and Ford finally merged their operations in Brazil and Argentina into a joint venture called Autolatina. Production was strong in Brazil, but financial results were weak. VW also took over the Seat company in Spain. VW began its connection with Seat by arranging for it to make VW's very small Polo model in Pamplona. Then, in 1986, the Spanish government, desperate to unload Seat, paid off Seat's $1.7 billion debt and promised to invest $500 million more and to pay the pensions for 4,500 surplus workers in return for VW taking control and investing another $500 million. By 1988 VW owned 83 percent of Seat, and this firm had regained production leadership in Spain from Fasa-Renault. In the early 1990s VW had plans to build a new assembly plant near Barcelona that would put together subassemblies shipped from Germany. Spain's entrance into the European Economic Community ended protectionism there.

At home, VW with its Audi subsidiary maintained production and sales leadership in Germany but suffered problems in the early 1980s. At its head, Carl H. Hahn replaced the ailing Toni Schmücker in 1982. Hahn had presided over VW of America's salad days of the 1960s, then went to the Continental rubber company to turn it around and came back to VW in time for the introduction of the Golf II model in 1984. It was a great success on the market and returned VW to profitability. VW gained a little more freedom of action in 1988 when the federal government of Germany sold its remaining 16 percent share of VW stock to the public. Although the state of Lower Saxony retained its 20 percent share, it seemed likely, in the early 1990s, that VW would have more flexibility in moving manufacturing operations out of Germany and discharging surplus labor. Autoworkers' wages and fringe benefits in Germany had become the highest in the world, after Sweden.

In the late 1980s Hahn began a series of major VW investments that would total the immense sum of about $38 billion by 1998. In addition to the preparation of new models by its German engineering staff, this involved a new car plant in East Germany; over $5 billion to be invested in the Czech Skoda works for a minority interest in that firm – an interest that would grow to a majority in a few years; a controlling share in the Bratislava, Czechoslovakia, auto concern; a new plant in Spain and the joint venture with Ford in Portugal; an assembly plant in Changchun, China; and a major expansion of its works in Puebla, Mexico. All this investment assumed that auto markets would continue to expand in Europe and the world and that VW would win its share despite vigorous competition in most of these markets. Although Japanese cars were taking 15 percent of the West German market by the mid-1980s, VW was willing to work with Japanese firms. It licensed Nissan to make a VW model for sale in Japan and in 1987 arranged to make a few thousand Toyota pickup trucks in Germany yearly, with a domestic content of about 50 percent.

RENAULT AND PEUGEOT

Renault did quite well in the 1970s as it had several small, fuel-efficient models. It continued to emphasize exports and tried to return to the U.S. market, working with the weakest of the American firms, American Motors Corporation, which had an extensive dealer network. By 1980 Renault had invested enough in AMC to own 46.4 percent of its equity, a controlling interest, and was selling about 20,000 annually of its subcompact, the R-5 (or Le Car), in North America. Thereafter Renault arranged to have a new model, the R-9 (the Alliance), put together in the main AMC plant in Kenosha, Wisconsin, with a locally made body. Renault aimed for annual sales of 200,000, which looked realistic when U.S. critics liked the car and its low price. The Alliance and its variant the Encore reached sales of 177,416 in 1984, but after a year or two owners of the car began to have mechanical problems with it, word spread, and sales dropped sharply.

Renault also bought a controlling interest in the Mack truck company by 1983 and sold several thousand vehicles a year through it. When Mack fell into financial difficulties in 1990 Renault bought full ownership.

In the increasingly competitive market of the 1980s, Renault began to have problems in Europe. To maintain its market share in cars it cut prices, but labor costs could not be cut, as labor was far from docile after Socialist François Mitterrand was elected president in 1981 and installed a Socialist cabinet with Communist participation. The result was large deficits for Renault that put its management at risk when the Mitterrand regime changed its policy from traditional socialist nationalization and welfare toward more freedom of enterprise. The government had taken over many of France's larger businesses, and now it expected them to become profitable. Weighed down by huge deficits, Bernard Hanon, Renault's president, had to resign in favor of Georges Besse, who had brought the large, recently nationalized aluminum and chemical firm Pechiney back to profitability. Besse was tough. In two years he slashed the labor force by 25 percent to 79,000, held wages steady and cut bonuses, reduced output, and eliminated such luxuries as racing. Employment at the mother plant at Billancourt, a stronghold of CGT and Communist power, was cut to 5,000 from its peak of 30,000. Then Besse, not a popular figure, was murdered by terrorists in November 1986. The killers appeared to be more concerned about Renault's policy in South Africa than in France. The government replaced him with Raymond Lévy, who continued the cost cutting and cast loose the money-losing AMC in March 1987, selling Renault's share to Chrysler for $200 million plus an additional sum to be determined later. Renault had invested $645 million in AMC since 1979, during which AMC had reported losses of $750 million.

Renault returned to profitability but lost market share in Europe, from 14.6 percent in 1982 to 10.6 percent in 1986 and 9.8 percent in 1990. Both Besse and Lévy began to place a higher priority on quality, where Renault had fallen behind some of its European and Japanese competition.

In 1987 the French government decided to convert Renault from a *régie* to an ordinary stock corporation, with the government, at least for a time, holding all the shares. The major obstacle this plan encountered was the large debt Renault owed to state-owned banks, about $2 billion. The government proposed to cancel this debt – which would amount to a subsidy–and in return cut production capacity in both cars (by 15 percent) and trucks (by 30 percent). After long negotiations and some changes in the plan, the European Economic Commission and the French parliament agreed to changing Renault's legal status. Thereupon Renault and Volvo agreed to a closer relationship in which each owned a substantial share of the other.

France's other major auto firm, Peugeot, grew to world importance and remained there despite some bumps in the road. Its acquisition of Citroën raised the company's total output to 1.4 million by 1976, slightly more than Renault. Jean-Paul Parayre, a young former civil servant, took over as chief executive in 1977 and picked up another presumed bargain the next year, Chrysler's European operations. The total output of the group made it Europe's largest producer in 1979. Peugeot retained Citroën's separate identity, for this firm had many loyal customers and an impressive engineering staff, but it gradually integrated the two divisions' manufacturing. The names Simca and Chrysler had little attraction in France or Europe, so Peugeot dropped them and resurrected the name Talbot, from an Anglo-French car company in the period 1904-38, for the former Chrysler European operations.

Peugeot did not have enough small cars to meet the shift in the market in 1980 after the second oil shock, so its sales dropped sharply. This required temporary worker layoffs and vigorous efforts to make permanent employment reductions. The most serious such contraction came in the former Ford-Simca-Chrysler factory at Poissy, west of Paris, where about half the workers were North African. Jacques Calvet, who became Peugeot's chief operating officer in 1984, was aggressive in cutting costs by reducing employment and simplifying Peugeot's model range. Ultimately, the group cut its employment from 218,000 to 160,000. Output hit bottom in 1984, but in that year Peugeot began to revive financially, at the same time Renault was approaching its most difficult years. In 1988 Peugeot dropped the Talbot name and the next year overtook Renault again as the largest French vehicle builder.

For decades Peugeot machines sold very well in Africa, but Japanese competition intensified there. Several times Peugeot launched attacks on the U.S. market but failed to take many sales from the Japanese or European specialist automakers. In Britain, Peugeot's Talbot UK division declined. It closed the factory in Linwood, Scotland, but Peugeot did invest a considerable sum to assemble one of its French models in the Ryton factory near Coventry. Its other plant in

Coventry reduced operations in 1987, when Peugeot ended the contract to sell kits of Hillman cars to Iran. Early in 1989, however, this relationship resumed when Peugeot agreed on a new 10-year contract to supply kits of Peugeot models from England for assembly in Tehran.

As the 1980s ended, six volume car producers remained in Western Europe, as BL-Rover dropped from this category. All had become profitable again after difficult restructurings forced by the end of the market's long expansion. The more competitive climate had required them to shed labor, introduce more mechanization, and raise quality. All of them saw the Japanese as their chief threat in the 1990s, but the 1989 Revolutions opened up Eastern Europe as a new area to develop.

THE SPECIALISTS

Although specialist car builders disappeared in the United States before and after the Second World War, in Europe a few succeeded in retaining their independence, although occasionally one would fall into the clutches of a volume carmaker – in the late 1980s, Alfa Romeo to Fiat, Jaguar to Ford, and Saab to General Motors. The specialist carmaker had to ask high prices and sell enough cars to periodically finance the development of a new model in order to maintain its image as a quality-conscious innovator. As development costs climbed with more government regulations on emissions and safety, and as consumer expectations rose, the specialist had to cut costs by obtaining more components either from subcontractors or from the volume producers. But as these firms came closer to being simple assemblers their unique appeal would wane. If perceptions of the quality of their cars dropped, trouble would quickly follow, as with Jaguar in the late 1970s. If the clientele disliked a new model it could mean disaster. In the face of all these looming risks, some of Europe's specialists stabilized their operations through diversification.

Daimler-Benz, the most successful of this group, made more Mercedes-Benz cars than BL-Rovers after 1980. The Mercedes-Benz's quality engineering and manufacturing, along with good marketing and service, won it a strong reputation throughout the world. Its American sales of about 80,000 per year in the 1980s accounted for some 16 percent of production. In Europe its best export markets were the other

TABLE 13.3   U.S. IMPORTS OF EUROPEAN CARS AND TRUCKS, 1980s*

1980		1988	
Volkswagen	92,382	Volkswagen-Audi	191,741
Mercedes-Benz	57,941	Volvo	98,497
Volvo	56,909	Mercedes-Benz	83,727
Audi	42,737	BMW	73,359
Fiat	37,184	Saab	38,490
BMW	37,017	Yugo	31,545
Renault	28,909	Jaguar	20,727
MG	13,688	Porsche	15,732
Saab	13,558	Sterling	8,901
Peugeot	12,930	Peugeot	6,712
Porsche	10,597	Alfa Romeo	4,476
Total Europe	661,801		574,540

* Imports by Ford and GM from European subsidiaries are not listed but are included in the totals along with small numbers from other European makers.

large countries, including Spain. Japan emerged as a sizable buyer of Mercedes-Benz cars, taking 31,500 in 1989.

Nevertheless, Daimler-Benz's primary importance lay in trucks and buses, where it became the world leader (excluding pickup and personal models). Here, as in cars, it was a leader in diesel technology. As tariff barriers fell it expanded truck sales in Europe and won a small share of the light-heavy market in the United States. In 1981 it bought the important Freightliner truck manufacturing firm of Portland, Oregon. Daimler-Benz did much of its truck assembly and some parts manufacturing overseas, with operations in 42 countries by 1988. In 1990 Daimler-Benz agreed to begin making trucks at the East German works in Ludwigsfelde.

Daimler-Benz also decided to diversify into other areas in the 1980s, especially under the leadership of Edzard Reuter (unusual for this firm in being a Social Democrat), the son of Ernst Reuter, former mayor of Berlin. Among German concerns, Daimler-Benz acquired the old electrical equipment firm AEG, the jet-engine maker MTU, and the aircraft manufacturers Dornier and Messerschmitt-Boelkow-Blohm. In 1990 it reached an open-ended agreement with the Japanese

TABLE 13.4   WEST EUROPEAN MOTOR-VEHICLE PRODUCTION, 1987

	Number	% of total
Passenger cars		
VW-Audi-Seat	2,179,735	17.9
Peugeot-Citroën	1,761,613	14.4
Fiat-Lancia-Alfa	1,692,932	13.9
Renault	1,520,253	12.5
Ford	1,487,683	12.2
GM-Opel	1,367,397	11.2
Mercedes-Benz	595,765	4.9
Rover	468,845	3.8
BMW	442,776	3.6
Volvo	422,912	3.5
Saab	134,112	1.1
Porsche	48,520	0.4
Jaguar	47,960	0.4
Others	27,785	0.2
Total	12,198,288	100.0
Trucks*		
Daimler-Benz	91,748	26.5
Iveco	69,811	20.1
Renault RVI	44,641	12.9
Volvo	35,399	10.2
Leyland Daf	28,765	8.3
Scania	27,261	7.9
MAN	21,023	6.1
Enasa-Pegaso	9,517	2.7
Motor Iberica	4,299	1.2
GM-Bedford	3,508	1.0
Others	10,807	3.1
Total	346,779	100.0

* over 3.5 tons gross vehicle weight

Source: World Motor Vehicle Data, 1989, 123. Various sources present different figures depending on how trucks are defined and how parts exports are accounted for.

conglomerate Mitsubishi to cooperate closely on industrial activities. The first production project of this entente is to jointly make a new four-wheel-drive vehicle.

The Munich-based BMW began to grow rapidly in the 1970s, selling largely in Germany first, then to the rest of Europe and the United States. In the late 1980s, 35 to 40 percent of BMWs were sold on the domestic market, a similar share in Europe outside Germany, and some 15 percent in the United States. Offering quality at high prices, like Mercedes, it found there was room for both companies.

The Porsche works in Stuttgart had been managed since the 1950s by Ferry Porsche, the son of Ferdinand. It engaged heavily in racing and managed to sell enough of its sports models (25,000 to 50,000 annually) to pay for this activity. Porsche developed its largest market in the United States.

As Volvo from the 1960s on expanded its output and solidified its markets in North America and the European Community, it tackled a growing problem of worker alienation as exhibited by high rates of turnover (30 percent) and absenteeism (20 percent). The company decided that the rising educational level of its workers had brought higher expectations, left unsatisfied by their current jobs. So at its various plants it changed operations to incorporate more content and responsibility into the workers' tasks. In many cases employees inspected their own work. Volvo then incorporated results from these experiments in a new assembly plant opened at Kalmar in 1974. In this small factory (600 employees making 30,000 cars a year) workers in teams of 15 or 20 were assigned to an area or "island" to perform some task of assembly, with tasks rotating among team members. Gone was the rigid assembly line, for the cars moved on individual battery-powered carriers. Computers kept track of each carrier and transmitted instructions about each car to the workers, permitting extensive flexibility. Numerous amenities made the factory a pleasant place to work. Although the result satisfied Volvo, absenteeism did not drop to the desired level. Many other auto firms in Europe and North America adopted parts of the Volvo scheme in their plants, especially the assembly islands.

In 1988 Volvo opened a second small assembly operation at Uddevalla in which the cars did not move at all; instead, 10-person teams put together major components, including engines and transmissions, and then assembled the car with readily available parts. Each team turned out four cars a shift. Forty-five percent of the workers were women, and there was only one robot in the entire plant.[11] This approach clearly was the opposite of the extreme automation of the Fiat Cassino works. Uddevalla resembled auto assembly of the pre-1914 period, of course, but with much greater mechanization of parts manufacture. Its flexibility turned out cars that were almost custom-built, a growing trend in the middle- and upper-price ranges.

The restless and imaginative chairman of Volvo since 1971, Pehr Gyllenhammar, pushed these changes in manufacturing, always in close consultation with the labor union. He announced, "I want the people in a team to be able to go home at night and really say, 'I built that car.' That is my dream."[12] By 1991, however, it appeared that the Uddevalla factory could not compete with more traditional auto plants, and it may have to be rebuilt.

Gyllenhammar tried in many ways to expand Volvo's markets and cut costs. Since the early 1970s Volvo has developed a close relationship with the Netherlands' DAF company, which in the 1980s made about 100,000 small Volvo cars a year, about as many as were assembled in Belgium. Volvo had also planned in the 1970s to assemble cars in the United States, in Virginia, but decided instead to use its facility there for its truck operations. Gyllenhammar tried to merge with Saab in 1977, but the two firms did not reach agreement. Later, he offered 40 percent of Volvo to Norway for rights to explore in a North Sea oil field, but his shareholders vetoed this scheme. In 1988 Volvo bought the bus operations of British Leyland, making it the largest bus manufacturer in Western Europe, about 5,000 capacity, ahead of Daimler-Benz. Then in 1989 Volvo and Renault reached a close technical and manufacturing arrangement. Volvo bought a 20 percent share in Renault and 45 percent of Renault Véhicules Industriels. Renault purchased 25 percent of Volvo cars and 45 percent of Volvo trucks.

Both of these companies had a strong interest in the American truck market. Renault owned Mack trucks; Volvo had begun to market trucks in the United States in the 1970s, then bought the bankrupt White truck company in 1981, which won it a valuable dealer network. Volvo continued making White trucks and assembled its own in the United States as well, about 2,000 a year. In 1986 General Motors relinquished control of its heavy-truck operations to Volvo, which made the Swedish firm one of the world leaders in heavy trucks, along with Daimler-Benz and Renault Mack. The Renault-Volvo arrangment makes it the largest heavy-truck group in the world and brings a top-of-the-line car to Renault. In the early 1990s, it was not yet clear how fruitful the cooperation would be between these two firms of quite different cultures. As an added complication, in 1991 Volvo announced that it would work with the Japanese firm Mitsubishi to make a car in the plant Volvo operated in the Netherlands; Renault would continue to be a major supplier of components to this factory.

Although the other Swedish specialist, Saab, scored well with its Scania heavy trucks in Europe, its cars lost money in the 1980s, and it searched for a partner with deep pockets who would not try to dominate the business. Approaches to Volvo and Fiat did not work out, but in November 1989 General Motors agreed to pay Saab $500 million for a half-interest in a joint venture to make Saab cars, called Saab Automobile. This cost GM one-fifth of the amount that Ford had paid for Jaguar, for a half-interest in a company that made about three times as many cars. GM gained badly needed manufacturing capacity and a luxury car name, something it desperately wanted in Europe. It hoped to employ Saab to challenge Mercedes and BMW, using Saab as Fiat used Lancia and as VW used Audi. Saab Automobile would benefit, in turn, from GM's financial strength and the opportunity to buy parts from it. It soon became clear that GM would dominate Saab Automobile. To stanch heavy financial losses, it closed the firm's new plant in Malmö, Sweden, built on the lines of Volvo's efforts to bring more humanism to car making.

The long-run prospects for the independent specialized automakers in Europe looked dim in the early 1990s. The most likely future for them seemed foreshadowed in the United States and Japan, where the volume car firms controlled this segment through separate divisions.

14

THE INDUSTRY'S PAST AND FUTURE

Over 100 years after the automobile industry began in Germany and France around 1890 it had become and would remain a major economic activity in Europe. The firms that succeeded in the motorcar business generally were the ones that identified a market and offered this market a product at a reasonable price–Renault with taxicabs before 1914, Citroën and Austin with small cars in the 1920s, VW and Fiat with small cars in the 1960s, Mercedes-Benz, BMW, and Volvo with quality cars (sometimes at inflated prices) for the affluent in the 1970s and 1980s. Reasonable price required a management that understood how to manufacture cars in large numbers, something the Europeans largely learned from American practice.

As the industry in Europe matured after 1945, those leaders who recognized its scientific character–as opposed to those who still acted according to marketing hunches and cut-and-try engineering–would be successful. But this science was expensive. With few exceptions, only large companies with deep financial resources would prevail. The Audis, Lancias, and Jaguars could not go it alone any more. Innovation paid off, but only when carefully tested. Rushing it to the market could lead to disaster.

Generally, Europe produced more innovation in the cars themselves than did the United States, and certainly this was the case after 1945. The strong product competition in Europe, especially toward the expensive end of the market where mechanically knowledgeable customers might reward engineering excellence, explains this, along with the marketing that emphasized cars' engineering qualities rather than brute horsepower or living-room comfort. After the Second World War, while U.S. automakers busied themselves with body styling and gadgets of tertiary importance, the Europeans developed steel-belted radial tires, disc brakes, fuel injection, turbo diesel engines, and other mechanical improvements. The drift of American companies away from

TABLE 14.1   MOTOR VEHICLES PER 1,000 POPULATION, 1974-1987

	1974	1978	1983	1987
West Germany	301	376	429	500
France	335	380	433	445
Italy	277	323	390	430
Britain	279	296	327	406
Spain	150	211	269	305
Czechoslovakia	104	153	187	201
Soviet Union	33	49	70	76
U.S.	622	678	700	723

Source: Calculated from *Facts & Figures* (Detroit: Motor Vehicle Manufacturers Association of the United States, various years).

advanced engineering cost them a large share of their own market in the 1970s and 1980s.

Americans had taught much to the European auto industry: mass-production methods from about 1910 into the 1950s, sophisticated techniques of planning, accounting, market research, and service after the sale. And the American-owned firms in Europe had shown that they could succeed there from the 1930s onward, helped by their strong capital resources and offering cars for that market produced and sold by American methods.

Many challenges confronted the European automobile industry in the 1990s. One was safety. With all the new drivers crowding onto European streets and highways in a single generation after 1950, it is not surprising that auto accidents and deaths became a major problem. The Soviet Union held the worst record, recording some 60,000 traffic deaths in 1989, eight to nine times the rate per million vehicles as in the major West European countries. As drivers matured and roads improved traffic fatality rates fell, but there were vigorous arguments about speed limits on expressways. Although such regulations came into force in most countries for reasons of safety and fuel economy, a political majority managed to detour such measures in Germany, accepting the argument that the open autobahn had helped bring engineering excellence to German motorcars. A deputy in the

Bundestag proclaimed that the lack of autobahn speed limits was a national treasure.

Traffic congestion continued to snarl activity in most European cities. Many banned auto traffic from certain areas and gave special preferences and subsidies to buses and subways. Few allowed the construction of expressways through the cities, for this would destroy neighborhoods of great historical interest. Exasperated by traffic problems, Madrid raised its penalties to as much as $900 a violation and threatened drunk drivers with six years in prison.

The governments in Europe were slower to act against automobile-caused air pollution than in the United States. This was because there were no major cases of severe pollution similar to Los Angeles to catalyze the issue, and because European car firms cleaned up their engines voluntarily in order to sell them in the United States. The growing environmental movement continued to push the pollution agenda. Eventually this may lead to the wide use of cars powered by electric batteries or hydrogen. Automotive engineers have been experimenting with electric- and hydrogen-powered vehicles for years but have had minimal success in developing a viable model. It appears that little will happen until either petroleum prices rise to double or triple the prices prevalent in the early 1990s or legislation requires automakers to sell vehicles with alternate power sources. A British regulation that delivery trucks cannot be left unattended with the engine running has led to tens of thousands of electric vehicles there, and the California state law requiring that some alternative-fuel-source cars be sold there by the mid-1990s may be the kinds of catalysts that will bring a major shift in automobile technology.

Labor-management conflicts will always be a problem, but for a time it appears that they will recede. With the political extreme Left in serious disarray from the Urals to the Atlantic in the 1980s and terrorism discredited, labor will be less likely to bring political ideologies into the factories. As socialist as well as conservative governments return nationalized firms to the private sector and unions become ever more reformist rather than revolutionary, ideological differences are in decline. Consequently, it will be easier to reach agreements. The appearance of Japanese-managed auto factories in Britain will provide another model of labor-management relations, in addition to the Volvo style of increasing labor's job content and responsibility for quality and the Fiat experiment of wholesale replacement of semiskilled workers by machines.

More vigorous competition will offer the greatest challenge to the European auto industry. In the decades after 1960 more and more automakers began to compete all over the world—nearly 20 by 1991. As this occurred, markets became more fragmented; the numbers of car models rose and the volume produced per model declined. Another Ford Model T or VW Beetle was not on the horizon. And there was a torrent of new technology in transmissions, materials, electronics, and other areas of automobile manufacture.[1] Can the European automakers handle all this change? It took them some 35 years to adopt the Fordist system of production from the United States. What about these recent challenges, especially the Japanese moving into the fragmenting market? Japanese cars, both imported and those produced in European factories, are the most visible signs of the stronger competition. Japanese automakers swiftly expanded their sales in Europe in the 1970s, concurrent with their invasion of North America. As Figure 14.1 shows, their sales to Europe leveled off in the 1980s as the major producing countries limited Japanese imports. Italy restricted them to a minuscule figure, 2,550 in the 1980s, although up to 40,000 may have been imported from elsewhere in Europe.[2] France set a limit of 3 percent of its market for Japanese cars. Under pressure the Japanese agreed to limit sales of their cars on the British market to about 11 percent and on the West German market to about 15 percent. Japanese sales in the smaller European states that did not levy high tariffs or set quotas strongly hint at their competitive threat. In 1987 the Japanese penetration of Ireland's market was 44 percent, of Finland's 41.8 percent, Norway's 37.8 percent, Greece's 35.1 percent, Denmark's 32.8 percent, Austria's 31.2 percent, and Switzerland's 28.9 percent.[3]

After bitter arguments within the European Community an agreement was reached in 1991 between it and the Japanese ministry of international trade and industry to limit Japanese auto imports to the Community to the 1990 level—1.25 million—until 1999. In addition, a gentlemen's agreement provided for a cap of 1.2 million on Japanese cars assembled in the Community. The total would reach about 16 percent of the expected European market in 1999.

The Japanese advantage over U.S. and European carmakers rested on a production system that their auto companies had worked out in the 1950s and 1960s.[4] Rather than the Fordist idea of making very large

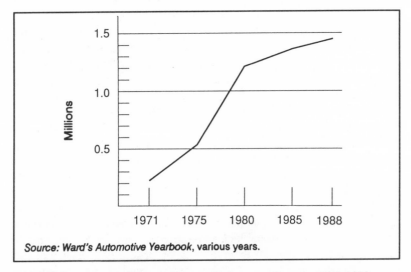

Source: *Ward's Automotive Yearbook*, various years.

FIGURE 14.1 JAPANESE MOTOR-VEHICLE EXPORTS TO EUROPE, 1971-1988

numbers of one model, taking advantage of economies of scale, using extreme division of labor, and mechanizing production and materials handling, the Japanese embraced a flexible post-Fordist system, demand-driven rather than supply-driven.

At first, in the late 1950s and early 1960s, the Japanese firms made cars for a rather small domestic market. To offer it a wide range of models and options, they evolved a flexible or "lean" production system. They organized strong product-development teams that could prepare a new model in slightly over half the time as a European or American firm. The manufacturing system was flexible, using machines that could be reset quickly to make parts on a batch scale rather than single-purpose machines dedicated to making one unchanging part for months on end. Therefore, it was possible to change models quickly and introduce innovations frequently. Widespread use of computers made this flexibility easier to manage. With cooperative labor unions, Japanese firms trained workers to be flexible also, capable of resetting or repairing machines themselves, performing several different jobs, and inspecting their own work. Labor became multiskilled, reversing the de-skilling associated with Fordism and Taylorism. Most workers received a guarantee of lifetime employment and seniority-based pay.

The flexible production system led to low parts inventories at the assembly and subassembly stages, and eventually to almost no inventories or a "just-in-time" delivery system for parts. This in turn required that there be no defective parts, for bad ones would immediately stop production. Here was a key element in the system: halting production immediately was better than building bad parts into dozens or hundreds of cars that would have to be repaired at high cost later. To ensure high-quality parts, the car assemblers developed very close working relationships with their suppliers, for they had to assume that all parts delivered would be perfect. This led to multiyear contracts and single sourcing of parts, and suppliers locating close to the assembler, rarely over two hours away, to ensure tight cooperation in designing parts and reliable delivery.

The various aspects of the Japanese system – rapid product development, flexible production, just-in-time parts delivery, a close working association between assemblers and suppliers, and increased worker responsibility – brought much greater labor productivity than was the case in North American or Europe. Recent scholarly comparisons of auto assembly factories demonstrate this. In 1989, for example, using a large sample of assembly plants in Western Europe, North America, and Japan, an international team of investigators found that the average Japanese volume producer required 16.8 assembly hours to make a car, in North America the average U.S.-owned plant took 24.9 hours, and in Europe the average European-owned plant required 35.5 hours. The study concluded that "average American performance – under unrelenting pressure from the Japanese transplants in North America – has improved dramatically, partly by closing the worst plants, . . . and partly by adopting lean production at others. Europe, by contrast, has not yet begun to close the competitive gap."[5]

In quality, as expressed by defects reported by owners, the Japanese average again led the United States and Europe.[6] The outcome of the Japanese system was high-quality cars that took a growing share of the market in Asia and Africa and could be delivered at competitive prices in North America and Europe. To beat the Japanese imports in Europe the local firms first tried to cut costs by carrying Fordism to an extreme. This is the usual reaction when an old technology is challenged by a new one. The old is refined and taken to

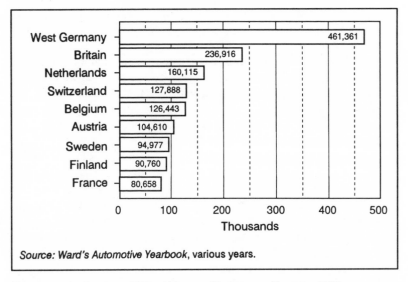

Source: *Ward's Automotive Yearbook*, various years.

FIGURE 14.2 JAPANESE MOTOR-VEHICLE EXPORTS TO EUROPE, 1988

extremes. European automakers created special plants making engines, transmissions, and other components in huge numbers and shipped them to one-product assembly plants that then sold them all over Europe. VW equipped a special production line in Wolfsburg–Halle 54–with robots to form a very mechanized system, but it was not very flexible. The Fiat assembly plant in Cassino has been mentioned. But consumers insisted on buying Japanese cars, so finally even the German government had to limit car imports from Japan.

In the early 1990s it appeared that neither the Volvo plant in Uddevalla nor the Fiat works at Cassino could meet the Japanese competition. Some of those in the European auto industry, after observing the Japanese advance for almost 30 years, could think of nothing better than to call for another 10 years of protection and large government subsidies. The above-mentioned study compares the productivity of average assembly plants, and averages are just that: they conceal individual differences. The same study found that the Ford company in the United States had moved a long way toward adopting the flexible or lean system and that its factory in Hermosillo, Mexico, ranked highest for quality–better than any Japanese plant–and high also in productivity. Transplanted Japanese firms in North America and Europe also ranked high in productivity and quality, demonstrating that the methods worked out by the Japanese companies are not culture-bound: they can work anywhere.[7]

Gradually, the flexible system has been understood by some U.S. and European automakers. The Japanese lead in productivity has been cut since 1980 as the others adopted some segments of their system, but (except in Sweden) they appear to have the greatest difficulty with changing the role of workers in the manufacturing process. This is an important component, but a long adversarial tradition held by both managers and workers will be difficult to overcome. The Japanese precedent suggests, nevertheless, that the day of the semiskilled autoworker will wane in Europe. The new worker will be well-trained and multiskilled. There will be many fewer of them in the new factories, and not many will be immigrants from southern Europe or Africa.

What will bring real change in the development and production of cars will be the presence of factories in Europe (probably Japanese-owned) using a flexible-production system. There are indications that the learning process has begun among auto parts suppliers in Britain, who have been selling to Japanese factories there.

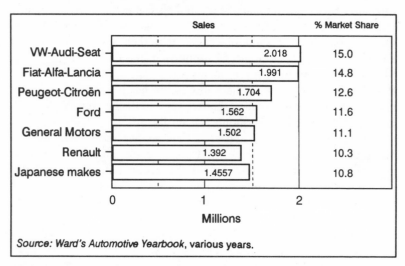

	Sales	% Market Share
VW-Audi-Seat	2.018	15.0
Fiat-Alfa-Lancia	1.991	14.8
Peugeot-Citroën	1.704	12.6
Ford	1.562	11.6
General Motors	1.502	11.1
Renault	1.392	10.3
Japanese makes	1.4557	10.8

Millions

Source: Ward's Automotive Yearbook, various years.

FIGURE 14.3   MANUFACTURER CAR SALES IN EUROPE, 1989

In this very competitive environment, European Community rules will make it harder for governments to bail out auto firms in financial trouble. Will this mean that the firms will follow more cautious policies and take fewer risks because no one will catch them if they fall? The West European auto companies are vigorous. If they maintain this stance and take the best from each other and their overseas competitors rather than retreat into protectionism, they will prosper into the twenty-first century. The sorry state of the East European and Soviet auto industries should be an object lesson on the dangers of protection.

In the late 1980s the Soviet auto industry produced a large number of mediocre cars and trucks. Its labor productivity was about one-fourth that of Western Europe and North America, and it had a poor record in designing vehicles and the factories in which to build them. It had depended on the West to begin its development in the 1930s, to expand it after the Second World War, and to modernize and further expand it in the 1970s. Its problems arose from a lack of competition that weakened efforts to raise efficiency and quality, from the ineffectiveness of central planning, and from a failure to assign enough good engineers to the industry.

The restructuring and privatizing that began in the Soviet states around 1990 aimed to bring autonomy to the productive units. For example, in 1991 the KamAZ truck-building complex was a stock corporation, with about 30 percent of its equity owned by other Soviet enterprises, 5 percent by its workers, and 38 percent by the ministry of automotive machinery, with 27 percent to be sold to other Soviet and foreign purchasers. A board of six presided over the firm, five of whom were from KamAZ management.[8] An early move by this board was to buy diesel engines from the Cummins company of Columbus, Indiana, and to arrange to make these engines itself in the future.

As Soviet firms try to compete in the world, their most difficult task will probably be to shrink their inflated labor forces to levels current elsewhere. The consequent social and political disgruntlement will probably encourage or force the political leadership to continue to protect the industry from foreign competition. At the same time, the automakers will have to import technology, as KamAZ and VAZ are doing. The latter has agreed to buy $1 billion of engine controls from General Motors over five years. The move toward free markets will bring more challenges to the Soviet auto industry, as it has done in Western Europe.

NOTES AND REFERENCES

CHAPTER 1

1. Jacques Ickx, *Ainsi naquit l'automobile* (Lausanne: Edita, 1961), 2: 152-56.

2. Reinhard Hanf, *Im Spannungsfeld zwischen Technik und Markt* (Wiesbaden: Steiner, 1980), 18, 46.

3. Paul Siebertz, *Karl Benz* (Stuttgart: Reclam, 1950), 170-72.

4. Georges Corlin, "Panhard-Levassor, ou cent ans d'industrie," manuscript in the Panhard archives in 1965, pp. 49-50.

CHAPTER 2

1. For a detailed account, see James M. Laux, *In First Gear: The French Automobile Industry to 1914* (Montreal: McGill-Queen's University Press, 1976).

2. *Automotor Journal* 6 (1902): 215.

3. See P. Fridenson, "Une industrie nouvelle: L'Automobile en France jusqu'en 1914," *Revue d'histoire moderne et contemporaine* 19 (1972): 560-62.

4. See W. J. K. Davies, *French Minor Railways* (Dawlish: David & Charles, 1965).

5. Corlin, "Panhard-Levassor," 61.

6. Laux, *In First Gear*, 99, 101.

7. Alexandre Nicolon, "Genèse et développement de l'automobile," *Esprit*, August 1983, 52-53.

CHAPTER 3

1. T. R. Nicholson, *The Birth of the British Motor Car, 1767-1897* (London: Macmillan, 1982), 3: 379.

2. Theo Barker, Introduction to *The Economic and Social Effects of the Spread of Motor Vehicles* (London: Macmillan, 1987), 8.

3. Lawson's activities are well-chronicled in Nicholson, *Birth of the British Motor Car*, vol. 3.

4. *Automotor Journal* 5 (March 1901): 280.

5. Roy Church, *Herbert Austin* (London: Europa, 1979), 1-16.

6. Great Britain, Royal Commission on Motor Cars, *Report* and *Minutes of Evidence*, c.d. 3080 and 3081 (London, 1906), 3081, 157; and *The Engineer* 101 (January-June 1906): 275. Some U.S. firms also imported French castings for engines before 1914.

7. Great Britain, *Parliamentary Papers*, c.d. 7574 (London, 1915), 60.

8. William Plowden, *The Motor Car and Politics (1896-1970)* (London: Bodley Head, 1971), 95n.

9. Ibid., 52.

10. R. J. Irving, "New Industries for Old: Some Investment Decisions of Armstrong Whitworth, 1900-1914," *Business History* 17 (1975): 150-75.

11. Mira Wilkins and Frank E. Hill, *American Business Abroad: Ford on Six Continents* (Detroit: Wayne State University Press, 1964), 51.

12. P. W. S. Andrews and Elizabeth Brunner, *The Life of Lord Nuffield* (Oxford: Basil Blackwell, 1959), and R. J. Overy, *William Morris, Viscount Nuffield* (London: Europa, 1976).

13. Roy Church, "Markets and Marketing in the British Motor Industry before 1914 with Some French Comparisons," *Journal of Transport History*, 3d ser., 3 (1982): 12-19.

14. Taxicab numbers from G. N. Georgano, *A History of the London Taxicab* (Newton Abbot: David & Charles, 1972), 59-60.

15. Robert A. Whitehead, *The Age of the Traction Engine* (London: Ian Allan, 1970).

16. *Automotor Journal* 19 (28 March 1914): 394.

17. John Hibbs, *The History of British Bus Services* (Newton Abbot: David & Charles, 1968), 47-48, 62-63.

18. James Foreman-Peck, "Tariff Protection and Economies of Scale: The British Motor Industry before 1939," *Oxford Economic Papers* 31 (1979): 237-57.

19. For Great Britain, Society of Motor Manufacturers and Traders, *Motor Industry of Great Britain* (London, 1932), 41, gives the higher figure, but this probably includes some double counting of trucks and hackneys. For France, see Laux, *In First Gear*, 196; for Germany, *Statistisches Jahrbuch* (1914), 137; for Italy, ANFIA, *Automobile in cifre* (Turin: ANFIA, 1982), 91.

20. Theodor Heuss, *Robert Bosch* (Tübingen: Wunderlich, 1946); Eugen Diesel, "Robert Bosch," in *From Engines to Autos*, by Eugen Diesel et al. (Chicago: Regnery, 1960), 233-65.

21. Stuart W. Leslie, *Boss Kettering* (New York: Columbia University Press, 1983), 38-50. Clearer descriptions of Kettering's system can be found in *The Automobile* 25 (October 1911): 606, 608, and in *The Horseless Age* 28 (September 1911): 351.

22. Karl Ludvigsen, *Opel: Wheels to the World* (Princeton, N.J.: Automobile Quarterly, 1975).

23. August Horch, *Ich Baute Autos* (Berlin: Schützen, 1937).

24. Annemarie Lange, *Das Wilhelmnische Berlin* (Berlin: Dietz, 1967), 140-41.

25. Werner Oswald, *Mercedes-Benz Personenwagen, 1886-1986* (Stuttgart: Motorbuch Verlag, 1986), 16-17.

26. Guy Jellinek-Mercedes, *My Father, Mr. Mercedes* (Philadelphia: Chilton, 1966).

27. Production numbers from Oswald, *Mercedes-Benz Personenwagen*, 17, 72, and private correspondence from Dr. Otto Nübel. Benz also made 428 trucks and buses in 1909 and Daimler 158.

28. *Statistisches Jahrbuch* (1914): 138.

29. Griffith Borgeson, *Bugatti by Borgeson* (London: Osprey, 1981), clarifies many legends.

30. *Statistisches Jahrbuch* (1914): 137.

31. Helmuth Albrecht et al., *H. Büssing: Mensch, Werk, Erbe* (Göttingen: Vandenhoeck & Rupprecht, 1986).

32. Bruno Bottiglieri, *I Primo quindici anni della Fiat* (Progetto Archivo Storico Fiat), 2d ed. (Milan: Franco Angeli, 1987), 1: 18-23.

33. Duccio Bigazzi, *Il Portello* (Milan: Franco Angeli, 1988), 40-45.

34. Angelo T. Anselmi, *Isotta Fraschini* (Milan: Editoriale Milani, 1977), 56-58, 252-318.

35. Carlo F. Z. Salazar, *Ottant'anni di camion Fiat* (Turin: Gruppo Editoriale Forma, 1983), 54-58, 81.

36. *The Automobile*, 2 August 1906, 146.

37. S. V. Voronkova, "Stroitelstvo Automobilnikh Zavodov . . . ," *Istoricheskiye Zapiske* 78 (1965): 148; William P. Baxter, "The Soviet Passenger Car Industry," *Survey* (London) 19, no. 3 (1973): 218.

CHAPTER 4

1. The British case has been brilliantly described and analyzed by Wayne Lewchuk in *American Technology and the British Vehicle Industry* (New York: Cambridge University Press, 1987).

2. Lewchuk, *British Vehicle Industry*, 72-77; Simonetta Ortaggi, "Cottimo e produttivita nell' industria del primo Novecento," *Rivista di storia contemporanea*, no. 1 (1978): 30.

3. Etienne Riché, *La Situation des ouvriers dans l'industrie automobile* (Paris: Rousseau, 1909), 60-73. A thorough and nuanced account of the French case can be found in P. Fridenson, "Un tournant taylorien de la société français," *Annales, E.S.C.* 42 (1987): 1031-60.

4. *Les Temps nouveaux* (Paris), 4 March and 1 April 1905.

5. David Hounshell, *From the American System to Mass Production, 1800-1932* (Baltimore: Johns Hopkins University Press, 1984), 249-53.

6. Heidrun Homburg, "Anfänge des Taylorsystems in Deutschland vor dem Ersten Weltkrieg," *Geschichte und Gesellschaft* 4 (1978): 180-93.

7. Stefano Musso, *Gli Operai do Torino, 1900-1920* (Milan: Feltrinelli Economica, 1980), 98-99.

8. Laux, *In First Gear*, 170-71.

9. Yves Cohen, "Ernest Mattern, les automobiles Peugeot et le pays de Montbéliard industriel avant et pendant la guerre de 1914-1918" (thesis, Université de Besançon, 1981); and "Ernest Mattern chez Peugeot (1906-1918)," in *Le Taylorisme*, ed. O. Montmollin and O. Pastré (Paris: La Découverte, 1984), 115-26.

10. Lewchuk, *British Vehicle Industry*, 121-30.

11. Paul Collins and Michael Stratton, "From Trestles to Trucks: The Influence of Motor Car Manufacturing on the Design of British Car Factories," *Journal of Transport History* 9 (September 1988): 202; Lewchuk, *British Vehicle Industry*, 156.

12. Anita Kugler, "Von den Werkstaat zum Fliessband," *Geschichte und Gesellschaft* 13 (1987): 316.

13. P. Fridenson, "Herrschaft im Wirtschaftsunternehmen," in *Bürgertum im 19. Jahrhundert*, ed. J. Kocka (Munich: Deutscher Taschenbuch, 1988), 2: 86; and Bernard P. Bellon, "The Workers of Daimler-Untertuerkheim, 1903-1945," Ph.D. diss., Columbia University, 1987, pp. 77, 85, 96.

14. Kugler, "Werkstaat zum Fliessband," 319-22.

15. "Der Fabrikerweiterungsbau der Wandererwerke A.G., Schonau bei Chemnitz," *Zeitschrift des Vereines deutscher Ingenieure* 58 (1914): 281-88.

16. Ortaggi, "Cottimo e produttivita," 51-52 and, more generally on changes at Fiat, 50-58.

17. Bigazzi, *Il Portello*, 50-90, describes in full detail the Darracq and Alfa factory in Milan.

18. Bellon, "Workers of Daimler-Untertuerkheim," 134.

19. Bigazzi, *Il Portello*, 64-65.

CHAPTER 5

1. Quoted in Kugler, "Von den Werkstaat zum Fliessband," 325.

2. Sylvie Schweitzer, *Des Engrenages à la chaîne* (Lyon: Presses universitaires de Lyon, 1982), 56-57.

3. Gilbert Hatry, *Renault usine de guerre* (Paris: Lafourcade, 1978), 68; and P. Fridenson, *Histoire des usines Renault* (Paris: Seuil, 1972), 1: 89-119.

4. P. Fridenson, "The Coming of the Assemby Line to Europe," in *The Dynamics of Science and Technology*, ed. W. Krohn et al. (Dordrecht: D. Reidel, 1978), 161.

5. Cohen, "Ernest Mattern, les automobiles Peugeot," 266-84.

6. Michel Laferrère, *Lyon: Ville industrielle* (Paris: P.U.F., 1960), 375-76, 380-81; Jacques Borgé and N. Viassnoff, *Berliet de Lyon* (Paris: E.P.A., 1981), 96-103.

7. Emmanuel Chadeau, *De Blériot à Dassault: Histoire de l'Industrie aéronautique en France, 1900-1950* (Paris: Fayard, 1987), 100.

8. Unpublished paper by John Morrow, Jr., "The French Automobile Industry in World War I Aviation," pp. 2-5.

9. Wilkins and Hill, *American Business Abroad*, 61-73.

10. Church, *Austin*, 43.

11. Lewchuk, *British Vehicle Industry*, 179.

12. Morrow, "The French Automobile Industry," 17-18; Ian Lloyd, *Rolls-Royce: The Growth of the Firm* (London: Macmillan, 1978), 63-89, 115-26.

13. Stefano Musso, *Gli Operai di Torino, 1900-1920* (Milan: Feltrinelli Economica, 1980), 137.

14. Centro Storico Fiat, "Automezzi Fiat nella guerra mondiale."

15. Centro Storico Fiat, "Il contributo della Fiat nella guerra mondiale."

16. Musso, *Gli Operai di Torino,* 135.

17. Duccio Bigazzi, "Gli operai della catena di montaggio: la Fiat 1922-1943," *Annali, Fondazione G. Feltrinelli* (1979-80): 897.

18. Morrow, "The French Automobile Industry," 18-19.

19. Voronkova, "Stroitelstvo Automobilnikh Zavodov . . . ," 168-69.

20. J. A. Gilles, *Flugmotoren 1910 bis 1918* (Frankfurt am Main: Mittler, 1971), 122-23.

21. Bellon, "Workers of Daimler-Untertuerkheim," 183, 202-5.

22. Ibid., 192.

23. Bellon details this little-remembered affair in "Workers of Daimler-Untertuerkheim," 206-33, 266.

24. E. von Ludendorff, *Ludendorff's Own Story* (New York: Harper, 1919), 2: 202-4.

25. Denis Bishop and C. Ellis, *Vehicles at War* (South Brunswick, N.J.: A. S. Barnes, 1979), 51.

26. H. C. von Seherr-Thoss, *Die deutsche Automibilindustrie* (Stuttgart: Deutsche Verlag, 1974), 62.

27. Kugler, "Von den Werkstaat zum Fliessband," 325.

28. W. F. Bradley, "German Automotive Factories Prepare for Competition," *Automotive Industries* 43 (25 November 1920): 1054.

29. Robert J. Wegs, *Die osterreichische Kriegswirtschaft, 1914-1918* (Wien: Schendl, 1979), 111.

30. For a discussion of the military use of trucks, see James M. Laux, "Trucks in the West during the First World War," *Journal of Transport History*, 3d ser., 6, no. 2 (September 1985): 64-70.

CHAPTER 6

1. See James Foreman-Peck, "The American Challenge of the Twenties," *Journal of Economic History* 42 (1982): 865-82.

2. Schweitzer, *Des Engrenages à la chaîne*, 21-26, 28-37, 57. A colorful memoir is Charles Rocherand, *L'Histoire d'André Citroën*, 2d ed. (Paris Christian, 1979).

3. Pierre Dumont, *Quai Javel, Quai André Citroën* (Paris: EPA, 1973), 427, appendices.

4. Hubert Bonin, "Les Banques face au cas Citroën (1919-1930)," *Revue d'histoire moderne et contemporaine* 32 (1985): 75-98.

5. Fridenson, *Usines Renault*, 1: 121-92, provides a wealth of information on and interpretation of Renault in the 1920s.

6. Daniel Henri, "La Société Anonyme des Automobile Peugeot de 1918 à 1930" (thesis, Université de Paris, 1983), is a thorough examination, summarized in D. Henri, "Comptes, mécomptes et redressment d'une gestion industrielle: Les Automobiles Peugeot de 1918 à 1930," *Revue d'histoire moderne et contemporaine* 32 (1985): 30-74.

7. Wilkins and Hill, *American Business Abroad*, 68, 97, 140.

8. *Machinery* (London), 15 September 1927, 738-39.

9. D. G. Rhys, "Concentration in the Interwar Motor Industry," *Journal of Transport History*, n.s. 3 (1976): 244.

10. Lewchuk, *British Vehicle Industry*, 155.

11. Wilkins and Hill, *American Business Abroad*, 189-99.

12. George Oliver, *The Rover* (London: Cassell, 1971), 68-81.

13. Lewchuk, *British Vehicle Industry*, 169.

14. Church, *Austin*, 76-77, 82, 84, 94-96.

15. Lewchuk, *British Vehicle Industry*, 160-92.

16. *Automobile Engineer* (London), 20 August 1930, 284.

17. F. M. L. Thompson, "Nineteenth Century Horse Sense," *Economic History Review* 29 (1976): 80.

18. Bellon, "Workers of Daimler-Untertuerkheim," 358-61.

19. "The Works of Adam Opel," *Automobile Engineer* (London), 18 September 1928, 314-19.

20. Bellon, "Workers of Daimler-Untertuerkheim," 321-28.

21. Werner Oswald, *Deutsche Autos, 1920-1945* (Stuttgart: Motorbuch Verlag, 1983), 403.

22. Gerhard Neumann, *Herman the German* (New York: Morrow, 1984), 19.

23. Oswald, *Deutsche Autos,* 401.

24. James M. Laux, "Les Moteurs Diesel pour les transports," *Culture technique,* no. 19 (March 1989): 20-23.

25. John M. Cammett, *Antonio Gramsci and the Origins of Italian Communism* (Stanford: Stanford University Press, 1967), 96-120, has an account of the 1920 struggles.

26. J. A. Lucas and F. E. Burdrof, "Fiat Automobile Production Methods," *American Machinist* 60 (24 April 1924): 605-7.

27. Michael Sedgwick, *Fiat* (New York: Arco, 1974), 114.

28. Duccio Bigazzi, "Management Strategies in the Italian Car Industry, 1906-1945," in *The Automobile Industry and Its Workers*, ed. S. Tolliday and J. Zeitlin (New York: St. Martin's Press, 1987), 81-85; idem., "Gli operai della catena di montaggio," *Annali, Fondazione G. Feltrinelli*, 948.

29. Piero Puricelli, "Autostrada," in *Enciclopedia Italiana* (Milan: Rizzoli, 1929); a thorough description is in Bruno Bolis, "Le Autostrade Italiane," *Strade*, n.s. 21 (1939): 574-84, 614-23.

30. Nils Kinch, "Volvo – Drömmen som Blev Verklighet," *Tvärsnitt* 2 (1988): 27-31; Christer Olsson, *Volvo: Sixty Years of Truckmaking* (Malmö: Förlagshuset Norden, 1987), 14-20, 218; and Bjorn Eric Lindh, *Volvo: The Cars from the 20s to the 80s* (Malmö: Förlagshuset Norden, 1984), 9-14.

CHAPTER 7

1. U.S. production in 1937 was much higher than in 1938, a recession year. In Europe the output was about the same in the two years. Almost all Canadian production in 1937 (207, 463) was controlled by U.S. firms.

2. Overy, *William Morris*, 23.

3. D. G. Rhys, *The Motor Industry* (London: Butterworths, 1972), 189.

4. Agatha Chapman and R. Knight, *Wages and Salaries in the United Kingdom, 1920-1938* (Cambridge: Cambridge University Press, 1953), 18, 22.

5. Martin Adeney, *The Motor Makers* (London: Collins, 1988), 136-41.

6. Hibbs, *British Bus Services*, 108-26; T. C. Barker and C. I. Savage, *An Economic History of Transport in Britain*, 3d ed. (London: Hutchinson, 1974), 161-210.

7. Price indexes from *Statistisches Jahrbuch*; wages from Gerhard Fry, *Wages in Germany* (Princeton, N.J.: Princeton University Press, 1960), assuming employment for 48 weeks in the year.

8. R. J. Overy, " Cars, Roads, and Economic Recovery in Germany, 1932-9," *Economic History Review* 28 (1975): 473-74.

9. Ibid., 475.

10. L. Rostas, "Industrial Production, Productivity and Distribution in Britain, Germany and the United States," *Economic Journal* 53 (1943): 46, 51.

11. Oswald, *Deutsche Autos,* 309.

12. Wilkins and Hill, *American Business Abroad,* 270-84.

13. K. B. Hopfinger, *The Volkswagen Story,* 3d ed. (Cambridge, Mass.: Bentley, 1971), and W. H. Nelson, *Small Wonder,* rev. ed. (Boston: Little Brown, 1967), are detailed accounts.

14. Nelson, *Small Wonder,* 67-71.

15. *Statistisches Jahrbuch* (1939-40), 237. Presumably, all or most of these vehicles were for civilian use.

16. Examples are Wolfgang Sauer, in K. D. Bracher et al., *Die National-sozialistische Machtergreifung* (Köln: Westdeutscher Verlag, 1960), 785, 801; Arthur Schweitzer, *Big Business in the Third Reich* (Bloomington: Indiana University Press, 1964), 297, 341-43; Karl Häuser in G. Stolper et al., *The German Economy, 1870 to the Present* (New York: Harcourt, Brace & World, 1967), 152; and Hans Peter Blauel, *Strength through Joy* (London: Secker & Warburg, 1973), 87. This issue is thoroughly ventilated in R. J. Overy, "Transportation and Rearmament in the Third Reich," *Historical Journal* 16 (1973): 389-409.

17. U.S. Strategic Bombing Survey (USSBS), *Report 77: German Motor Vehicles Industry* (Washington, D.C., 1947), 2-3. This source gives somewhat larger numbers for total trucks made in the 1930s than those presented in the *Statistisches Jahrbuch.* Probably some military trucks were not included in the latter's totals.

18. Sauer, *Die Nationalsozialistische Machtergreifung,* 785, 801; Schweitzer, *Big Business in the Third Reich,* 297, 341-43; T. L. Jarman, *The Rise and Fall of Nazi Germany* (London: Cresset, 1955), 192; Hannah Vogt, *The Burden of Guilt* (New York: Oxford University Press, 1964), 149. For a corrective, see Overy, "Transportation and Rearmament."

19. P. Kandaouroff, "Les Autoroutes en Allemagne," *Génie Civil* 116 (23 March 1940): 193-94.

20. T. H. MacDonald (U.S. commissioner of public roads), "Highways and National Defense," *American Highways* 19, no. 4 (October 1940): 12.

21. USSBS, *The Effects of Strategic Bombing on the German War Economy* (Washington, D.C., 1945), 73-75; Arnold Krammer, "Fueling the Third Reich," *Technology and Culture* 19 (1978): 394-407.

22. Fridenson, *Usines Renault,* 1: 199-200.

23. Reliable information on the fall of André Citroën is difficult to find. Among the better discussions are Fabien Sabates and S. Schweitzer, *André Citroën: Les Chevrons de la gloire* (Paris: EPA, 1980), 287-313; Hubert Bonin, "Les Banques ont-elles sauvé Citroën? (1933-1935)," *Histoire, Economie et Société* 3

(1984): 453-72; Rocherand, *L'Histoire d'André Citroën*, 231-57; and J. A. Grégoire, *50 ans d'Automobile* (Paris: Flammarion, 1974), 231-338. Press reports that quote official documents include *Le Temps* (Paris), 22 December 1934, 4 February 1935, and 21 December 1935; *Financial Times* (London), 22 and 24 December 1934, 4 and 8 February 1935, 24 June 1935, 2 October 1935.

24. Grégoire, *50 ans d'Automobile*, 326.

25. Wilkins and Hill, *American Business Abroad*, 248-50, 263-69.

26. Joseph Jones, *The Politics of Transport in Twentieth-Century France* (Montreal: McGill-Queen's University Press, 1984), 28-98, 234.

27. Bernard Badie, "Les Grèves de 1936 aux usines Renault," *Le Mouvement Social*, no. 81 (1972): 69-109.

28. J. P. Depretto and Sylvie V. Schweitzer, *Le Communisme à l'usine* (Roubaix: EDIRES, 1984), 207-79.

29. Wilkins and Hill, *American Business Abroad*, 266-67.

30. Bigazzi, "Management Strategies,"86; idem., "Gli operai della catena di montaggio," *Annali, Fondazione G. Feltrinelli*, 938-47; Valerio Castronovo, *Giovanni Agnelli* (Turin: UTET, 1971), 549-55.

31. Dante Giacosa, *I miei 40 anni di progettazione alla Fiat* (Milan: Automobilia, 1979), 27-40. Although the Topolino was cheaper for Italians than the Balilla, the prices of the two in dollars do not reflect this because of the U.S. devaluation of the dollar in 1933.

32. The anecdotes are reported in Sedgwick, *Fiat*, 218-19.

33. Giovanni Contini, "Politics, Law and Shop Floor Bargaining in Postwar Italy," in *Shop Floor Bargaining and the State*, ed. S. Tolliday and J. Zeitlin (Cambridge: Cambridge University Press, 1985), 195-96.

34. Kinch, "Volvo," 31; Olsson, "Truckmaking," 218.

35. Wilkins and Hill, *American Business Abroad*, 208-27; Christine White, "Ford in Russia: In Pursuit of the Chimerical Market," *Business History* 28, no. 4 (October 1986): 77-104; Antony C. Sutton, *Western Technology and Soviet Economic Development* (Stanford, Calif.: Stanford University Press/Hoover Institution, 1967-68), 1: 243-49, 2: 177-94; and George D. Holliday, *Technology Transfer to the USSR, 1927-37 and 1966-75* (Boulder, Colo.: Westview Press, 1979), 114-36.

36. J. V. Stalin, *Works* (Moscow: Foreign Languages Publishing House, 1955), 13: 121.

37. Robert Conquest, ed., *Industrial Workers in the U.S.S.R.* (New York: Praeger, 1967), 45-123; Bruno Grancelli, *Soviet Management and Labor Relations* (Boston: Allen & Unwin, 1988), 35-54; Lewis H. Siegelbaum, *Stakhanovism and the Politics of Productivity in the U.S.S.R., 1935-1941* (New York: Cambridge University Press, 1988).

CHAPTER 8

1. Quoted in Martin Van Creveld, *Supplying War* (Cambridge: Cambridge University Press, 1977), 231.

2. The following numbers are from Hans Adolf Jacobsen, "Motorisierungprobleme im Winter, 1939-1940," *Wehrwissenschaftliche Rundschau* (September 1956): 513; Matthew Cooper, *The German Army, 1933-1945* (London: Macdonald and Jane's, 1978), 162-63, 210-11; and Van Creveld, *Supplying War*, 143-45.

3. USSBS, *The Effects of Strategic Bombing on the German War Economy*, 282.

4. Information on motor-vehicle firms can be found in USSBS reports on specific plants – for example, *Auto Union A.G.* and *Maybach Motor Works*.

5. Bellon, "Workers of Daimler-Untertuerkheim," 493-502, 511-13.

6. Ibid. and USSBS, *Daimler-Benz, Untertuerkheim*.

7. Wilkins and Hill, *American Business Abroad*, 282, 330-31.

8. Maurice Olley, *The Motor Car Industry in Germany during the Period 1939-1945*, BIOS Report 21 (London: HMSO, 1950), 7.

9. USSBS, *German Motor Vehicles Industry*, 24.

10. Ibid., Exhibit C.

11. USSBS, *Oil Division Report*, 14-39, 121.

12. Richard M. Daniel, "The Little Can That Could," *American Heritage of Invention and Technology* 3, no. 2 (Fall 1987): 62, 64.

13. Richard Ogorkiewicz, *Armor* (New York: Praeger, 1960), 247; John Sweet, *Iron Arm: The Mechanization of Mussolini's Army, 1920-1940* (Westport, Conn.: Greenwood Press, 1980), 181.

14. Carlo Salazar, *Ottant'anni di camion Fiat* (Turin: Gruppo Editoriale Forma, 1983), 109.

15. S. Harvey, "L'Effort de guerre italien et le bombardement stratégique de l'Italie," *Revue d'histoire de la deuxième guerre mondiale* 36, no. 143 (July 1986): 62, 77.

16. Colonel Philibert, "Les Arrières dans l'attente (de fin septembre 1939 à début mai 1940)," *Revue historique des armées* 1, no. 4 (1974): 92-94; André Duvignac, *Histoire de l'armée motorisée* (Paris: Imprimerie nationale, 1947), 462-65.

17. The best account of this disputed episode appears to be Gilbert Hatry, *Louis Renault: Patron absolu* (Paris: Lafourcade, 1982), 365-69.

18. P. Fridenson in J.-P. Bardou et al., *La Révolution automobile* (Paris: Albin Michel, 1977), 191; J.-L. Loubet-Loche, "Les Automobiles Peugeot: Histoire d'un enterprise, 1945-1973" (doctoral thesis, ANRT, Lille, 1988), 26; Peter Lessmann, "Abschlussbericht zum 'Frankreich-Komplex' " (on Peugeot), 65-66; and M. R. D. Foot, *SOE in France* (London: HMSO, 1966), 286-88.

19. Saint-Loup, *Marius Berliet: L'Inflexible* (Paris: Presses de la cité, 1962), 248-49.

20. William Hornby, *Factories and Plant* (London: HMSO, 1958), 200, 220-22, 253-62; C. M. Kochan, *Works and Buildings* (London: HMSO, 1952), 312-15.

21. David Thoms and Tom Donnelly, *The Motor Car Industry in Coventry since the 1890s* (New York: St. Martin's Press, 1985), 115-18.

22. Ian Lloyd, *Rolls-Royce: The Merlin at War* (London: Macmillan, 1978).

23. Ian Lloyd, *Rolls-Royce: The Years of Endeavour* (London: Macmillan, 1978), 233.

24. Lloyd, *The Merlin at War*, 84-115, 174.

25. Correlli Barnett, *The Audit of War* (London: Macmillan, 1986), 164.

26. Great Britain, *Statistical Digest of the War* (London: Central Statistical Office, 1951), 149, 159; Hornby, *Factories and Plant*, 193; USSBS, *German Motor Vehicles Industry Report*, 7, 13.

27. Eugene Zaleski, *Stalinist Planning for Economic Growth, 1933-1952* (Chapel Hill: University of North Carolina Press, 1980), 604.

28. Mark Harrison, *Soviet Planning in Peace and War, 1938-1945* (Cambridge: Cambridge University Press, 1985), 250-51; Klaus Segbers, *Die Sowjetunion im Zweiten Weltkrieg* (Munich: Oldenbourg, 1987), 90-121, 134-66; and Sydney L. Mayer, ed., *The Russian War Machine* (London: Arms & Armour, 1977), 177-79.

29. Harrison, *Soviet Planning*, 80-81. Segbers, *Sowjetunion im Weltkrieg*, 290-93, describes Soviet modernization of tank production during the war.

30. Alexander Boyd, *The Soviet Air Force since 1989* (New York: Stein & Day, 1977) 38-39, 199.

31. Sutton, *Western Technology and Soviet Economic Development*, 3: 5-6.

32. T. H. Vail Motter, *The Persian Corridor and Aid to Russia* (Washington, D.C.: Department of the Army, 1952).

CHAPTER 9

1. The Soviet Union received a very large number of machine tools, valued at $405 million, through the Lend-Lease program during the war. Soviet reparations from Germany after the war included a much larger but uncounted number of machine tools. For German machine tools, see USSBS, *Machine Tools and Machinery as Capital Investment*, 1, 15, 90.

2. Peter Dunnett, *The Decline of the British Motor Car Industry* (London: Croom Helm, 1980), 31-40; Barnett, *The Audit of War*, 272-75.

3. Loubet-Loche, "Automobiles Peugeot," 35, 47-50.

4. Ibid., 60-62.

5. Hatry, *Louis Renault*, 401-26.

6. P. Fridenson, "Les Cas Renault," unpublished paper of 24 May 1984; Fernand Picard, *L'Epopée de Renault* (Paris: Albin Michel, 1976), 255-74.

7. Picard, *Renault*, 105, 138, 181, 215, 279-89.

8. The most informative account is Marcel Peyrenet, *Nous prendrons les usines: Berliet* (Geneva: Slatkine, 1980), which is quite critical of the Berliet family. Sympathetic to the Berliets are Robert Aron, *Histoire de l'épuration* (Paris: Fayard, 1974), book 3, vol. 1, 202-32, and Saint-Loup, *Marius Berliet*, 261-312.

9. Peyrenet, *Nous prendrons les usines,* 61-111.

10. Ibid., 78.

11. The quotations are from Alain Pinol, "Travail, travailleurs et production aux usines Berliet (1912-1947)" (thesis, Université de Lyon, 1980), 196-97.

12. Peyrenet, *Nous prendrons les usines,* 118-19.

13. *Wall Street Journal*, 11 July 1984, 20, recounts some 2 CV stories.

14. Nelson, *Small Wonder*, 101.

15. Castronovo, *Agnelli*, 675.

16. Michel Burnier, *Fiat, Conseils ouvriers et syndicat* (Paris: Editions ouvrières, 1980), 90.

17. Ibid., 92.

18. Sutton, *Western Technology and Soviet Economic Development, 1945 to 1965*, 3: 199-200.

19. Ibid., 3: 16-22, 29, 38, 194-98.

CHAPTER 10

1. Karel Williams et al., *Why Are the British Bad at Manufacturing?* (London: Routledge & Kegan Paul, 1983), 219-23.

2. Jonathan Wood, *Wheels of Misfortune* (London: Sidgwick & Jackson, 1988), 139.

3. Williams et al., *Why Are the British Bad at Manufacturing?*, 226-34, 238.

4. H. A. Turner et al., *Labour Relations in the Motor Industry* (London: Allen & Unwin, 1967), 224.

5. Steven Tolliday, "Government, Employers and Shop Floor Organisation in the British Motor Industry, 1939-69," in *Shop Floor Bargaining and the State*, 108-10.

6. Hugh Scanlon, quoted in Adeney, *The Motor Makers*, 266.

CHAPTER 11

1. P. Fridenson, "L'Usine de Flins," *Monuments historiques*, no. 134 (August 1984): 7-14.

2. See the 1952 lecture by P. Lefaucheux quoted by Aron in *Histoire de l'épuration*, book 3, vol. 1, 40-41.

3. His point of view can be found in Pierre Dreyfus, *Une Nationalisation réussie: Renault* (Paris: Fayard, 1981).

4. Loubet-Loche, "Automobiles Peugeot," 220.

5. Ibid., 244.

6. Pierre Bercot, *Mes Années aux usines Citroën* (Paris: Pensée universelle, 1977), and Alain Jemain, *Michelin* (Paris: Calman-Lévy, 1982), 187-207.

7. A biography is Alan Friedman, *Agnelli* (New York: New American Library, 1989).

8. Giorgio Spriano, *Technological Choices and Spatial Organization of Production in the Fiat System* (London: Department of Geography, London School of Economics, 1985), is an excellent brief discussion.

9. Mark Chatterton, *Saab: The Innovator* (Newton Abbot: David & Charles, 1980); *The Saab-Scania Story* (Stockholm: published by the company, 1987).

10. A fine survey of the European auto industry in the 1970s, including the smaller countries, can be found in Gerald Bloomfield, *The World Automotive Industry* (Newton Abbot: David & Charles, 1978).

CHAPTER 12

1. Imogene U. Edwards, "Automotive Trends in the U.S.S.R.," in U.S. Congress, Joint Economic Committee, *Soviet Economic Prospects for the Seventies,* 93d cong., 1st sess. (Washington, D.C., 1973), 293-97; Holliday, *Technology Transfer to the USSR*, 137-70; Mikael Sandberg, "Fiat Auto Technology and Soviet Motor Industry Reorganization," *Nordic Journal of Soviet and East European Studies* 1, no. 4 (1984): 31-53.

2. *Izvestia*, 7 December 1974, as reported in *Current Digest of the Soviet Press*, 1 January 1975, 15-16.

3. W. H. Parker, "The Soviet Motor Industry," *Soviet Studies* 32 (1980): 534-37.

4. *Izvestia*, 12 September 1988, as reported in *Current Digest of the Soviet Press*, 12 October 1988, 18.

5. William J. Conyngham, *The Modernization of Soviet Industrial Management* (Cambridge: Cambridge University Press, 1982), 160.

6. Parker, "The Soviet Motor Industry," 538.

7. *Izvestia*, 14 August 1988, as reported in *Current Digest of the Soviet Press*, 14 September 1988, 17.

8. *Izvestia*, 30 April 1987, as reported in *Current Digest of the Soviet Press*, 27 May 1987, 17.

9. Useful information on the East European auto industries can be found in A. Tiraspolsky, "Camions et autobus en Europe orientale," *Courrier des pays de L'Est*, April 1977, 19-36; A. Tiraspolsky and I. Kamenka, "Le Développement de la voiture de tourisme en Europe orientale," *Courrier des pays de L'Est*, January 1976, E42-E53; and Vladimir Sobell, *The Red Market* (Aldershot, England: Gower, 1984), 172-82.

10. See the comments in O. Bogomolov et al., *The World Socialist Economy* (Moscow: Soviet Academy of Sciences, 1936), 247-59, where the merits of international trade and the division of of labor are pointed out, with appropriate endorsements from Marx and Lenin.

11. Kálmán Pécsi, *The Future of Socialist Integration* (Armonk, N.Y.: Sharpe, 1981), 16-20.

12. Sobell, *The Red Market,* 178-79.

CHAPTER 13

1. J.-J. Chanaron, in *Die Automobil-Revolution* (Gerlingen: Bleicher, 1989), 156.

2. Edouard Seidler, *Let's Call It Fiesta* (Lausanne: Edita, 1976), 77-83.

3. The average annual output of cars per employee at Dagenham and Halewood dropped from 17 in 1970-74 to 13 in 1975-79, while at Ford's continental plants at Genk and Saarlouis, making similar cars, the average output over the same period rose from 25 to 31 (Adeney, *Motor Makers*, 271, 311).

4. *New York Times*, 28 November 1989.

5. Adeney, *Motor Makers*, 315-17, 337; Wood, *Wheels of Misfortune*, 202-3, 237-38.

6. Barbara Castle, *The Castle Diaries: 1974-1976* (London: Weidenfeld & Nicolson, 1980), 374. The nearly 1 million unemployed was a gross exaggeration.

7. Michael Edwardes's own account is *Back from the Brink* (London: Collins, 1983). A good outside analysis is Karel Williams et al., *The Breakdown of Austin Rover* (New York: St. Martin's Press, 1987).

8. Wood, *Wheels of Misfortune*, 231.

9. Friedman, *Agnelli*.

10. Richard Johnson, in *Automotive News*, 10 July 1989, 26. See also Kurt Hoffman and Raphael Kaplinsky, *Driving Force* (Boulder, Colo.: Westview Press, 1988), 206-9.

11. *Automotive News*, 10 July 1989, 22.

12. *New York Times*, 25 June 1987, D5.

CHAPTER 14

1. Kim B. Clark and Takahiro Fujimoto, *Product Development Performance* (Boston: Harvard Business School Press, 1991), 36.

2. Friedman, *Agnelli*, 158.

3. *World Motor Vehicle Data Book* (Detroit: Motor Vehicle Manufacturers Association of the United States, 1989), 125.

4. Hoffman and Kaplinsky, *Driving Force*, 121-38; James P. Womack et al., *The Machine That Changed the World* (New York: Rawson Associates, 1990).

5. Womack, *The Machine That Changed the World*, assembly hours from 85; quoted from pp. 86-87.

6. Ibid., 86.

7. Ibid., 87-88.

8. *Izvestia*, 17 August 1991, as reported in *Current Digest of the Soviet Press*, 25 September 1991, 46.

BIBLIOGRAPHIC ESSAY

This essay includes major treatments of the European automobile industry and aspects of it. As it is quite selective, many of the items cited in the Notes and References are not mentioned.

GENERAL STUDIES

There are few serious studies of the automobile industry throughout the world or in Europe as a whole. J.-P. Bardou, J.-J. Chanaron, P. Fridenson, and J. Laux try to cover its world history in *La Révolution automobile* (Paris: Albin Michel, 1977), updated in *The Automobile Revolution* (Chapel Hill: University of North Carolina Press, 1982) and in *Die Automobil-Revolution* (Gerlingen: Bleicher, 1989). All editions of this book have extensive bibliographies. Gerald Bloomfield, *The World Automobile Industry* (Newton Abbot: David & Charles, 1978), surveys it in the 1970s, and its situation in the 1980s is analyzed in Alan Altshuler et al., *The Future of the Automobile* (Cambridge: MIT Press, 1984). Kurt Hoffman and Raphael Kaplinsky, *Driving Force* (Boulder, Colo.: Westview Press, 1988); James P. Womack et al., *The Machine That Changed the World* (New York: Rawson Associates, 1990); and Kim B. Clark and Takahiro Fujimoto, *Product Development Performance* (Boston: Harvard Business School Press, 1991), all deal with the Japanese challenge to the European and American auto industry. *The Economic and Social Effects of the Spread of Motor Vehicles*, ed. Theo Barker (London: Macmillan, 1987), presents a group of studies on the reception of motorcars and trucks.

For particular aspects of the European picture, Jacques Ickx offers a very detailed account of the invention of the automobile in *Ainsi naquit l'automobile*, 2 vols. (Lausanne: Edita, 1961); the emergence of trucks is described in J. Laux, "Trucks in the West during the First World War," *Journal of Transport History* 6 (September 1985): 64-70; and Patrick Fridenson deals with production in "The Coming of the Assembly Line to Europe," in *The Dynamics of Science and Technol-*

ogy, ed. W. Krohn (Dordrecht: Reidel, 1978), 159-75. Ford best exemplified the early American challenge to Europe, as seen by Mira Wilkins and F. E. Hill in *American Business Abroad: Ford on Six Continents* (Detroit: Wayne State University Press, 1964). Europe led America in automotive diesel engines, as summarized in J. Laux, "Les Moteurs Diesel pour les transports," *Culture technique*, no. 19 (March 1989): 20-28.

Two periodicals that provide news and statistics are *Automotive News* and the *Ward's Automotive Yearbook*.

FRANCE

A general study is J. Laux, *In First Gear: The French Automobile Industry to 1914* (Montreal: McGill-Queen's University Press, 1976). Renault is thoroughly examined in P. Fridenson, *Histoire des usines Renault*, vol. 1 (Paris: Seuil, 1972), and Gilbert Hatry, *Louis Renault* (Paris: Lafourcade, 1982). For Citroën, see Fabien Sabates and S. Schweitzer, *André Citroën* (Paris: EPA, 1980), and S. Schweitzer, *Des Engrenages à la chaine: Les Usines Citroën, 1915-1935* (Lyon: Presses universitaires de Lyon, 1982). Studies of Peugeot have begun to appear, including Yves Cohen, "Ernest Mattern, les automobiles Peugeot et le pays de Montbéliard . . ." (thesis, Université de Besançon, 1981), and Jean-Louis Loubet-Loche, *Les Automobiles Peugeot* (Paris: Economica, 1990), based on the thesis cited in the Notes and covering the years 1945-75.

Several accounts treat Berliet, including Jacques Borgé and N. Viasnoff, *Berliet de Lyon* (Paris: EPA, 1981), and Saint-Loup, *Marius Berliet: L'Inflexible* (Paris: Presses de la cité, 1962). Marcel Peyrenet, *Nous prendrons les usines* (Geneva: Slatkine, 1980), is a full discussion of the "worker-management" episode at Berliet, 1944-49. Griffith Borgeson, *Bugatti by Borgeson* (London: Osprey, 1981), carefully studies this overpraised entrepreneur.

The many discussions of automobile labor include Etienne Riché, *La Situation des ouvriers dans l'industrie automobile* (Paris: Rousseau, 1909); P. Fridenson, "Un Tournant taylorien de la société française," *Annales E.S.C.* 42 (1987): 1031-60; and Bertrand Badie, "Les Grèves du Front populaire aux usines Renault," *Mouvement social*, no. 81 (1972):

69-109. An interesting and somewhat self-serving memoir is J. A. Grégoire, *50 ans d'automobile* (Paris: Flammarion, 1974).

BRITAIN

Two journalistic surveys are Martin Adeney, *The Motor Makers* (London: Collins, 1988), and Jonathan Wood, *Wheels of Misfortune* (London: Sidgwick & Jackson, 1988). The careers of two leaders are traced in Roy Church, *Herbert Austin* (London: Europa, 1979), and R. J. Overy, *William Morris: Viscount Nuffield* (London: Europa, 1976). Wayne Lewchuk, *American Technology and the British Vehicle Industry* (Cambridge: Cambridge University Press, 1987), is an outstanding work on labor and management in the British car business until the 1930s. Karel Williams et al., *The Breakdown of Austin Rover* (New York: St. Martin's Press, 1987), is a persuasive account of the 1970s and 1980s, deemphasizing labor disputes. Michael Edwardes, *Back from the Brink* (London: Collins, 1983), tells the story of the decline of BL from its top management's point of view, with much emphasis on labor disputes.

GERMANY

Jan Norbye, *German Car* (New York: Portland House, 1987), is well-illustrated and encyclopedic on the car firms, with little analysis. Werner Oswald, *Deutsche Autos, 1920-1945* (Stuttgart: Motorbuch Verlag, 1983), is one of several catalog-type volumes by this author. Good accounts of auto firms include Karl Ludvigsen, *Opel: Wheels to the World* (Princeton: Automobile Quarterly, 1975); on VW, Walter Nelson, *Small Wonder*, rev. ed. (Boston: Little, Brown, 1967); Gerhard Mirsching, *Audi* (Gerlingen: Bleicher, 1988); and Halwart Schrader, *100 Jahre Porsche* (Stuttgart: Porsche, 1975). Two important articles by R. J. Overy that treat the 1930s and the war are "Cars, Roads, and Economic Recovery in Germany, 1932-8," *Economic History Review* 28 (1975): 466-83, and "Transportation and Rearmament in the Third Reich," *Historical Journal* 16 (1973): 389-409. A valuable resource for the Second World War years are the United States Strategic Bombing Survey reports on the German economy and on war plants (Washington, D.C., 1945). A rare discussion of plant organization and labor at Daimler in the early days is Fritz Schumann, *Auslese und*

Anpassung der Arbeiterschaft in der Automobilindustrie (Leipzig: Duncker & Humblot, 1911).

ITALY

The big book here, based on Fiat archives, is *Giovanni Agnelli* (Turin: UTET, 1971), by Valerio Castronovo. It is supplemented by a biography of this man's grandson, *Agnelli* (New York: New American Library, 1989), by Alan Friedman. The memoirs of a leading Fiat design engineer are Dante Giacosa, *I miei 40 anni di progettazione alla Fiat* (Milan: Automobilia, 1979). Michael Sedgwick, *Fiat* (New York: Arco, 1974), emphasizes cars and racing. Duccio Bigazzi, *Il Portello* (Milan: Franco Angeli, 1988), is an outstanding scholarly volume on Alfa-Romeo to 1926. Good treatments of labor include Stefano Musso, *Gli Operai di Torino, 1900-1920* (Milan: Feltrinelli economica, 1980), and Simonetta Ortaggi, "Cottimo e produttivita nel' industria italiana des primo novecento," *Rivista di storia contemporanea*, no. 1 (1978): 15-58.

SOVIET UNION

The history of the Soviet industry can be gleaned from several articles: William P. Baxter, "The Soviet Passenger Car Industry," *Survey* 19 (1973): 218-40; W. H. Parker, "The Soviet Motor Industry," *Soviet Studies* 32 (1980): 515-41; and the well-informed Imogene U. Edwards, "Automotive Trends in the U.S.S.R.," in U.S. Congress, Joint Economic Committee, *Soviet Economic Prospects for the Seventies*, 93rd cong., 1st sess. (Washington, D.C., 1973): 291-314. There are some discussions of this industry in Antony Sutton, *Western Technology and Soviet Economic Development*, 3 vols. (Stanford, Calif.: Stanford University Press/Hoover Institution, 1968-73). S. V. Voronkova, "Stroitelstvo Automobilnikh Zavodov...," *Istoricheskiye Zapiski* 78 (1965), 147-69, treats the First World War period. Eugene Zaleski, *Stalinist Planning for Economic Growth, 1933-1952* (Chapel Hill: University of North Carolina Press, 1980), has information on wartime output.

ELSEWHERE IN EUROPE

Volvo has sponsored two useful books on its history: Björn Eric Lindh, *Volvo* (Malmö: Förlagshuset Norden, 1984), and Christer Olsson, *Volvo: Sixty Years of Truckmaking* (Malmö: Förlagshuset Norden, 1987). Nils Kinch, "Volvo–Drommen som Blev Verklighet," *Tvärsnitt* 2 (1988): 27-34, is one of a number of studies by this author on Volvo. Mark Chatterton emphasizes the cars in his *Saab: The Innovator* (Newton Abbot: David & Charles, 1980). For the industry in other parts of Europe, one can consult J. Ciuro, *Historia del automóbil en España* (Barcelona: C.E.A.C., 1972); Hans Seper, *Damals als die Pferde scheuten: Die Geschichte der Oesterreichischen Kraftfahrt* (Vienna: Oesterreichischer Wirtschaftsverlag, 1968); Jaromir Vlasimsky, *75 Years of Czechoslovak Automobile Manufacture, 1897-1972* (Bratislava, 1972); and comments in Kálmán Pécsi, *The Future of Socialist Integration* (Armonk, N.Y.: Sharpe, 1981).

INDEX

THE AUTHOR

James M. Laux is Professor of History Emeritus at the University of Cincinnati, where he taught from 1957 to 1989. His publications on automotive history include *In First Gear: The French Automobile Industry to 1914* (1976), *The Automobile Revolution*, with J. P. Bardou and others (1982), and articles for such journals as *Mouvement Social, Journal of Transport History, Aerospace Historian, Culture Technique,* and *French Historical Studies.*